Imperfect Solidarities

FLASHPOINTS

The FlashPoints series is devoted to books that consider literature beyond strictly national and disciplinary frameworks and that are distinguished both by their historical grounding and by their theoretical and conceptual strength. Our books engage theory without losing touch with history and work historically without falling into uncritical positivism. FlashPoints aims for a broad audience within the humanities and the social sciences concerned with moments of cultural emergence and transformation. In a Benjaminian mode, FlashPoints is interested in how literature contributes to forming new constellations of culture and history and in how such formations function critically and politically in the present. Series titles are available online at http://escholarship.org/uc/flashpoints.

A complete list of titles begins on page 208.

Imperfect Solidarities

Tagore, Gandhi, Du Bois, and the Global Anglophone

Madhumita Lahiri

NORTHWESTERN UNIVERSITY PRESS | EVANSTON, ILLINOIS

Northwestern University Press
www.nupress.northwestern.edu

This book is freely available in an open access edition thanks to the TOME (Toward an Open Monograph Ecosystem)—a collaboration of the Association of American Universities, the Association of University Presses, and the Association of Research Libraries—and the generous support of the University of Michigan. Learn more at the TOME website: openmonographs.org.

Portions of chapter 3 previously appeared in "Gandhian Fictions: Rereading Satyagraha," *South Africa Social Dynamics* 38, no. 1 (2012): 104–16; and in "World Romance: Genre, Internationalism, and W. E. B. Du Bois," *Callaloo* 33, no. 2 (2010): 537–52.

Printed in the United States of America

10 9 8 7 6 5 4 3 2 1

Library of Congress Cataloging-in-Publication Data

Names: Lahiri, Madhumita, author.
Title: Imperfect solidarities : Tagore, Gandhi, du Bois, and the forging of the global Anglophone / Madhumita Lahiri.
Other titles: FlashPoints (Evanston, Ill.)
Description: Evanston, Illinois : Northwestern University Press, 2021. | Series: Flashpoints | Includes bibliographical references and index.
Identifiers: LCCN 2020019191 | ISBN 9780810142664 (paperback) | ISBN 9780810142671 (cloth) | ISBN 9780810142688 (ebook)
Subjects: LCSH: Tagore, Rabindranath, 1861–1941—Criticism and interpretation. | Gandhi, Mahatma, 1869–1948—Criticism and interpretation. | Du Bois, W. E. B. (William Edward Burghardt), 1868–1963—Criticism and interpretation. | English literature—Foreign countries—20th century—History and criticism. | American literature—African American authors—20th century—History and criticism. | Internationalism in literature.
Classification: LCC PR9080.5 .L34 2021 | DDC 820.9358—dc23
LC record available at https://lccn.loc.gov/2020019191

For my mother, Rita Lahiri: in solidarity

Lola welcomes onto the stage: Victoria, Elena,
    Francie, lamé pumps and stockings and always
the rippling night pulled down over broad shoulders
    and flounced around the hips, liquid,
the black silk of esta noche
    proving that perfection and beauty are so alien
they almost never touch. Tonight, she says,
    put it on. The costume is license
and calling. She says you could wear the whole damn
    black sky and all its spangles. It's the only night
we have to stand on. Put it on,
    it's the only thing we have to wear.

— Mark Doty, "Esta Noche"

Contents

Note to the Reader

Whereas words and quotations from other languages are italicized, I have chosen not to italicize non-English terms that are repeatedly used or that, like "gitanjali" and "satyagraha," are themselves central to my analysis. All translations are my own unless otherwise specified. For all languages, I have provided the original script whenever possible.

Given the century-old nature of the material under discussion, I have retained the terms of the time—"Negro," "Asiatic," "Oriental," and so on—when necessary to avoid the confusions of anachronism. In referring to actually existing persons, however, I have chosen to capitalize racial indicators—for example, "White people and Black people"—to honor the evolving consensus around such usage and to serve the clarifying function of indicating when the terms refer to racial categories rather than chromatic ones.[1]

The progressive U.S. consensus of capitalizing one term but not the other seems to be constitutively linked to U.S. politics. The most common argument holds that "Black" marks a positive ethno-national recognition for a long-oppressed people who may not be able to claim other ethnic or national markers (which is often assumed for European-descended Americans). However, this leads to serious difficulties in applying "Black" and "white" to non-U.S. persons: citizens of African nations, for instance, may much prefer to be recognized by national or ethnic markers. To capitalize "Black" without also capitalizing "White" is to extrapolate a U.S. experience of race and recognition well beyond its relevant contours.

Lowercasing the racial term "white," on the other hand, risks trivializing an entire world of ethnonationalism, together with its serious and ongoing historical consequences. I capitalize "White" because it is a term of ethnic and national identification, whether we like it or not. Capitalizing "White" draws our attentions to the operations of Whiteness: not as a racial fact, but as a constructed category within which many people are categorized, and with whom only some identify. Given that my book includes Black people who would find being called "Black" a flattening misrecognition, it seems acceptable to place White people who may not appreciate that marker in the same position.

Finally, the antiracist capitalization of "Black" but not "white" has led to a predictable racist response: capitalizing "White," but not "black." It seems to me that both are constructed categories, in keeping with our understandings of race, and therefore both are deserving of capitalization as a way of highlighting their powerful effects. The capital "W" may remind some readers of White supremacist usage—and given that this book tells, in part, the story of White supremacism, that reminder is both intentional and desirable.

Illustrations

Acknowledgments

This project has been with me for a very long time, and it is a pleasure to thank the many mentors, interlocutors, and friends who made this book possible.

This project originated in my graduate studies in the English Department at Duke University, with the support of the Program in Women's Studies and the Franklin Humanities Institute. Jane Gaines insisted that I locate the central theoretical question; Maurice Wallace connected African Americanist queries to postcolonial ones; Ian Baucom knew the Gandhi chapter would be necessary; and Sean Metzger taught me how to spawn that most elusive of academic beasts: a strong argument. The late Srinivas Aravamudan encouraged my linguistic interests; Negar Mottahedeh demonstrated what postcolonial formalism could be. Ranjana Khanna transformed me into an academic, and her extraordinary intellectual perspicacity has shaped my knowledge of what postcolonial studies has been, should be, and might someday become. Ignacio Adriasola, Anne Gulick, Chase Foster, LaTarsha Pough, and Shilyh Warren are as smart as they are companionable: without our conversations, this book would not have been possible.

A summer at the School of Criticism and Theory significantly strengthened this book's theoretical claims. Haun Saussy taught me about bilingualism, and I became friends with Katherine Baxter in the process. Her intellectual adventures continue to inform my own, whether in Ithaca, Hong Kong, or the Lake District. My Bengali skills were polished during a summer at the American Institute for Indian Studies' program in Kolkata: I thank my instructors for their patience with my poor spelling, and Bridget Kustin for the kind of friendship that can traverse three continents.

Much of my work on Gandhi was undertaken during a postdoctoral fellowship at the Centre for Indian Studies in Africa at the University of the Witwatersrand, South Africa. I thank Dilip Menon for his leadership of that interdisciplinary conversation. Pamila Gupta, Megan Jones, Jedi Ramalapa, Kirk Sides, Micaela Smith, Jon Soske, and Tim Wright provided academic solidarity and good cheer, and they helped me consider what internationalist solidarity must become. Achille Mbembe encouraged me to move to South Africa; Sarah Nuttall made me understand the value of being there. To them, and to their lovely children, I am most grateful. Isabel Hofmeyr showed me how to make archivally grounded work theoretically compelling: her intellect, and her friendship, continue to inspire.

Part of this manuscript was undertaken at Brown University, where I benefited greatly from Timothy Bewes's talent for theoretical accuracy. I thank Stuart Burrows, Michelle Clayton, Olakunle George, Sohini Kar, Tamar Katz, Aniruddha Maitra, Thangam Ravindranathan, and Zachary Sng for their friendship and their feedback, and Michael Steinberg for his leadership of our conversations at the Cogut Center for the Humanities. At the University of Warwick I delighted in an ongoing conversation around postcolonial theory and world literary studies, for which I thank Neil Lazarus, Gurminder Bhambra, Christina Britzolakis, Tina Lupton, and Rashmi Varma. Joe Jackson, Carina Hart, Mike Niblett, and Rochelle Sibley are the best pub companions one could imagine: I thank them for political rants, theoretical debates, and rambles in the Cotswolds.

I completed this manuscript at the University of Michigan, Ann Arbor, with the support of the Institute for Research on Women and Gender, the Center for South Asian Studies, and the Department of English Language and Literature. I thank Micah Auerback, Sara Blair, Julie Ellison, Farina Mir, Jonathan Freedman, Linda Gregerson, Danny Hack, Lucy Hartley, Matt Hull, Christi Merrill, Scotti Parrish, Derek Peterson, Adela Pinch, Aswin Punathambekar, Sid Smith, Xiaobing Tang, Tessa Tinkle, Valerie Traub, Gillian White, and Jonathan Zwicker for engaging with this manuscript in its formative stages. Michael Awkward has been a mentor, and occasionally a provocateur; David Porter has engaged my work at every stage, and with crucial queries that only he could devise. Gaurav Desai and Supriya Nair are astute guides to our shared and varied subfield: I thank both of them for their engagement with this work, their continued encouragement throughout the writing process, and (of course) their fabulous parties. I thank librarians Sigrid Cordell and Jeffrey Martin for their research guidance, and Matt Liberti and Alex Ramsey for their research assistance.

I went to graduate school at Vilashini Cooppan's suggestion, and I revised this book with the benefit of her guidance. For both, I am most grateful. Mrinalini Sinha has read this manuscript in its entirety not once but twice: her generosity is both intellectual and personal. Manan Desai and Aliyah Khan have been solid comrades on the tenure track and enthusiastic coconspirators in postcolonial studies. I thank Amanda Armstrong-Price, Eliezer Ben Asher, Elizabeth Bruch, Miranda Brown, Deirdre de la Cruz, Clem Hawes, Tung-Hu Hui, Webb Keane, Aida and Ari Levy-Hussen, Victor Mendoza, Joshua Miller, Alana Price, Cathy Sanok, Meg Sweeney, Ruby Tapia, Kira Thurman, Melanie Yergeau, and Andrea Zemgulys for making Ann Arbor feel like home. Toy Basu, Varuni Bhatia, Erin Brightwell, and Jatin Dua deserve special commendation for their tailgating skills.

Working with the team at Flashpoints and at Northwestern University Press has been a pleasure: I thank Michelle Clayton, Susan Gillman, Trevor Perri, and Maia Rigas for their guidance, and two anonymous reviewers for their comments. The epigraph for this volume is from *My Alexandria: Poems*, copyright 1993 by Mark Doty, used by permission of the University of Illinois Press. I thank the Crisis Publishing Co., the publisher of the magazine of the National Association for the Advancement of Colored People, for the use of material first published in the July and October 1929 issues of *The Crisis* magazine.

Ashok and Rita Lahiri have built their lives in four countries and on three different continents: their fearlessness, their love, and their unending enthusiasm for, well, the entire world have shaped the argument on every page. I thank Arjun for Dr. Bakwaswala, and Amrita for Tungavidhya. Madhav, Kartik, and Shlok Kapoor have radiated their support in person and in video; Wren Fei-Ming Armstrong-Price, Mira Anahita, Nico Fox Elhanan Hu, and Sophia McDonald have brought joy on even the hardest days. AKPK's love has been transcontinental, and unconditional; Rinu and Tanu have humored my attempts to understand the young. Mashi, Mesho, Vini, and Anuj have provided love and encouragement from fourteen hours in the future; Ishita, Dennis, and Meera have done the same from four hours' drive south. Chinyere

Ezie and Po-Ching Chen have been true friends, whether in laudable accomplishments or in unpublishable adventures.

S. E. Kile remains endlessly skeptical of the present: his linguistic enthusiasm, and his personal existence in deep time, means that our conversations regularly cross continents and span millennia. This book has benefited profoundly from our ongoing conversation; I continue to delight in his companionship and love.

Imperfect Solidarities

Introduction

What happens when you make up a word? Every language teems with unexpected innovations—whether made up by babbling toddlers, hip teenagers, or distracted adults—and most of these made-up words will quickly disappear. But every so often, an invented word can change history. This book examines three neologisms that transformed our ongoing struggle against colonialism and racism: "gitanjali," coined by Rabindranath Tagore; "satyagraha," devised by M. K. Gandhi; and "brownies," deployed by W. E. B. Du Bois. Inheritors of a world shaped by colonialism and slavery, these three men chose the eccentric allegiances of internationalism over the essentialized loyalties of nationalism. Whereas nationalism claims its origins, internationalism champions an idealized future—and so they invented new words to make an interconnected future imaginable.

The novelty of the words examined here is somewhat disguised by their reliance on earlier concepts. "Gitanjali" is a recognizably Bengali amalgam; "satyagraha" is an ostentatiously Sanskrit term; and a brownie is an established figure in British folklore. In each case, however, the neologism acquired a very different meaning than its preexisting associations would suggest. Tagore reformulated "gitanjali," which literally means "song offering," into a pan-Asian approach to aesthetics. Gandhi redefined "satyagraha," which lexically denotes holding to the truth, as meaning "passive resistance." Du Bois recast the brownie, then famous as a White imperial sprite, as a magical mixed-race child. By strategically claiming their precedents, their creators disavowed radical innovation, even as they decisively transformed existing concepts through their unprecedented uses of these terms.

Print internationalism, in my theorization, names a strategy within the worldwide hegemony of the English language (signaled in the phrase "the global Anglophone"). This strategy works to create alternate geographies (such as "the Global South") and to summon new collectivities (such as "people of color") through the creation of new words. It is a phenomenon that is at once linguistic and literary. Periodicals are central to my study, but so are pamphlets, books, and published letters, for these are the genres that comprise the varied and exuberant world of early twentieth-century print culture.

Print internationalism was particularly influential in the early twentieth century, when activists from marginalized groups frequently sought worldwide solutions to the pervasive problems of racism and colonialism. The historical framework of this monograph begins with the South African War (also known as the Second Anglo-Boer War, 1899–1902), which led to the formation of an explicitly White South African state; it spans World War I (1914–18), whose unprecedented mobilization of African American soldiers led, on their return to the United States, to both antiracist mobilization and racist violence; and it ends with the advent of World War II (1939–45), when Japan's aggressive expansion demolished hopes of a beneficial pan-Asian order. Given this bounded but eventful timeframe, the chapters are organized relationally, with significant chronological overlap. We begin with Tagore's expansive rejection of nationalism and move, via their contentious public correspondence, to Gandhi's harnessing of print internationalism in the service of an increasingly nationalist politics. Via Du Bois's framing and publication of both Tagore and Gandhi, I conclude with Du Bois's antiracist project as it was forged through print internationalism.

Situations of cultural intermixture frequently generated radical novelty, whether in linguistic terms or identarian ones. In centering on the new words of internationalism, coined chiefly by famous men, we encounter as well the women of internationalism, whose rapidly changing status in the currents of early twentieth-century feminist movements sometimes enabled their innovations across the boundaries of race and nation. Thus, Sonja Schlesin, a Russian Jewish woman, lived and worked with Indians in South Africa; Sister Nivedita, an Irish woman, converted to Hinduism and connected Bengali intellectuals with Japanese ones; and Jessie Redmon Fauset, an African American woman, tutored her young readers on

South and Southeast Asia. The worldwide interests and flexible identities of these women thus resemble the suspect philology behind many of these new words, which diverges from the focus on purity, authenticity, and inheritance often central to nationalism. In developing these observations into a feminist method, I encourage attentiveness to innovation—as seen in the new words coined by internationalist activists—rather than to origins or etymologies. By moving us from a focus on authenticity to a focus on novelty, I demonstrate a process of postcolonial reading that can concatenate textual surfaces in the pursuit of historical depths.

THE WORD AND THE WORLD

My argument builds on Benedict Anderson's theorization of nationalism as an imagined community, an intervention that has transformed our studies of the novel and the newspaper. Given the familiarity of Anderson's claims to many scholarly readers, I will use his argument here as a productive contrast to my own. His argument begins in the modern period, where the capacity of both time and space to be mapped and measured rendered them both potentially gridded and possibly knowable, features that were further developed by the print technologies of the newspaper and the novel. Through these two genres, as well as though nonprint technologies like the museum and the census, print nationalism generated an imagined community through the production of an imagined "meanwhile," wherein readers imagined themselves as coexisting and interchangeable with their fellow citizens. Print internationalism, by contrast, produces the discrepant and unpredictable associations of a world that is invoked rather than graphed. Whereas print nationalism is fraternal, suggesting readers' interchangeability, print internationalism is familial, emphasizing the natural reconciliation of significant differences. National print media asserts a homogeneous, empty time for the nation, producing simultaneity and the "meanwhile"; internationalist print media, acknowledging its spatial and historical discontinuities, emphasizes transformations yet to come.

Print nationalism's key genres are the novel and the newspaper, generally purchased in the marketplace at a set price. Print internationalism's central genres are the fictionalized history and the print periodical, both as likely to be sold in the market as to be acquired through subscription (not at a standard price, but with a pledge of support). These periodicals include the South Africa–based weekly *Indian Opinion* and the U.S.-based monthly *The Crisis*, each of which, as we see in chapters 2 and 3, blurred the distinction between a newsletter—a publication promoting ongoing political activities—and a newspaper—a publication providing reportage. The fictionalized histories, such as Tagore's *Talks in China* and Gandhi's *Satyagraha in South Africa*, analogously blurred the boundaries between public evidence and personal experience, as discussed in chapters 1 and 2. Where newspapers are marked by regularity in their publication and circulation, the periodicals of print internationalism frequently reflect a more erratic temporality, published on an uneven schedule that also informs their pages. And whereas novels can encourage nationalism by providing characters who might seem just like us, the fictionalized histories of print internationalism encourage us to read historical personages differently. Through print internationalism, we learn to see them as the protagonists of ongoing struggles, whose goals, though possibly different, are nonetheless relevant to our own.

In contrast to the individualized reader of the imagined community, the reader of print internationalism is a social creature, approaching texts through collaboratively defined norms. Print internationalism in my theorization activates "an open network of people who share ways of reading texts": that is, an interpretive community.[2] Famously associated with the work of Stanley Fish, the paradigm of an interpretive community emphasizes the role of implicit understandings, acquired through social participation, that inform every act of reading and render any text intelligible.[3] Its social emphasis means that the interpretive community is strongly associated with arguments for cultural relativism, making it particularly apposite for the kinds of worldwide inquiry pursued here. While the term "interpretive community" remains familiar to many literary scholars, two closely related concepts are more widely used today: "discourse community" and "textual community." Scholars of rhetoric and sociolinguistics are more likely to use the term "discourse community," which describes a group of people linked by written communication and organized around shared goals. While the print internationalism that I theorize resembles a discourse community in its voluntary membership and its orientation around particular objectives, its members are more likely to share a general disposition—against racism, for instance, or against imperialism—than to "actively share goals."[4] (To the extent that the interpretive community is convened for particular political purposes, however, we might say that print internationalism creates an interpretive community that, if all goes as planned, might also become a discursive community.)

The interpretive community as developed here, moreover, does not necessarily emphasize direct interaction with written texts, as is the case in most models of discursive community. The "reader" of print internationalism may be not a direct reader at all but, instead, a nonliterate person who nonetheless participates in print culture through a social context. In this respect, it resembles what scholars of premodern literatures and cultures term a "textual community." Often associated with the work of Brian Stock, a textual community is a form of social organization whose members find a prized text meaningful, even as they have varying levels of literacy. The print object thus forms a key aspect of these members' lives, even though they may interact with it in a variety of ways. These participants in print internationalism might browse a publication primarily for its images and layout, using these to puzzle over what the words might say; or they might encounter the textual object when it is read aloud to them, positioning the interpretive community of print internationalism within existing social structures. For these reasons, my analysis in this volume will attend not only to words but also to formatting, photographs, and illustrations: print internationalism, as I demonstrate, creates new words by investing them in very particular published forms.

Readers who attended one of Tagore's lectures in China, or heard Gandhi address a rally in South Africa, or encountered Du Bois at the Universal Races Congress in London likely left those events with an understanding of those thinkers' politics. It would be their texts, however, that gave solidity to these conceptions, for the materiality of print rendered these ephemeral convergences tangible. The political movement—lived networks of interpersonal association and activism—provides an institutional context for reading, while the reading act in turn reinforces otherwise ephemeral interpersonal connections. The texts thus both benefit from and contribute to these socially constituted understandings: the print object, like the public convention, would inculcate the interpretive protocols that make internationalism both imaginable and desirable. Unlike nationalism, which must represent the nation (however conceived), internationalism predicates itself on a loosely defined expansiveness; if framed at all in representational terms, it highlights an existing conundrum, not a preexisting inheritance. By focusing on creating an interpretive community, print internationalism can build on shared political experiences without requiring a belief in their commonality of experience, for it works instead to cultivate a shared interpretive code.

The neologism of print internationalism demands new regimes of interpretation to render itself comprehensible, and it creates an interpretive community rather than, as with print nationalism, an imagined community. The distinction is important: despite its name, an interpretive community is hardly a community in our commonly used sense of the word, for it generally lacks the sense of commonality that we associate with the experience of community in our everyday lives. That imagined commonality, however, is precisely what can be generated by an imagined community, despite its inclusion of persons never to be known. While an interpretive community can be coterminous or isomorphic with an imagined community, this occurs only under specific circumstances.[5] Neither shared experience nor imagined commonality is required, however, to be part of the interpretive community that can read a phrase and comprehend its most useful meaning.

To accomplish these pedagogical ends, print internationalism designs its strategies in accordance with the specific materiality of its printed objects, whether bound as a codex or published as a broadsheet. As these internationalists were well aware, literacies vary, and reading is a widely discrepant affair. In this context, the scriptive functions of a print periodical—copying, folding, and clipping—or of a printed book—turning pages, preserving wholeness, storing on a shelf—become key considerations in the writing process. As a consequence, I further situate print internationalism within the scholarship on everyday life and the material world. As we witness in the repeated didacticism of these authors, print internationalism frequently forged an interpretive community through explicit instruction. They wished to teach their readers how to interpret differently: first the printed text, then the historical record, and finally, thereby, the contemporary world. Insofar as our ability to follow a phrase requires understanding the objects involved, being part of this interpretive community necessitates apprehending a print object as a "scriptive thing," a term Robin Bernstein has used to theorize an object that carries its own limited possibilities of manipulation, and hence its own implied instructions for our use.[6] And being part of the interpretive community, moreover, requires a modicum of skill, rendering it akin to Pierre Bourdieu's concept of a habitus: that is, a form of embodied history that indicates fully internalized knowledge. Consequently, the interpretive communities of print internationalism are created by modifying what Michel de Certeau theorized as the practices of everyday life, through the internalization of new practices not only of reading but also of clipping, circulation, and self-presentation.

To understand what "gitanjali," "satyagraha," or "brownies" means is not simply to have learned a new word but to have entered a new understanding of the world, and a new lived relationship to it as well.

An understanding of internationalism as generating interpretive communities carries with it spatial and temporal implications. Because every interpretation is already governed by an implied interpretive community of varying utility, the pedagogical impetus of print internationalism works to change the implied contexts that result in certain interpretations. Consequently, print internationalism reshapes its readers' perceptions of the world, and of categories like the local, the regional, and the ethnic. It does not simply add an extra-national awareness to its readers' existing national consciousness. After all, even the most seemingly particular nationalism makes broad though implicit claims about the world as a whole. As studies of nationalism have exhaustively demonstrated, nationalism frequently claims autochthony—that is, it claims to represent a community so essentially of that national territory that its members seem as though sprung organically from its rocks and soil. Yet these claims of local authenticity are themselves subtended by a worldwide imaginary: Each nation is authentic because nations themselves are multiple, even as each nation imagines itself distinctive in its own particular way. This vision of a world composed of coexisting nations was given institutional form after World War II, through organizations like the United Nations and the International Monetary Fund. In contrast to this official internationalism, which seeks to manage the inevitable rivalries among various nationally constituted communities, the print internationalisms of my inquiry seek to upend this national framework—that is, our now taken-for-granted vision of the world that makes nationalism appear both natural and inevitable. Whether criticizing the U.S.-led League of Nations or the British Empire, the print internationalisms of Tagore, Gandhi, and Du Bois seek to dismantle the typical rubrics for apprehending the world and replace them with new interpretive protocols.

Attending to the neologism, as I demonstrate in this monograph, provides several methodological advantages. By commencing my inquiry with an attention to new words, I shift our attention away from the border-crossing concerns of translation to the future-oriented dreams of linguistic innovation. In attending to words and their peculiar trajectories, as well as those of the famous men with whom they are associated, I situate the revolutionary work of great men within a larger social and intellectual milieu: one that is crucially peopled with relatively forgotten women. Through this combination of formalist excavation and historicist contextualization, I propose a theory of print internationalism that originates in the shifting global dynamics of the early twentieth century, even as it evades the political structures that emerged from that period.

READING PRINT INTERNATIONALISM

Although this monograph is organized around three great men, the centering of each chapter around a particular neologism enables us to displace or at least suspend considerations of their intentions, accomplishments, and failings. Writing about celebrated icons, after all, poses a familiar peril: in many cases, the political urgency of the subject material intertwines with the extraordinary accomplishments of anticolonial icons to produce an account filled with heroes and villains. Hoping to avoid this well-trodden path, I undertook extensive archival research, interweaving my close analyses of famous texts with scrupulous readings of texts previously unstudied. These lesser-known materials were published, circulated, and still exist right beside those that are well-known today—and in many instances I found that the less-studied publications heavily reflect the authorial and editorial work of women. Drawing on these findings, I highlight how print internationalism among non-White peoples in the early twentieth century was crucially enabled by women, whose oft-indeterminate and rapidly shifting social standing meant that they could intervene, in surprising and strategic ways, in the transformation of an imperial world order. Thus an Irish convert to Hinduism, Sister Nivedita, oversaw the publication of an Asianist manifesto that closely resembled Tagore's later politics; a Jewish woman, Sonja Schlesin, inscribed Gandhi's South African practices; and an African American author, Jessie Redmon Fauset, edited Du Bois's international children's publication. In examining the interventions of these women as well as those of the more famous men with whom they collaborated, I rely on feminist methodologies for literary study, reading beyond narrow definitions of authorship and strict boundaries of genre.[7] As this monograph demonstrates, once we approach texts as objects congealed within an ongoing flow of conversation and collaboration, a far larger cast of creative actors becomes evident.

Yet even as my research on print internationalism unearthed these treasured stories of women's contributions, it also surfaced uncomfortable details of these print internationalisms' substantial political limitations. Gandhi's writing on South Africa contributes to Indian politics but sidelines South African concerns; Du Bois's Indian interests are, in the end, African American in their priorities; and Tagore, despite his expertise, seeks China only to support his native Bengal. In approaching these less-than-admirable realities, I have drawn on recent disciplinary debates on reading, sometimes traced to the hermeneutic dichotomy described by Paul Ricoeur in his study of Sigmund Freud. In Ricoeur's famous theorization, the hermeneutic field is organized around the poles of faith, which seeks to restore a fullness of meaning to the object under interpretation, and of suspicion, which works to strip it of false meanings and illusions. Ricoeur argues that these seemingly opposed hermeneutic poles are part of a single project, which he describes as the "never-ending task of distinguishing between the faith of religion," which exists beyond human-made expressions, and "belief in the religious object," which is human-made and hence fallible.[8] Consequently, he explains, whereas the hermeneutics of faith may be seen as working from a naive faith in the object's plenitude, the hermeneutics of suspicion instead "seeks, through interpretation, a second naïveté."[9] Thus, suspicion is not simply the opposite of faith but the pursuit of "faith that has undergone criticism, postcritical faith."[10]

Postcolonial studies has long sought this "postcritical faith," interrogating its treasured narratives and figures in search of an optimism that might hold up to a "second naïveté." But this critical disposition of attachment, care, and concern for the objects of postcolonial cultural production has coexisted, sometimes uneasily, with a strain of postcolonial studies that focuses on metropolitan and imperial cultural productions, where critical negativity often prevails. In the colonized culture, scholars find artworks that become the objects of faith, recollection, and reparation; in the colonizing culture, already-canonized texts frequently become objects for suspicious reading and demystification. The polarization that Ricoeur registers within the hermeneutic field thus maps onto the polarization that colonialism introduces to social life: a need to have faith in the culture that has been colonized, no matter how badly it has been disparaged in the official record, and a need to be suspicious of the colonizing culture, despite its status as both official and reasonable. In trying to navigate these poles, I want to suggest, the postcolonial critic frequently oscillates between a positive critical disposition and a negative one—between what Eve Sedgwick famously termed the paranoid and reparative critical modes.[11]

Theorizing print internationalism offers a particularly rich context in which to navigate this polarity, which, as I have suggested, exists for the postcolonial critic simultaneously as a hermeneutic dichotomy and a geopolitical one. The works examined here, after all, are writing about at least two marginalized and dispossessed cultures at once: one to which they belong, which is inevitably treated with care, and one to which they do not, which is frequently instrumentalized. Tagore exoticizes semicolonial China, and Gandhi primitivizes Black South Africa, yet they both do so in order to benefit colonized India, while Du Bois essentializes colonized India in order to benefit Black Americans' struggles against racism. These texts, consequently, cannot be immediately allied to an exploitative culture nor to an exploited one: they call at once for our attachment and our demystification.

The reparative impulse in *Imperfect Solidarities* is most evident in my pairing of the three central neologisms with a second triptych of much more recent coinages. The examination of Tagore's neologism "gitanjali" is paired with an excavation of its role in what we now call "the global Anglophone"; Gandhi's "satyagraha" is positioned within his recognition of the commonalities enshrined in our concept of "people of color"; and Du Bois's "brownies" is considered alongside his understanding of what we know as "the Global South." In each case, the insertion of a second term—each a neologism from the late twentieth century—serves two intellectual purposes. First, by naming the relevant framework with an intentionally anachronistic term, I highlight how our thinking about the past is necessarily expanded and restrained by the words of our own time. And second, by linking a key neologism of the early twentieth century to another coined nearly a century after, I suggest directions for further inquiry, for the politically urgent neologisms of our own time are likely similar in their operations to those of Tagore, Gandhi, and Du Bois a century ago.

In reading these works of print internationalism, consequently, I have heeded recent critical calls to attend scrupulously to the surfaces of texts, and I frequently examine references with a literal approach to that period's historical and social realities.[12] I read these writers' failures along the surface of these texts, which is to say that I read them for their rhetorical effects, rather than as symptoms of larger social realities. Despite such strong superficial attachments, however, this monograph remains firmly within postcolonial studies: a field which, as I understand it, is by definition incapable of turning postcritical.[13] Consequently, my interest in a form of surface attention most closely resembles that of Anne Anlin

Cheng, for whom the surface is most interesting for its role in essentialized discourses of racial difference.[14] The surface is essentially political; it is worthy of our attention precisely because it has been historically effective. *Imperfect Solidarities* situates Tagore's exoticization of China within his dismissal of particular aesthetic differences in an artwork, analyzes Gandhi's belittling of Black South Africans alongside his use of an allegorical narrative mode, and studies Du Bois's evocation of caste prejudices as part of his strategy for wider U.S. readership. These are surface-focused explanations to complex political and historical failures, yet they are not already familiar in the scholarship. In avoiding a primarily symptomatic reading method, which would read these problems as indications ("symptoms") of a larger social structure (such as "the political unconscious"), I have sought to avoid that which, here, is less unconscious than obvious. To argue instead, for instance, that these failures are symptoms of widespread racism in the early twentieth century, would be to provide a below-the-surface analysis whose conclusions are nonetheless already evident.

Despite this monograph's tilt away from symptomatic reading methods, some readers may notice that each of the neologisms "satyagraha," "gitanjali," and "brownies" operates akin to a representative unit of ideology. Each neologism is arguably "the smallest intelligible unit of the essentially antagonistic collective discourses of social classes" that Fredric Jameson sought in *The Political Unconscious*—and which he named, in a worthy neologism of his own, an ideologeme.[15] Much as the ideologeme in Jameson's influential theory of symptomatic reading resolved the semiotic square and imbued stability to textual meanings, so too do these neologisms indicate a seemingly latent meaning that is a problem's apparent resolution.[16] These neologisms can thus serve at once as idea and as narrative: as both abstract value and structuring fantasy.[17] My readings certainly follow what I see as Jameson's foundational assumption: that in sites of textual rupture we can identify the constraining conditions of a particular historical moment. From there, however, I diverge from Jameson's model. Instead of seeking what he famously termed the political unconscious, I read print internationalism as itself an agent of historical transformation. By thus embracing a print-cultural materialism, I read symptomatically, but with critical complicity rather than critical distance. Insofar as symptomatic reading still prevails in this monograph, it emanates from a presentist political imperative: *Imperfect Solidarities* thus reads most symptomatically when it reads for political guidance.[18]

Jameson, like the New Critics before him, assumed a completeness within the individual work of art, whereas I approach the texts of print internationalism as an uneven yet interconnected realm. What kind of reading method applies when the text is not assumed as a discrete and continuous whole? The chapters presented here, while centering on a notable individual, take as their analytic point of coherence the new coinage itself. Neither the author nor the artwork is seen, in my method, as intrinsically contained, consistent, or stable. While my destabilization of the author here is theoretically informed by poststructuralism, my focus on writers from marginalized backgrounds means that I am interested not in the death of the subject but, rather, in recognizing that subject's constitutive instability. I am uninterested in the death of the author but remain fascinated by the operations of the author function, and I consequently rely on a performative understanding of authorship: that is, I approach authorship not only as a question of creation but also as one of creative recognition.[19]

Despite much writing on its possible demise, close reading remains the method of literary studies, and of this monograph as well. Semiotic closure, central to the study of the political unconscious, remains central here as well, even as I detach the operations of narrative from always implying the novelistic plot. The work of narrative here coheres not only in the book-length texts under consideration, many of which rely on the fictionalization of history and politics—Gandhi's *Satyagraha in South Africa*, Du Bois's *Dark Princess*, Tagore's *Talks in China*—but also in the ersatz historical narratives—of Africa, India, and China—that each of these intellectuals constructs.

Readers may notice here the resonance of a Foucauldian notion of discourse—popularized in postcolonial studies through the foundational work of Edward Said—even as the approach I have chosen prioritizes detailed accounts of localized albeit dispersed textual phenomena over magisterial accounts of historical transformation. I accordingly utilize a network model for the social, which has received much positive interest within recent literary studies.[20] While the network is not a guiding metaphor for writers in the early twentieth century, an analogous metaphor does surface repeatedly in the print internationalism under consideration, perhaps most obviously in the first chapter: that of a web, then associated with spiders and not, as today, with the internet. Approaching print internationalism as a web is particularly apposite for this study, enabling us to grasp its unpredictable correspondences and complex allegiances without disregarding the gaps that make such connections possible. This approach can recalibrate the completeness of the text as envisaged by New Criticism—wherein the aesthetic object attains considerable cultural powers—with the interwoven texts of New Historicism—wherein the text intertwines with its historical moment.

Imperfect Solidarities demonstrates how flawed connections across continents can, through the unpredictable medium of the global Anglophone, generate dramatic transformations in how we understand our world. In invoking solidarity, this book acknowledges the profound influence of Marxist internationalism, as well as Karl Marx's concerns about the fluid nature of modernity. In the modern world, Marx famously decreed in 1848, "all that is solid melts into air." That quote from *The Communist Manifesto* became the title of a now-classic study by Marshall Berman, who argued that the constant disappearance of solidity is the defining feature of our modern condition. In Berman's hands, Marx's diagnosis is apt but his optimism is misplaced: writing in 1982, he argued that the solidarity of which Marx dreams will be "like everything else here, only temporary, provisional, built for obsolescence."[21]

In naming this monograph *Imperfect Solidarities*, I have sought to emphasize not only these allegiances' ephemerality but also their imperfections. The epigraph for this book is taken from Mark Doty's poem "Esta Noche," first published in his 1993 collection *My Alexandria*. Doty's poem summons the beauty and power of imperfection, from its Spanish title to its mainly English text, celebrating *la fabulosa Lola* as she moves between cultures and subverts conventions. In Doty's vision, an evening—*esta noche*—becomes poetry through "the artifice of the awkward or lovely": through a scene as temporary as it is transformative. In coining "gitanjali," "satyagraha," and "brownies," the central figures in *Imperfect Solidarities* fell far short of perfection, but they did transform the world. Like *la fabulosa Lola* "shifting in and out of two languages like gowns / or genders," they devised for us both "license / and calling": they put on, we might say, "the only thing we have to wear."

TRANSLATION, PHILOLOGY, AND NEOLOGY

Contemporary literary studies has often deployed translation studies to analyze cultural contact, yet that rubric, as this book demonstrates, is ill suited to the study of print internationalism. Translation—with its Latin root *translatio*, "to carry across"—is essentially a *spatial* practice: the translator shifts a set of meanings from one sign system to another, whether linguistically (as from Japanese to English), mathematically (as when moving a shape), or metaphorically (as in "cultural translation"). Beyond a Latinate context, understandings of translation such as the Sanskritic *anuvaad* (literally, "to say again") are often more attuned to its iterative—and hence temporal—implications, but in all cases the relationship to that which exists before translation is revolutionary by coincidence, rarely by intention. A "good" translation is faithful to the original language text, and not, as with the neologisms here, most concerned with possible political effects. Translation connects existing languages and renders them commensurable, and as a result, any act of translation impacts *both* languages in one way or another. However, this mutual transformation is generally seen as an associated effect of the act of translation, not as its guiding motivation. Even the individual who undertakes translation as part of a revolutionary politics, for instance, is most likely to see the revolutionary aspect of her efforts in the importation and dissemination of the concepts—that is, the signifieds. The recalibration of existing signs—or more precisely, the signifiers—is viewed as incidental.

Because translation emphasizes the carrying across of meaning between different languages (or, to be precise, differently articulated sign systems), it is poorly equipped to address this transformation of meanings within a discontinuous but connected world. It cannot, for instance, theorize the invention of a new and unprecedented language—a project epitomized in the period under discussion in the invention of Esperanto. The neologisms in this book, like Esperanto, dream of new language forms that might render the world better connected and thereby harmonious—but unlike Esperanto, which publicized its disruption of the existing order of national languages, these neologisms contain their disruptive novelty within the increasingly worldwide reach of the English language.

By flaunting their novelty, these neologisms—"gitanjali," "satyagraha," "brownies"—emphasize temporal disruption in addition to geographical motion, even when their disruptions are also those of etymology. The neologisms here are transportable from the first, proving not so much resistant to translation but beyond translation's purview. This renders them decisively different from what Emily Apter has termed an Untranslatable, which she defines as "an incorruptible or intransigent nub of meaning that triggers endless translating in response to its resistant singularity."[22] While the work of translation requires us to attach existing signifiers to unfamiliar signifieds, the practice of coining neologisms demands the production of *new* signifiers. This is both an obvious distinction and a consequential one. As the very term for the coining of new words—"neology"—implies, the practice embraces a temporal orientation: the speaker or writer produces a term that has not previously existed, in the hopes that it will persist into an uncertain future. Failure, in this instance, is the risk of immediate obsolescence, because every neologism, at its inception, is simply a solitary errant usage. (We can compare this to the concept of a "failed" translation, which is usually defined by its failure to adhere to the meanings of the original text, no matter how lasting or consequential the translation itself may prove.) By tracing these neologisms back to their initial emergence, we witness a durational anxiety, and hence a historical one: between the new word, resonant with its possibilities, and the nonce-word, unremarkable in its transience.

My focus on neology—the coining of new words—proposes a new direction for the flourish of recent scholarly interest in philology—a love of words that is particularly attentive to their pasts. In the first decade of the twenty-first century, the return to world literature in the U.S. academy sought to address the limitations of the comparative literature paradigm. Now, at the close of the second decade, a series of publications seek to return to philology, arguing that this earlier discipline can reinvigorate the humanities today. Philology has been declared "the forgotten origins of the modern humanities" and the "colonial foundation of the humanities"; it has been championed as a solution for the provincialism of literary studies, and it has been discouraged for encouraging racist fantasies of pure origins.[23] Its political significance seems to be a matter of consensus, even if its political impact remains a topic of debate. Whereas philology orients us to the past of words, and to the histories contained within language itself, neology directs us, as its very name suggests, toward the future, intimating the latent meanings that are activated when new words are found. This book reflects the philological impulse to attend to textual fragments and seek linguistic origins; at the same time, the words at the heart of my inquiry are from the first beset with opportunism and impurity. Whereas philology, for better and worse, can reveal the ancestry of present words, the neology of my study dispenses with precise origins for the romance of unpredictable possibilities.

The neologism may be most familiar to the humanities scholar through its prevalence in contemporary scholarship, where new words are frequently coined to explain a research innovation. The neologism thus points the way to future scholarly endeavors, much as the neologisms detailed here suggest internationalist activities yet to be realized. Despite this overlap, the scholarly use of the neologism is fundamentally different from the uses explored in this monograph. First, whereas the neologisms of humanities scholarship are carefully articulated in their philological associations, the neologisms of the intellectuals here display a pointed disregard for accuracy and antecedents. They rely on ersatz etymologies and opportunistic cultural borrowings, ignoring questions of authenticity for aspirations of political resonance. Instead of the professional humanist's attentive engagement with preexisting scholarly conversations, these activist intellectuals dream of international conversations not yet in existence. The scholarly neologism usually advertises its innovation, in the hopes of being added to an existing critical corpus; the neologisms here disguise their disruption, in the hopes of creating an understanding readership—as I proposed earlier, an interpretive community—as though by accident.

These are not coinages like *différance*, carried into English by Jacques Derrida, or "womanism," originating in the political philosophy of Alice Walker, whose originality is foregrounded and which remain strongly associated with their authors. Such new coinages contain a strong example of what Michel Foucault termed the author function, often through the incursion of the authorial first person. In the neologisms studied here, by contrast, the author fades away in order to strengthen the word itself. By removing the author, and rendering the word seemingly authorless, the textual incursion obtains the abstract validity of a commonly accepted truth. Think of terms like "neurotypical" and "cisgender": neologisms that seek to transform lived experience by renaming it, and that hide their authorship, despite their recent provenance, in the pursuit of powerfully widespread social use.[24] The forgetting of the provenance of the neologism through the erasure of authorship thus enables the new coinage to acquire the status of objective truth.

STRUCTURE OF THE BOOK

The print internationalisms studied here emerged in the context of two influential worldwide movements. The first movement is centered on the series of meetings known as the Second International (1889–1916), which comprised a vast array of activists seeking to unite the workers of the world through the analytics of Marxist internationalism. After the

First World War, that movement became subordinate to Soviet leadership with the advent of the Third International (or ComIntern, 1919–43). The second major worldwide movement of this period is international feminism, which in this period prominently featured the struggle for women's suffrage. Because of the profound influence of these two movements on the words at the center of our story, I pay particular attention to the analytics of class and gender that formed the basis of Marxist and feminist internationalisms, respectively. The first, that of class, is evident in my discussions of Tagore's desired unity between the folk and the elite, Gandhi's changing views of "coolies," and Du Bois's ambivalent invocations of caste. The second, that of gender, manifests itself in the consideration of women like Sister Nivedita, Sonja Schlesin, and Jessie Redmon Fauset, whose editorial and authorial labors made these print internationalisms possible.

The first chapter offers a history of "the global Anglophone" by focusing on the internationalist poet whom I claim as its progenitor: Rabindranath Tagore. In his powerful deployment of English for the circulation and appreciation of Asian poetry, whether originally written in Chinese or in Bengali, Tagore offers, I argue, a provocative point of origin from which to articulate a robust conception of the global Anglophone. Tagore works to reconnect India and China by highlighting their shared spiritual linkage, which historically includes writing itself. Tagore's persona was central to his reputation, especially outside India, yet as I demonstrate, his tour in China was much less effective than his circulation in print. This pattern will continue in the following chapter with Gandhi, whose writings about Africans can only be understood through his limited engagements with them, and with Du Bois, who argues that print circulation, and not personal exchange, can best build international solidarity.

The second chapter excavates the development of the term "people of color" by focusing on an anticolonial internationalist whose impact has been cross-racial but whose antiracist politics were racially singular: M. K. "Mahatma" Gandhi. As the historical record shows, Gandhi demonstrated that the practices of nonviolent protest he named satyagraha were transportable, replicating his South African innovations in India and changing the course of world history in the process. Even though Gandhi's strategies were later deployed by Black Americans, Gandhi's record is often read, not without reason, as a cautionary tale of the difficulties of cross-racial solidarity. Gandhi's early writings were sometimes derogatory of Black people, and his activism against anti-

Indian racism in South Africa largely ignored that directed against Black South Africans. Much as Tagore's print internationalism reflected the limits of a civilizational claim for constructing internationalist solidarity, Gandhi's reflects the limitations of one based on the experience of racism alone.

The third chapter creates a longer history for the concept of "the Global South" by focusing on the antiracist internationalist who is frequently championed as its visionary: W. E. B. Du Bois. Through his careful incorporation of Indian politics in both his fiction and nonfiction writing, Du Bois facilitated a print internationalism that could simultaneously articulate the oppressions of racism and colonialism (in keeping with his vision of "the global color line"). In doing so, however, he subordinated Indian politics to African American priorities, frequently invoking caste as an indication of India's degeneracy—and drawing on time-worn Orientalist tropes in the process. In this manner, Du Bois's print internationalism prefigures both the potential and the pitfalls of our contemporary category of "the Global South": its ability to consider multiple interlocking systems of oppression across the world, as well as its inability to give all regions equal priority.

Whereas these chapters of *Imperfect Solidarities* explore print internationalisms to which we might be broadly sympathetic, in the conclusion I turn briefly to a print internationalism that was unambiguously abhorrent: what Hannah Arendt termed, in 1945, the "fascist international." In ending on this darker note, I explore how the print internationalism of the early twentieth century continues to have implications for our understandings of the early twenty-first. Print internationalism, as this study demonstrates, can be a powerful force in the world: It is my hope that it will be a force for good.

CHAPTER 1

The Global Anglophone

Rabindranath Tagore's Gitanjali

In 1913 the Bengali poet Rabindranath Tagore won the Nobel Prize for Literature. In its award, the committee cited Tagore's 1912 *Gitanjali: Song Offerings*, a collection of English-language versions—created by Tagore himself—of his Bengali poetry and published from London in 1912. Even though Tagore was best known for his copious writings in the Bengali language, the prize was widely seen as indicative of the beneficial effects of Britain's worldwide rule. After all, Tagore's collection of free verse poems had been framed for publication by a preface from another British colonial subject, the Irish poet W. B. Yeats (1865–1939); furthermore, the poems in *Gitanjali* had first appeared to the public a few months earlier, published in the new U.S. magazine *Poetry* thanks to the Anglophile poet Ezra Pound (1885–1972).[1] Both Yeats and Pound, in their own ways, had praised *Gitanjali* for what it brought not only to poetry but specifically to the English language. In reading Tagore's volume, Yeats hears "our own voice as in a dream," while Pound finds "that sort of metric which we awhile predicted or hoped for in English."[2] In citing Tagore's *Gitanjali* collection to award his Nobel Prize, as I demonstrate, the committee signaled Tagore's pivotal role in the worldwide literary sphere that we now call the global Anglophone.

"The global Anglophone" is now a fairly common term in U.S. literary studies, albeit a frequently disparaged one. The successor in many regards to terms like "commonwealth literature" or "postcolonial literature," "the global Anglophone" replaces those terms' explicit acknowledgment of the political legacy of the British Empire by instead foregrounding that empire's linguistic legacy. It is, however, almost always overshadowed by the well-established term "postcolonial," which boasts both theoretical and political credentials. A special issue of the postcolonial studies journal *Interventions* in 2018, "From Postcolonial to World Anglophone," concludes with a response titled "Postcolonial, by Any Other Name?";[3] a special issue of the Americanist journal *Post45*, "Forms of the Global Anglophone," ends with a response titled "Postcolonial, Still";[4] while a panel slated for the Modern Language Association's (MLA) annual conference in 2020, itself organized by the forum named Global Anglophone, declares its intentions of "decolonizing global Anglophone literature."[5] While I am informed by these widespread concerns about the global Anglophone as a depoliticizing classification, my account of the global Anglophone in this chapter more closely resembles the small but growing body of scholarship that argues for its conceptual utility.[6]

Whereas another twenty-first-century competitor, "world literature," traces its ancestry to the concerns of nineteenth-century German intellectuals in an increasingly connected and market-driven world, "the global Anglophone" is of more recent coinage. According to the *Oxford English Dictionary*, the word "Anglophone" originated in the imperial and linguistic specificities of early twentieth-century Canada. Because French speakers, following the French term for language users outside France itself, were termed "Francophones," their fellow Europeans who were English speakers came to be called "Anglophones." The term was thus useful in distinguishing between the language spheres marked by French and British colonialism, and this led to its expanded usage with the advent of decolonization. Thus, in the 1960s, what used to be termed "French Africa" and "British Africa" became a variety of independent postcolonial nations; when these regions nonetheless were described in their linguistic and historical commonality, they would be called "Francophone Africa" and "Anglophone Africa." As this shift suggests, a history of European colonialism was thereby signaled by highlighting the main European language in use: the "Anglophone" in this sense did not erase colonialism but, rather, highlighted its lasting effects. The word "Anglophone" thus evolved from a noun ("an Anglophone in Canada") to an adjective ("Anglophone Canada"). Within U.S. literary studies as indexed by the MLA International Bibliography, the term began to appear in the 1970s, with its utility as a linguistic modifier of a regional name—"Anglophone African literature"—transforming into an adjective that could modify literature itself—"Anglophone literature" (perhaps from Africa). In this shift, the adjective "Anglophone" came to stand in the place of the national descriptor—as in the phrases "British literature" and "American literature"—and, through a kind of self-authoring, a new noun form was born—"the Anglophone." Unlike the original noun, however, this one meant *not* an individual who speaks English but a *region*, real or imagined, where English is spoken. An additional modifier—usually "global," but sometimes "world"—was added to differentiate the older regional usage, making the regional a subset of a larger linguistic sphere. Thus, for instance, "Anglophone South Asian literature" is part of "the global Anglophone." As U.S. English departments in the late twentieth century increased their research, teaching, and (if modestly) hiring in English-language literatures beyond the United States and the United Kingdom, this broad category of "the global Anglophone" became increasingly prevalent in describing these literary interests. As this institutional utility indicates, it was defined by the absence of certain regions (the United States and the United Kingdom), but it nevertheless suggested expansiveness in its terminology rather than lack. In 2014, for instance, the MLA converted the "Division for the Study of English Literatures Other Than British and American" into a "Comparative Literary and Cultural Studies" forum called "Global Anglophone": a shorter name, and a contested one.[7]

In claiming "the global Anglophone" as central to this monograph, I thus approach a category that has a robust administrative and institutional life within literary studies, but less of a conceptual or scholarly purchase. "The global Anglophone" as I use it denotes an elastic space of discussion and exchange: thus, for instance, it includes writers from the Anglophone countries usually excluded (such as the then-U.S.-based W. E. B. Du Bois) as well as Anglophone writers from decidedly non-Anglophone regions (such as the Chinese intellectual Liang Qichao). To use "the global Anglophone" as I do for the early twentieth century is to commit a serious anachronism—and I do so in order to evidence what we may have already known. The linguistic dominance of English may seem a foregone conclusion only in the twenty-first century, but signs of its global reach, and the consequent global possibilities, were vibrant and varied even in the early twentieth century.

The study of the emergence of the global Anglophone, moreover, is particularly relevant to scholars concerned with the history of White supremacy. Anglophone colonies, and not Francophone, Hispanophone, or Lusophone ones, decisively spawned the concept of "White men's countries" and thereby created a strictly binarized White supremacism that became particularly influential in the twentieth century. Unlike the elaborate racial gradations of Spanish and Portuguese colonialism, or the *evolué* status selectively offered within French colonialism, Anglophone imperialism explicitly articulated a divide between White people and the rest of humanity. The Anglophone settler colonies (and later countries) of Canada, Australia, South Africa, and the United States became increasingly insistent on this division in their immigration and citizenship policies of the late nineteenth and early twentieth centuries. These countries, which remain central to the global Anglophone, consolidated Whiteness as a criterion of citizenship and, crucially, as a unifying category, alleviating conflicts between settlers of different European ancestry and enabling a rapprochement between British and U.S. imperialisms.[8]

In naming the current global dominance of the English language as a literary conceit, the global Anglophone thus recognizes in name what Tagore's 1913 prize announced in practice. The Nobel Prize, after all, may recognize authors working in any language and do so under the auspices of the Swedish Academy, yet its first recognition of non-European literature was of Tagore's *translated* collection: it only occurred once that literature was circulating in English. As a pioneering institution in the literary field, the Nobel Prize transformed the terrain of literary production into one of competition on a worldwide scale. With its conceit—that a worthy litterateur might be found every single year, through a process of worldwide comparison—the Nobel Prize rearticulated literature itself as a kind of sporting contest among nations, not unlike the sporting competitions of the Olympic Games, revived in 1894. Its advent in 1901 was contemporaneous with worldwide cultural expos like the World's Fair, but those stupendous demonstrations of the world's varied populations served a different purpose. Even as they assembled various peoples side by side for convenient comparison and imperial observation, the World's Fairs nonetheless championed cultural particularity and authenticity, usually through a focus on folk arts and popular forms. The Nobel Prize for Literature, by contrast, asserted that literature was a universal activity at its most rarefied level. Consequently, even as the prize celebrated individual authors, it showcased them as representative of a common human capacity for literature, transcending their cultural particulars precisely through their exemplarity for all. In

1913, the awarding of the prize to Tagore marked its transformation into a truly international competition: all of the dozen prior recipients had been European. Because Britain still ruled over India, however, Tagore's prize was regarded not only as an award to a British subject but also as evidence of the cultural and civilizational benefits of British rule in India. In this confusing juncture, his Nobel Prize made both British imperialists and Indian nationalists very proud. This vexed reception foreshadows the analogous contradictions in Tagore's subsequent embrace of an Asianist print internationalism.

Born in 1861 to a wealthy and influential family in an increasingly restive Bengal, Tagore soon became politically active, playing a crucial role in the Swadeshi movement against the partition of Bengal (1905–8). This agitation was successful in its demands and profoundly influenced later all-India campaigns—yet it marks the apex of Tagore's career as an anticolonial nationalist leader rather than its opening triumph. The Swadeshi agitation between 1905 and 1908, Tagore later lamented, was coercive in its methods even as it championed liberation. Whether in fiction or in prose, Tagore dramatized his disillusionment with Indian nationalism, and he did so in the colloquial Bengali of ordinary life, disclaiming any dreams of linguistic or cultural purity. When he won the Nobel in 1913, however, he had not yet committed his criticism of the West to print. In 1913, then, observers may have concluded that Tagore had abandoned anticolonialism along with political agitation. In 1916, King George V anointed Tagore a Knight of the British Empire, and that same year he delivered English-language lectures about—or, rather, against—nationalism in Japan and the United States, publishing them the following year in book form.[9] His novel *Ghare Baire* (*The Home and the World*), also published in 1916, appeared in English translation the following year, and it was widely read, in India as in Europe, as a critique of Indian nationalism. In conjunction, these events of 1916 suggested a clear moral: Tagore, critical of nationalism, had embraced instead the worldwide ambit of the British Empire.

"Sir Rabindranath," however, would not prove a sustainable persona, for Tagore soon articulated a trenchant anti-imperialism. In 1919, British troops massacred hundreds of unarmed Indian civilians who had peacefully congregated in Jallianwala Bagh, a walled garden in the northern city of Amritsar. Tagore protested, in part, by returning his knighthood. In a letter to the viceroy explaining his decision, Tagore's dissent was patriotic and his concerns partly national. In the published version of the letter, which appeared in the leading Indian periodical the

Modern Review, Tagore wrote of "the helplessness of our position as British subjects in India," claiming an undifferentiated colonial subjection as his own.[10] His role, he argued, required "giving voice to the protest of the millions of my countrymen, surprised into a dumb anguish of terror."[11] Thus assuming both solidarity and spokesmanship, Tagore returned his knighthood and declared: "I for my part wish to stand, shorn of all special distinctions, by the side of those of my countrymen who, for their so-called insignificance, are liable to suffer a degradation not fit for human beings."[12] Even during this explicitly patriotic action, however, Tagore grounded his nationalist commitment within humanist universals. His countrymen deserve his companionship in this particular crisis, but not simply because of their shared nationality. Rather, his actions reflect the nature of the violation: not simply the oppression of his fellow Indians, but "a degradation not fit for human beings." Commenting approvingly on Tagore's published letter, the editor of the *Modern Review*, Ramananda Chatterjee, drew two "lessons for us": that we should "acquire the power of helping ourselves" and simultaneously cultivate "a feeling of true brotherliness towards all."[13] Tagore's politics reflected this twofold structure, for he simultaneously rejected both of the era's reigning ideologies—anticolonial nationalism, with its privileging of "ourselves," and imperial globalism, with its false claims of including "all." Whether in print and in person, he instead developed an internationalism that could recalibrate the relations between the universal and the particular. He did so through a print internationalism that emphasized Asia, both in rhetoric and in practice, even as it operated through the English language.

I propose that Tagore can be positioned as the originator of a disruptive model for what we now know as "the global Anglophone": not only because of his 1913 Nobel Prize, which cited his English translation of his poetry, but also through his use of English to build an emphatically non-Eurocentric internationalism. In a global Anglophone that foregrounds Tagore's gitanjali, English is revealed as a conduit for other language cultures that can work through English to build a better—and not necessarily, in the end, Anglophone—world. In this recentering of the global Anglophone, moreover, I hope to displace its less flattering associations, as for instance its parallels to the literary usage of "the Francophone." The concept of "Francophone literature" originates in racial and geographical marginalization: it refers, within French-language literature, to writing in French by those outside continental France. Given this unpleasant act of boundary demarcation signaled in the term, "Francophonie" is often decried by the most celebrated of "Francophone" authors, many of whom would prefer to work within a linguistically and regionally unmarked remit like "Littérature-monde."[14]

The global Anglophone as I conceive it, however, reflects the difference in writing in English outside that language's imperial centers. Instead of naming, as in the Francophone model, the persistent desire for an isomorphism of language and nation, as in the confusing term "English literature"—from England? or in English? or both?—the global Anglophone can visualize the imperial continuities across the modern world. Whereas terms like "postcolonial literature" frequently necessitate distinctions between colonialisms old and new, the term "global Anglophone" emphasizes the effects of Anglo-American hegemony without demarcating its historical contours. The now-extensive scholarship on Tagore's *Nationalism* (1917) and *The Home and the World* has yielded a sophisticated understanding of Tagore's critique of nationalism.[15] By attending instead to his lesser-known texts, both published and unpublished, I theorize what he championed in nationalism's place: an Asia-centered print internationalism. Given Asia's linguistic diversity, this internationalism relied of necessity on the English language, even as it acknowledged that language's inextricability from Western imperialism. Consequently, this print practice reoriented the English language by using it for pan-Asianist purposes—creating, as I demonstrate, a vision for the global Anglophone in the process.

Tagore created an Asia-centered print internationalism within the global Anglophone by articulating interpretive protocols that he coded as quintessentially Asian. These protocols crystallize most powerfully, I argue, in the curious neologism that Tagore uses as the title of his famed 1912 poetry collection, *Gitanjali: Song Offerings*. Tagore's term "gitanjali" melds the Sanskritic Bengali words for song (*geet*) and religious offering (*anjali*) to invent a new, particularly literary and emphatically international, form of devotional practice. *Anjali* is a religious term, but "gitanjali"—Tagore's neologism—is not religious in any familiar sense. While Tagore's writings draw heavily on Hindu and folk forms of addressing the divine, his offerings, ultimately, are not to any divinity but to a humanist universalism—what he will describe in a 1927 preface to a Chinese poem as "an offering to the universal feast of mind."[16] The word *gitanjali* thus frames cultural particularity as an object of aesthetic contemplation—rather than, for instance, anthropological investigation or historical analysis. Through such contemplation, Tagore suggests, one can produce perceptual, and thereby political, transformations, using the offerings of widely different cultures as they circulate across the global Anglophone. *Gitanjali's* openly religious phrasing deploys the assumed ancient wisdom of the spiritual East, and its usage of an untranslated foreign word for its title likely suggested to its readers a text that would be authentically different. Importantly, Tagore's volume retains its untranslated neologism even in its existence as a translated collection of English-language texts.

The performance of linguistic recalcitrance in the bilingual title—*Gitanjali: Song Offerings*—is thus reaffirmed by what Tagore undertakes between *Gitanjali's* covers. The poems that he presents as translations of an original Bengali collection are not, on closer inspection, what we would consider translations at all. Yet the collection's poems proclaim an original that has been translated even as it refuses to maintain fidelity or even consistency in that act of translation, thus becoming, as William Radice puts it, a work "conceiv[ed] in translation without a precisely defined source."[17] As I demonstrate, the kinds of literary interpretation championed by Tagore, which he coded through the neologism crowning this collection, were uniquely suited to his conception of the global Anglophone as a vehicle for a liberatory print internationalism. I use the conceptual work thus undertaken by *Gitanjali*, both collection and neologism, to explore the intersection through which Tagore's print internationalism operated.

CREATING *THE IDEALS OF THE EAST*

Tagore's interest in the liberatory potential of Asia, and what he valorized as the essentially spiritual nature of Eastern civilization, is often attributed to his immersion in Western discourses of the exotic Orient. Tagore certainly associated the West with industrialization and mechanization, and he frequently denounced Western civilization as prizing the efficiency of the machinic over the magnitude of the spiritual. Yet Tagore's description of Eastern civilization is not simply that of an alternative to the West, wherein "the East" primarily names an inversion of Western priorities: feminine rather than manly, spiritual rather than materialistic, collectivist rather than individualistic, and so forth. His vision of Asia, rather, made specific claims of commonality, generated through his conversations with other Asians (and, in some key instances, non-Asian converts to Asian religions). Tagore deployed many of the existing stereotypes of Eastern mysticism and spirituality, and his Asianism can be justly criticized for its reification of these tropes. He built on these tropes, however, to situate Asia's legendary spirituality in interpretive practices rather than in embodied instincts. Through this process, the tropes became the evidence of practiced skills, for Tagore emphasized the aesthetic as a means of international transformation. This project was facilitated, in *Gitanjali* as elsewhere, by his deployment of Sanskritic words within Anglophone texts.[18] These untranslated words, which included existing terms as well as the key neologism "gitanjali," served as metonymic representations of Asia's shared religious inheritance.

Tagore's approach to pan-Asianism was shaped by an Anglophone manifesto of political aesthetics called *The Ideals of the East*, written in Kolkata (then spelled Calcutta) by the Japanese art historian Okakura Kakuzō and published in London with a preface by the Irish-born Hindu leader Sister Nivedita. Shaped by Okakura's expertise in Japanese art and Nivedita's knowledge of reformist Hinduism, this 1903 text would define the emphases of Tagore's print internationalism. Making Okakura's and Nivedita's emphases his own, Tagore located the fundamental unity of Asia in our ability to interpret, across borders, the values of seemingly disparate aesthetic signs. To set up this chapter's analysis of the print internationalism signaled in Tagore's neologism "gitanjali," I will first discuss the one created by Okakura and Nivedita.

Although this print internationalism is now remembered in association with Asian men, it was crucially facilitated from its very inception by a seemingly unrelated demographic: White women. In 1900, the Japanese art historian Okakura Kakuzō (岡倉覚三, also known as Okakura Tenshin, 1863–1913) gave a series of lectures on Asian art at his Tokyo home.[19] In the audience was an American convert to Hinduism, Josephine MacLeod, who had moved to India in 1898. After the talk, McLeod invited Okakura to India to meet her guru, Swami Vivekananda (né Narendranath Datta, 1863–1902), the Kolkata-based champion of a muscular Hinduism marked by nationalism, evangelism, and a theory of nondualism called *advaita*. Okakura arrived in Kolkata on January 6, 1902, and stayed in India for nine months, residing for most of that time at the Tagore family home. He struck up what would become an extended conversation with Rabindranath Tagore, and their friendship has often been credited for the versions of pan-Asianism espoused by both thinkers.[20]

Tagore's Asianist internationalism, much like Okakura's before him, was not a narrative of native expression, whether Bengali, Japanese, or simply "Asian." Rather, it embraced the possibilities of reinvention, wherein for instance a simple book of poems in English translation could become a gitanjali: an aesthetic act of transcendental devotion. While Tagore was undoubtedly influenced by Okakura, his print internationalism equally suggests the influence of Okakura's most sustained collaborator in India: Sister Nivedita (1867–1911). Born Margaret Elizabeth Noble to a Scottish family in what is now Northern Ireland, she worked as an activist and educator in the United Kingdom before moving to India in 1898. A devotee of Vivekananda, she assumed the name "Sister Nivedita." In person and in print, Nivedita powerfully expressed the ideal of India as more a civilizational principle than a racial inheritance. Asian by conversion if not by descent, Nivedita dreamed of a spiritually enlightened Asia, one in which India, Japan, and China would delight in their commonly defined religious inheritance. Although this commonality lay in the connections between Hinduism and Buddhism, as a fervent Hindu, she named it simply Hinduism. Nivedita's nonracial yet Indian essentialism was crucial for Okakura's vision of pan-Asianism, and it would come in turn to decisively shape Tagore's print internationalism. While the dominant narrative of a private friendship between Okakura and Tagore suggests a reassuring authenticity in these influential Asians' expressions of pan-Asianism, it does so by ignoring the copious contributions of Nivedita. Such elision may be in keeping with the biases of both cultural authenticity and transcultural patriarchy, but it jars uncomfortably with the priorities of the Asianist vision under discussion. Both Okakura and Tagore, after all, labored to demonstrate that the values they attributed to Asia were transmitted not through blood but through cultivation. This emphasis informs my decision here to highlight Nivedita's contribution, for she was after all that which both men encouraged: Asian by choice, not simply by birth.

During Okakura's yearlong residence in Tagore's Kolkata home, his close collaboration with Nivedita resulted in two book-length manuscripts. Only one of these, *The Ideals of the East*, would be published in either of their lifetimes. (Their second manuscript, now known as *The Awakening of the East*, was "discovered" only in 1938 and circulated primarily in the context of aggressive Japanese expansion in Asia.) *The Ideals of the East* was published from London in 1903 under Okakura's name, with an introduction by Nivedita. The publisher, John Murray, added his own prefatory note: "Mr. Murray wishes to point out that this book is written in English by a native of Japan." As this note suggests, the authorship of this text was itself a prized performance. As an English-language text "by a native of Japan," *The Ideals of the*

East promised both authenticity and accessibility, much as Tagore's self-translated *Gitanjali* would a decade later.

Yet whereas *Gitanjali* expressed its print internationalism through its approach to inhabiting the global Anglophone—in the untranslated neologism of its title, for instance, or its iconoclastic approach to poetry translation—*The Ideals of the East* hewed to the existing practices of English-language writing. It was written from the start in English, which it used in an accessible and conventional fashion: no translation, disruptive or otherwise, was required. Consequently, the print internationalism of *The Ideals of the East* was easily obscured, evident only to those who knew to look for it, perhaps because they knew of Okakura's Indian sojourn and his collaboration with Nivedita. For all other readers, however, the text could easily serve, as John Murray prominently claimed, as a text "in English" by a Japanese "native."

My reading makes that latent print internationalism evident, highlighting the print internationalism of Okakura's text by delineating Nivedita's crucial contributions. Nivedita's introduction asserts that an understanding of Asia's transcendent wholeness can have immediate effects, for instance in one's ability to effectively preserve cultural heritage. To prove her point, she narrates Okakura's trip to the Ajanta caves in western India, famed for their Buddhist sculptures. Likely made between the second century B.C.E. and the sixth century C.E., these Indian sculptures found their salvation in this Japanese visitor, for Okakura's

> acquaintance with the art of the same period in Southern China enabled him to see at once that the stone figures now remaining in the caves had been intended originally merely as the bone or foundation of the statues, all the life and movement of the portrayal having been left to be worked into a deep layer of plaster with which they were afterwards covered.[21]

Okakura, according to Nivedita, can thus distinguish "the bone or foundation" of an artwork from its "life or movement": through his familiarity not only with his native Japan but also the neighboring country of China, he can travel to yet another Asian location, India, and immediately apprehend the essential forms of Asian art from earlier millennia. Because he understands, as the title puts it, "the ideals of the East," he can "see at once" what "had been intended" by Asian artists now long dead.

The superior perception of Asia can thus overcome divides of space and time, and it has lasting consequences as well. Approaching these sculptures in India as though they were exclusively a part of Indian art would have led to their damaging misrecognition, resulting in what Nivedita describes as "an unfortunate amount of 'cleaning' and unintentional disfigurement."[22] But thanks to his internationalist sensibility, Okakura recognizes the true forms of art and thus saves the artwork from a disastrous fate, not only for Indians but for Asians everywhere.

Whether in Nivedita's introduction or in Okakura's main text, *The Ideals of the East* thus posits a perception that bridges the sacred and the secular. This explicit embrace of religious modes makes their print internationalism decisively different from the operations of print nationalism. The emergence of print nationalism, in Anderson's formulation, required the supersession of the singular languages of religious communities by the interchangeable languages of the imagined communities of nationalism. The emergence of this Asianist internationalism, however, posits the sacred as immersive, essential to print internationalism's interpretive community. This is a singular semiotics that can interpret the remnants of an Asia that once was, thereby rendering evident an Asian unity yet to come. Such an explicit melding of the sacred and the secular becomes a key aspect of Tagore's print internationalism. We find this melding signaled in the sacral tones of Tagore's gitanjali, whose guiding notion of devotional aesthetics Tagore drew from Okakura and Nivedita. Gitanjali, with its iconoclastic linguistic sensibility, enables the formation of communities at once more extensive than the nation and still immediate in their concerns.

Tagore's gitanjali further builds on *The Ideals of the East* in invoking its reshaping of a continent into a conceptual geography. Whether in Nivedita's introduction or Okakura's main text, *The Ideals of the East* embraces a flexible geography for Asia, suggesting that it is at once oceanic, in their repeated use of aquatic metaphors, and terrestrial, as in Okakura's famous opening paragraph:

> ASIA is one. The Himalayas divide, only to accentuate, two mighty civilizations, the Chinese with its communism of Confucius, and the Indian with its individualism of the Vedas. But not even the snowy barriers can interrupt for one moment that broad expanse of love for the Ultimate and Universal, which is the common thought-inheritance of every Asiatic race, . . . distinguishing them from those maritime peoples of

> the Mediterranean and the Baltic, who love to dwell on the Particular, and to search out the means, not the end, of life.[23]

The commonalities of "every Asiatic race" distinguish them from another collective category, the "maritime peoples of the Mediterranean and the Baltic." Despite their presently limited political power and lack of military prowess, *The Ideals of the East* suggests, their love of the "Universal" and the "Ultimate" is superior to the latter's pursuit of the "Particular" and the expedient. Before dividing East and West, however, we are first told of the divide within that single Asia, separating two civilizations—Chinese and Indian—marked by "communism" and "individualism," respectively. Okakura refers to them later as "the two great poles of Asiatic civilization,"[24] thus spreading out a single Asia without splitting it apart. Whereas Gandhi would write, six years later, of exactly two civilizations—Indian and Western—Okakura's innovation, heavily informed by Nivedita's Hindu faith, is to assert that civilizations can be binarized but not enumerated. This claim is maintained in Tagore's Asianist enthusiasms, and it enables a productive fuzziness at the center of his conception of Asia. Much as premodern dynastic societies were defined around a radiating center of power rather than through the demarcated borders of nation-states, so too this Asia has "two great poles" and a "broad expanse" surrounding them—another crucial difference from the imagined spatial consistency of Anderson's print nationalism, where borders define the imagined community's shared geography. The text moves from this assertion of singularity and dualities to a description of various racial migrations. These remarks culminate in the text's articulation of Asia's racial linkages: "For if Asia be one, it is also true that the Asiatic races form a single mighty web."[25] As the web metaphor suggests, the inter-Asian connections are multiple and often discontinuous, even as the final reality is "a single mighty" unity across races. This is not quite the network metaphor so prevalent in our twenty-first-century moment, but it possesses many of its conceptual strengths, enabling the gaps between its various nodes (in this case, races) to be constitutive of an apprehensible whole.

In creating a "web" model of Asia's interconnected differences, moreover, both Okakura and Nivedita rely on an eclectic understanding of Asia's religious inheritance, combining Buddhism, Confucianism, Daoism, and Hinduism. Okakura explains in his opening pages that "we forget, in an age of classification, that types are after all but shining points of distinctness in an ocean of approximations, false gods deliberately set up to be worshipped, for the sake of mental convenience."[26] This vivid image of light glinting on water renders cultural variation at once stunning and insubstantial: an optical illusion manifesting itself on a surface that betokens unfathomed depths. In understanding nations as merely "false gods," moreover, Okakura draws on nineteenth-century Bengali debates around the essential monotheism of Hinduism's lived polytheism, debates in which Nivedita herself had participated.

These religiously informed discussions reveal Nivedita's most substantial contribution to the book: the nondualist school of Hindu philosophy known as *advaita*, which constitutes just a minor strain in Japanese Buddhism but nonetheless became essential to Okakura's Asianism. In *advaita* philosophy, the recognition that the differentiation experienced in daily life was an illusion (*maya*) enabled an individual to seek greater unity with the universe. As Okakura glossed the concept in his diary from Kolkata in 1902:

> The word *adwaita* [*sic*] means the state of not being two, and is the name applied to the great Indian doctrine that all which exists, though apparently manifold, is really one. Hence all truth must be discoverable in any single differentiation, the whole universe involved in every detail. All thus becomes equally precious.[27]

The *advaita* framework of *The Ideals of the East* led to a marked conceptual difference between Nivedita's and Okakura's, and later Tagore's, Asia-centered print internationalism and the pan-Asianisms of their contemporaries. Whereas other versions of pan-Asianism in the same period would draw on linguistic history (such as that of classical Chinese), or on the Confucian and Daoist notion of the kingly way (*wangdao* 王道), the Asianism spawned by Nivedita and Okakura and, as I discuss in the following pages, spread by Tagore would always emphasize the single entity that merely appears to be multiple. This Asia is a "united breathing organism" in Nivedita's introduction, and "a single mighty web" in Okakura's text: it is an "ocean of approximations" that is "divide[d] only to accentuate" its unity.

Most importantly, *The Ideals of the East* produces an interpretive matrix which will come to animate Tagore's sustained interest in East Asian art and literature. The difficulties of distinguishing between the good and the bad of modernity can be resolved, Okakura suggests, through a distinction between technique and ideals. This claim echoes Okakura's famous 1882 disagreement with the painter Koyama Shōtarō (小山正太郎, 1857–1916), who claimed, in a manifesto of this title, that "calligraphy is not art." Okakura intervened to defend one of Japan's most esteemed art forms, and he did so by shifting the emphasis away from the methods of artistic expression—such as calligraphy, painting, or sculpture. Rather than debate how Japan's calligraphic tradition would fit within the genre taxonomies of Western art, Okakura argued that art should be judged not by how it is made, but by the ethical vision expressed in the final work. Twenty years later, writing from India for all of Asia, Okakura would repeat this move in *Ideals of the East*, presenting the difference between technique and ideals as a widely available route for cultural revitalization. He explains: "Technique is thus but the weapon of artistic warfare; scientific knowledge of anatomy and perspective, the commissariat that sustains the army. . . . Ideals, in turn, are the modes in which the artistic mind moves, a plan of campaign which the nature of the country imposes on war."[28] By establishing this distinction between the techniques of art and its substantive ideals, Okakura laid the groundwork for much of Tagore's project. His division authorized Tagore's later investment in the global Anglophone as the medium for his Asia-centered print internationalism. Nivedita's work with Okakura, written and published in English, demonstrated that *The Ideals of the East* could, quite literally, deploy "the weapon" of the English language in service of Asia's "artistic mind." Despite the European origins of the English language, the global Anglophone thus became a legitimate "weapon of artistic warfare," expressing an Asian-centered vision of the future by Okakura and Nivedita, and by Tagore as well. *Gitanjali*'s more complex inhabitation of the global Anglophone would thus fulfill the articulation that Okakura and Nivedita's text had expressed, giving that vision an aesthetic form.

SANSKRIT FOR THE GLOBAL ANGLOPHONE

Why did Tagore reach through English to Sanskrit to accomplish his print internationalism, as he did with his collection's title, *Gitanjali*? While this strategy may seem at first glance designed chiefly to appeal to the Western reader, we find Tagore using the same method in his most crucial *Indian* discussion: his published disagreements with M. K. "Mahatma" Gandhi. Even as Tagore moved from nationalism to internationalism in the second decade of the twentieth century, the Indian anticolonial movement expanded massively in its scale and its ambitions during this same period—a shift often attributed to Gandhi's return to India in 1915. Gandhi had invented his methods of nonviolent resistance, known as satyagraha, while in South Africa, and on returning to India he led several smaller protests on the same model. Tagore was both a friend and a comrade, an interlocutor and an admirer, of Gandhi's, but as Gandhi's politics evolved, Tagore's admiration came to be accompanied by skepticism. In 1919, Gandhi organized his first all-India satyagraha, and in 1920, fusing the energies of the Khilafat movement and the outrage against the Jallianwala Bagh massacre, he launched an all-India satyagraha campaign called the noncooperation movement.[29] Centering on the boycott of all things foreign, the noncooperation movement particularly advocated the mass abandonment of British institutions of education and the public immolation of foreign fabrics. Whereas the first two tactics had been used with some success in the Swadeshi movement of 1905 to 1908—which, as we saw earlier, Tagore had prominently supported—Gandhi added a new component that came to decisively distinguish his mobilizations from earlier Indian protests. The Swadeshi agitation of 1905–8 had asked its supporters to replace their foreign fabrics with those made in Indian textile mills. Gandhi's noncooperation movement of 1920 to 1922, by contrast, asked its supporters to abandon industrial mills altogether, regardless of the mill's ownership or location. Instead, supporters were told to make and wear the homespun fabric known as *khadi*.

As Gandhi's noncooperation movement gained in strength and influence, Tagore launched a public critique of Gandhi's political strategy. In a series of published exchanges in 1921 and 1925, Tagore and Gandhi engaged in an increasingly acrimonious debate, one interrupted only by Gandhi's imprisonment from 1922 to 1924 and by Tagore's trip to China in 1924.[30] Despite both leaders' preference for Indian languages—Tagore for Bengali, and Gandhi for Gujarati—their much-publicized debate took place within the language of English. The irony was considerable: Tagore began this debate, for instance, with a salvo that dismissed nationalism on the basis of linguistic evidence. He proclaimed: "We have no word for 'Nation' in our language. When we borrow this word from other people, it never fits us."[31] Lexicographers may or may not concur with Tagore's philological assertion, yet the phrasing of his objection only generates more questions. Who comprises Tagore's imagined collectivity of "us," for which the word "nation" cannot serve? The plural pronoun "we" is undefined, and it is further confused by the confident use of the singular noun with the plural possessive, for he writes of "our language" in reference to a subcontinent that is famously multilingual.

For Tagore, even the repackaging of nationalist concepts under Indic names is insufficient: "However we may delude ourselves with the phrases learnt from the West, Swaraj is not our objective."[32] The simplicity of Tagore's sentence belies its strategic obfuscation: what, exactly, are "the phrases learnt from the West" that would lead to the adoption of "Swaraj," an ostentatiously non-Western word, as "our objective"? Leaving this ambiguity unresolved, Tagore continues to dismantle the term "Swaraj," a key term in Gandhi's version of anticolonialism, which is usually translated as "self-rule," and which Gandhi preferred to terms like "swatantra," a common competitor with a more obvious emphasis on governance. Tagore argues, in this English-language essay, that "swaraj" is just "maya," a Sanskrit word with cosmic significance that indicates the illusory nature of what we perceive as reality.[33] He thus provides Sanskrit to Sanskrit translation, but within the language of English. This is a nexus of linguistic interchange that defies our existing theorizations of the translated and the untranslated.

As these examples suggest, even when debating his compatriots, Tagore relied on the strategy of linguistic interruption through untranslated words that he had first devised in his print internationalism. In these debates with Gandhi, the English language serves Tagore as both a medium and a metaphor. For instance, Tagore asserts that whereas previous nationalist leaders had deluded the country with their inflated rhetoric, Gandhi communicated in a substantial fashion that exceeded elite language:

> Previously, the vision of our political leaders had never reached beyond the English-knowing classes, because the country meant for them only that bookish aspect of it which is to be found in the pages of the Englishman's history. Such a country was merely a mirage born of vapourings in the English language. . . . At this juncture, Mahatma Gandhi came and stood at the cottage door of the destitute millions, clad as one of themselves, and talking to them at last in their own language. Here was the truth at last, not a mere quotation out of a book.[34]

The transformation here is both of medium and of language: rather than a country represented by "a mirage born of vapourings in the English language" and praised by "a mere quotation out of a book," Gandhi presents "the truth at last" and does so to "the destitute millions" in "their own language." The linguistic reference is metaphorical—India's millions, after all, speak many different languages—as is the framing device of Gandhi standing "at the cottage door." Yet with this metaphor Tagore praises Gandhi as embodying "the truth at last," through clothing and perhaps through speech.

Tagore's contributions were all published in the *Modern Review*, a Kolkata-based monthly periodical edited by Ramananda Chatterjee whose content, circulation, and cosmopolitan sensibility register it indubitably, I would suggest, as part of the global Anglophone. Widely regarded as the premier English-language periodical of late colonial India, it served as both a literary revue and a political newspaper. Tagore's views consequently appeared in volumes of well over a hundred pages in length, amid features that varied widely across politics, literature, science, archaeology, and the arts; a smattering of full-page advertisements; and a cover image of strikingly original contemporary art.

Tagore first published his misgivings about the noncooperation movement in May 1921, and he did so in an intimate first-person voice explicitly addressed neither to Gandhi nor to his readers.[35] He published, instead, three letters that he had written, while in Chicago and then New York, to the Anglican priest and anticolonial activist Charles Freer Andrews (1871–1940).[36] Tagore's opening salvo in the debate thus mimicked the format of an epistolary novel, appearing under the minimalist title "Letters from Rabindranath Tagore." He opened the first letter by explaining that he has been unable to "tune my mood of mind to be in accord with the great feeling of excitement sweeping across my country," so he has turned instead to poetry, "playing with inventing new metres."[37] This seemingly trivial artistic activity has wider political significance, he explains, because inventing metres is akin to a social principle that he terms "the law of co-operation." Tagore writes that this law "was what the metre is in poetry, which is not a mere system of enclosure for keeping ideas from running away in disorder, but for vitalising them, making them indivisible in a unity of creation."[38] Gandhi's movement of noncooperation to which Tagore objects is thus a violation of laws both social and aesthetic: by severing the ordering principles of human existence, it yields not politics but chaos. It creates poetry bereft of meter—which, as Tagore suggests, lacks any "unity of creation" that would give it meaning. As elsewhere in his print internationalism, Tagore's understanding of Indian politics remains animated by gitanjali: poetry, not practicality, is a guiding principle. He consistently advances a musical understanding of anticolonialism, writing of "the music of this wonderful awakening of India by love."[39] In trying to join this awakening, though, he discovered a "mighty volume" of "shouts":

> And what is this noise about me? If it is a song, then my own *sitar* [stringed instrument] can catch the tune and I join in the chorus, for I am a singer. But if it is a shout, then my voice is wrecked and I am lost in bewilderment. I have been trying all these days to find in it a melody, straining my ear, but the idea of non-cooperation with its mighty volume of sound does not sing to me, its congregated menace of negation shouts.[40]

Despite Tagore's perception of a "congregated menace of negation," the noncooperation movement did mark a significant positive moment of collaboration, as non-Muslims rallied around the Muslim-identified Khilafat cause. The "negation" of British goods, moreover, was paired with the emphatic affirmation of homespun *khadi* fabric, as Gandhi encouraged not only the wearing of *khadi* but its creation within the home. By spinning on the *charkha* (spinning wheel) to make *khadi*—a practice that would become iconic of Gandhi himself—any individual could join Gandhi's agitation, without even leaving home.

And yet, Tagore's advocacy of a musical and poetic project of anticolonial liberation could not incorporate the advocacy of hand-spinning. Much like Okakura and Nivedita, who argued that the final vision in a created work was more important than its techniques of creation, so too Tagore condemned Gandhi's advocacy of spinning as the advocacy of a mere method, no matter how indigenous, rather than the expression of ideals through an appropriate creative means. Gandhi called on all Indians to spin for half an hour every day, regardless of their aptitude, disposition, or profession. Tagore was a champion of the folk arts, yet he vehemently refused to spin, much to the dismay of his contemporaries. The spinning of *khadi* failed to qualify for him as a form of worshipful aesthetic activity: that is, as a gitanjali that might contribute to collective advancement. In his published disagreement, Tagore described Gandhi's followers as at once "immensely busy" and "intensely afraid," motivated by "an unquestioning obedience" to what he termed Gandhi's magical formula: boycotts and spinning.[41] Spinning, in Tagore's opinion, provided a distracting "relief" from the difficulties of anticolonial liberation, enabling Gandhi's followers to ignore "the defects of character and the perversions of social custom" that are the real obstacles to meaningful liberation.[42] He argued that "the whole attention is concentrated on home spun thread, no surprise is felt but rather relief." Tagore laments that Gandhi's politics, while opposed to the standardizing impulses of modernity in its intentions, retains an impersonal standardization in its message: "To one and all he simply says: Spin and weave, spin and weave."[43] Spinning creates thread, but is not a creative act, "for in turning the wheel man merely becomes an appendage of the *charkha*; that is to say, he but does himself what a machine might have done: he converts his living energy into a dead turning movement."[44]

Spinning thus marks the limits of the devotional aesthetics that Tagore championed as gitanjali. Instead of producing various forms that figure an underlying unity of spirit, as in his approach to Asian literature, spinning produces a single product—the thread that becomes the homespun fabric *khadi*—through a single activity. It thereby dulls the individual spirit into a mechanical or animalistic uniformity, rendering humans akin to bees, spiders, and "mill-turning bullock[s]."[45] This criticism of Gandhi's agenda can help us to understand the particularity of Tagore's Asianist aesthetics, not only in comparison to his Indian contemporaries but also in relation to Western aesthetic theory. In Western philosophy, art has long been defined by the value of purposelessness, a criterion that distinguishes the useful realm of craft from the valorized realm of art, whether in the cherished disinterest of Immanuel Kant's critique of aesthetic judgment or the championed autonomy of Theodor Adorno's work of art. Tagore's critique, however, concerned monotony and consistency, not utility or necessity. The aesthetic for him required humans' reshaping of the material world in the process of creation, regardless of the nature of the original materials. His advocacy of Asian aesthetics could, consequently, accommodate works that were poorly made, or even made using foreign materials, as long as they still expressed ideals—perhaps, we might say, expressed *The Ideals of the East*. Tagore's Asianism could not include the indigenous monotony of *khadi* cloth, no matter how much it enabled Asia's political liberation, nor how faithfully it used the Asian mechanism of the *charkha*.

As these two Indian icons debated Indian politics in the Anglophone public sphere, they resorted to quoting extensively from the language that leveled regional differences but magnified those of caste, class, and religion: Sanskrit. Through these Sanskritisms, they created within their English-language debate a frisson of the secretive knowledge of a Brahmin past. Whereas Tagore inserted untranslated Sanskrit to suggest that his quotidian objections would enable the consideration of ultimate ideals, Gandhi incorporated Sanskrit quotations only to transform those abstractions into concrete commandments. For instance, Tagore concluded his essay "The Call of Truth" (August 1921) with a quotation from Sanskrit verse: it is transliterated into Roman script but not translated into English, and is devoid of any attribution:

> Yo ékōvarno vahudā shakti yōgāt
> Varnānanekān nihitārthodadhāti
> Vichaiti chānte vishwamādau
> Sa no buddhyā subhayā samyunaktu![46]

As only the most elite of his readers would have recognized, Tagore's entirely unexplained culminating quotation is taken from the *Shvetashvatara Upanishad*, one of a set of ancient texts composed in the first and second millennia B.C.E. Intended for careful recitation, these verses were preserved primarily through oral transmission and only secondarily through textual inscription. The verse in its most conventional form reads:

> य एकोऽवर्णो बहुधा शक्तियोगाद्वर्णाननेकान्निहितार्थो दधाति ।
> विचैति चान्ते विश्वमादौ च देवः स नो बुद्ध्या शुभया संयुनक्तु ॥
> (*Shvetashvatara Upanishad* 4.1)
>
> Who alone, himself without color, wielding his power creates variously countless colors, and in whom the universe comes together at the beginning and dissolves in the end—may he furnish us with lucid intelligence.[47]

Given this Upanishad's focus on a theistic argument for the unity of the divine, Tagore's deployment of this verse, untranslated, moved his essay from a concrete discussion of contemporary nationalism into the epochal contemplation of divinity itself. As this example demonstrates, even Tagore's most explicitly political publications culminate in a chant of prayer. There is no form of truly creative writing, it seems, that does not in Tagore's hands become a form of gitanjali.

Tagore quotes scripture again in 1925, this time to argue for an internal vision of liberation that will be more than the "heaps of thread and piles of cloth" that he dismisses as Gandhi's platform.[48] Instead of a single activity that can be replicated individually across all of India, Tagore champions the initial fulfillment of a comprehensive ideal for what liberation would mean, even if only on a limited scale. Tagore declares:

> That which we would achieve for the whole of India must be actually made true even in some small corner of it. . . . Then only shall we know the real value of self-determination, *na medhaya na bahudha srutena*, not by reasoning nor by listening to lectures, but by direct experience.[49]

The "small corner" thus serves as an inspirational example, enabling Indians to generate a vision that is positive in its aspirations, not merely anti-Western in its goals. This ideal, once realized, can reverberate through "the whole of India." In making this pragmatic suggestion, Tagore quotes from the *Mundaka Upanishad*, which is known for its attack on ritual and its valorization of an internal approach to the divine.

Whereas Tagore in his earlier quotation from the Upanishads presented a verse in its entirety without any explanation, in this later instance he includes only part of the line and also provides a faithful gloss of its contents. The original verse reads:

> नायमात्मा प्रवचनेन लभ्यो
> न मेधया न बहुना श्रुतेन
> (*Mundaka Upanishad*, 3.2.3)
>
> This self cannot be grasped,
> by teachings or by intelligence,
> or even by great learning.[50]

In both instances, Tagore chooses one of the later verses in the Upanishads, and in each he quotes a section which transformed his worldly discussion of political strategy into a metaphorical image for a larger spiritual process. The passage in which this quotation occurs valorizes a self that is cosmic, whose transcendental connections Tagore associates with "the real value of self-determination," more so than mere political autonomy.

TAGORE'S CHINA

Toward the end of these debates with Gandhi, Tagore undertook a trip of which he had long dreamed: to China. China was a sustained interest for Tagore, one that culminated in his establishment of an institute for Chinese studies (Cheena-Bhavana) at his Visva-Bharati University in 1937. Whereas his travel diaries for his other Asian voyages, such as his trips to Japan and to Indonesia, would be published in Bengali, for his China trip Tagore published his talks in English, a choice which makes that volume particularly apposite to our discussion. Tagore emerged on the Chinese literary scene amid discussions of India as a cautionary tale of Asian decline, for instance in the work of the reformer Kang Youwei (康有為 1858–1927). Yet Tagore's international celebrity generated considerable interest, with some Chinese reformers wondering if he might serve as a cultural exemplar and potential model for a rapidly changing China. His work was first published in China in 1915; less than fifteen years later, he had been the subject of at least 350 essays and eighteen book-length translations, not to mention a considerable number of shorter published translations.[51]

To take Tagore in China seriously, we must first dismiss an assumption commonplace in much contemporary criticism—that translation, via the circuit of the global Anglophone, delimits all future reception. Even though Tagore's works were mediated through English, in Asia as in Europe, they were often differently understood in those two continents. *The Home and the World*, for instance, was read in diametrically opposite ways by Western and Chinese Marxists. Georg Lukács's polemical review of *The Home and the World*, which he published in 1920 under the title "Tagore's Gandhi novel," famously condemned it as a libelous pamphlet, understanding it as a long attack on Gandhi and describing Tagore as England's "intellectual agent in the struggle against the Indian freedom movement."[52] Chinese readers, by contrast, read Tagore's works only to conclude that his politics were synonymous with those of Gandhi.[53] Chinese-language readers of *The Home and the World* might have read any one of three different Chinese translations, but all three translators worked from the translation (into English) that Tagore and his nephew Surendranath Tagore had generated. Whereas recent scholars have worked to reconcile Chinese understandings of Tagore's novel with Bengali ones,[54] what is more interesting, for our purposes, is the divergence enabled through multiple moments of translation. As this example demonstrates, translation not only creates equivalences across languages but also, and simultaneously, generates new forms of incommensurability. This is not the incommensurability of untranslatability, wherein a term or concept cannot find its equivalent in another language world, but an incommensurability born of the unpredictable *consequences* of translation: an effect of translation, and perhaps a history of untranslatability, but not an impediment to it. When it comes to Tagore in China, activities of translation produce not standardization but a seemingly endless multiplication of possibilities (a pattern evident as recently as 2013, when Feng Tang's [冯唐 b. 1971] new Chinese translation of Tagore's *Stray Birds* generated outrage and controversy). The translation of Tagore from English into Chinese sometimes echoed the choices made in the earlier translation of Tagore's Bengali manuscripts into the English language. For instance, much as *Gitanjali* had been untranslated in the title of its English text and transliterated phonetically into the Roman alphabet, it was similarly untranslated for the Chinese edition and transliterated as *Jitanjiali* 吉檀迦利. In this instance, moreover, the process of transliteration offered its own resources for shaping meaning and conditioning reception: the title was transliterated through the method used for transporting Buddhist terminology into Chinese. Because of these nontranslational methods, Chinese-language readers, perhaps even more than their English-language peers, approached *Gitanjali* anticipating, from its very title, to read a spiritual text.

The most significant Tagore collection in China, however, was neither the *Gitanjali* of his Nobel Prize citation, nor the novel *Ghare Baire* (*The Home and the World*, 1916), which has received so much attention in recent U.S. scholarship.[55] The greatest literary impact of Tagore in China was made by *The Crescent Moon* (*Xinyue ji* 新月集) poetry collection of 1913, with the 1916 collection *Stray Birds* (*Feiniao ji* 飛鳥集) a close second. These two collections, unlike *Gitanjali*, circulated in Chinese under translated titles (and not transliterated ones). Both *The Crescent Moon* and *Stray Birds* were only modestly successful in the West, and they are relatively unknown outside China even today. Unlike the more somber and explicitly theological *Gitanjali*, *The Crescent Moon* contained what the subtitle termed "child-poems": brief prose poems, usually centered around a single evocative image or a simple narrative about two characters. Like *Gitanjali* the previous year, these poems were translated by Tagore himself, yet they were conspicuously devoid of the archaic English diction (such as the use of "thou") and the direct address to the Divine found in the performed anachronism of Tagore's *Gitanjali*. Whereas the English-language *Gitanjali* included an influential preface by the Irish poet W. B. Yeats, the English-language *The Crescent Moon* collection lacked any framing by other writers. It did, however, contain eight color illustrations by Nandalal Bose (1882–1966), Asit Kumar Haldar (1890–1964), Abanindranath Tagore (1871–1951), and Surendranath Ganguly (1885–1909). These paintings were all in the Orientalist style of the Bengal School of Art, which rejected Western styles of perspective and mimesis in favor of a flat plane of representation and the figural methods of Japanese wash painting. In picking up *The Crescent Moon*, the Chinese reader of Tagore's Anglophone volume would have found a book that, despite its use of English, was at once distinctively new and recognizably Asian. Through the inclusion of these images, Tagore once again positioned his English-language poetry within the global Anglophone even as it pulled readers outside it: much as the untranslated title, anachronistic phrasing, and iconoclastic translations of *Gitanjali* performed the disruptive presence of other languages, elsewhere, so too the Asianist illustrations of *The Crescent Moon* disturbed its pages of otherwise conventional English-language usage.

Sisir Kumar Das has described in detail the relations between the English poems of *The Crescent Moon* and its Bengali sources, foremost among them the 1903 collection *Shishu* (*The Child*), where one finds the originals for thirty-five of the forty poems.[56] This divergence reflects, in part, the considerable temporal gap between these poems' composition and their translation into English. *Shishu* was written in 1903, shortly after the death of Tagore's wife, and it was intended to console his twelve-year-old daughter, who herself was sick with an illness that would prove fatal. A decade later, Tagore was working at the height of his worldwide acclaim, translating thirty-five of these poems for entry into the global Anglophone, at a time when U.S. and U.K. publishers were clamoring for his material.[57]

While *Shishu* is a text suitable for reading aloud to children, *The Crescent Moon* is intended for an adult reader, its complete sentences inviting solitary and silent contemplation. The Bengali poems frequently rely on the consistent rhythmic patterns typical of children's poetry, in keeping with Tagore's sustained interest in the improvisational women's genre known as *chhara*. The English poems, by contrast, provide the reassuring repetition of assonance, not the steady patter of children's rhyme. An indicative example can be found in the poem "Birpurush" (literally, "Valiant Man") in *Shishu*, translated as "Hero" in *The Crescent Moon*:

মনে করো যেন বিদেশ ঘুরে
    মাকে নিয়ে যাচ্ছি অনেক দূরে।
তুমি যাচ্ছ পালকিতে মা চড়ে
দরজা দুটো একটুকু ফাঁক করে,
আমি যাচ্ছি রাঙা ঘোড়ার 'পরে
    টগবগিয়ে তোমার পাশে পাশে।

রাস্তা থেকে ঘোড়ার খুরে খুরে
    রাঙা ধুলোয় মেঘ উড়িয়ে আসে।

Mone koro jano bidesh ghure
    Maake niye jacchi onek dure.
Tumi jaccho palkite ma chore
Dorja duto ektuku phank kore,
Ami jacchi ranga ghorar pore
    Togbagiye tomar pashe pashe.
Rasta theke ghorar khure khure
    Ranga dhuloy megh uriye ashe.

The simple rhyme scheme unfolds in eight even lines, usually a trochaic pentameter but with the occasional dactyl or spondee thrown in. The overall effect is that of a galloping horse, with the nontrochaic feet occurring on onomatopoeic or descriptive words (*ektuku*, *togbagiye*). In *The Crescent Moon*, however, Tagore removes the rhyme scheme entirely, creating a poignant opening passage marked by fear. Whereas the meter of his Bengali poem places us in the action, the complete sentences of his English poem, combined with an early introduction of images that occur later in the Bengali, relay a languid scene instead:

> Mother, let us imagine we are travelling, and passing through a strange and dangerous country.
>
> You are riding in a palanquin and I am trotting by you on a red horse.
>
> It is evening and the sun goes down. The waste of *Joradighi* lies wan and grey before us. The land is desolate and barren.
>
> You are frightened and thinking—"I know not where we have come to."
>
> I say to you, "Mother, do not be afraid."[58]

Whereas the Bengali poem can be easily read to, or even read by, a child, the English poem is intended for an adult reader, who might from that position contemplate the fantasies of childhood. Joradighi is simply the name of a particular place in Bengal, but by italicizing its name for the Anglophone reader the unfamiliar word gains the potent resonances of a mysterious and perhaps mythical wasteland.

It was this adult-oriented poetry about childhood, and not the child-oriented poems of *Shishu*, that captured the Chinese imagination in the early twentieth century. *The Crescent Moon* is the only one of Tagore's English-language poetry collections in which all of the poems are titled, including several poems originally published (in different forms) in *Gitanjali*. The modifications of poem 62 in *Gitanjali*, which becomes "When and Why," the ninth poem in *The Crescent Moon*, are indicative of the pattern of revisions. Whereas the opening lines of *Gitanjali*'s poem 62 read:

> When I bring to you
> What the pleasure is that streams
> What delight that is which the summer breeze brings

The Crescent Moon's "When and Why" begins:

> When I bring you
> What pleasure streams
> What delight the summer breeze brings

As this example indicates, *The Crescent Moon* frequently simplified the style of the earlier *Gitanjali*, removing the articles and pronouns that so impressed early readers and so frustrated that text's later audiences. This shift in style, however, was poorly received in the West: the *Times Literary Supplement*, for instance, described the collection as "more childish than childlike."[59]

Whereas the child focus in *Shishu* suggests possibilities for performance and play, the childlike focus in *The Crescent Moon* generally opens out onto larger spiritual and political considerations. Whatever the motivations behind his translation choices, Tagore's pattern of translation into English fortuitously encouraged *The Crescent Moon*'s positive reception in China, for Tagore's choices shifted the poems away from the genre of children's literature to a register reminiscent of that associated with the Neo-Confucian philosopher Li Zhi (李贄, 1527–1602). Li Zhi had championed the "childlike heart-mind" (*tongxin* 童心) as an innate human talent whose sincere expression authorized political and religious dissent. Tagore was likely unfamiliar with Li Zhi's work, but at a time when the legitimacy of revolution was a key concern, Tagore's "child-poems" may have struck his Chinese audience like a similar resource: a performed simplicity that critiqued corruption and ostentation, and that was simultaneously ethical and political.

The resemblance to Li Zhi's philosophic ideal was almost certainly inadvertent, but the consequences were significant: by embodying in the English-language *Crescent Moon* collection the Chinese ideal of the childlike heart-mind, Tagore's poetry became associated with Li Zhi's stance, wherein the succinct expression of ostentatious naïveté could express a trenchant call to political revolution. Li Zhi concludes his most famous essay on the childlike heart-mind (*tongxin shuo* 童心說) with an anguished exclamation, itself a reworking of a line from the third century B.C.E. Daoist text *Zhuangzi* 莊子: "Oh! Wherever can I find a genuine great sage who has not yet lost his childlike heart-mind and have a word with him about writing?"[60] Chinese readers of *The Crescent Moon* may well have found in Tagore an answer to Li Zhi's query.

The Crescent Moon had an extraordinary career in China, where it was widely read and admired by the elite, many of whom read it in English while studying in Japan, England, or the United States. For this reason, it is an exemplary instance of how print internationalism can work within the global Anglophone, for its effects were enabled by Anglo-American hegemony and yet not reducible to its politics. As Gal Gvili has demonstrated, Chinese readers found in Tagore's works the potential of poetry to unify society, while religion, refracted through Tagore's spiritual aesthetics, came to be seen in sentimental terms. Consequently, while British and American readers generally understood gitanjali as a spiritual aesthetics that might remedy the ills of Western civilization, Chinese intellectuals usually understood gitanjali to describe aesthetics and poetics deployed as a transcendent offering to the universal. In 1923, in admiration and emulation of Tagore's collection, Xu Zhimo (徐志摩, 1897–1931) founded the Crescent Moon Society (*xinyue she* 新月社) to promote the Chinese new poetry (*xin shi* 新詩). The society's members included literary luminaries like Hu Shi (胡適, 1891–1962), Wen Yiduo (聞一多, 1899–1946), and Shen Congwen (沈從文, 1902–88), and it sought to create a new poetry marked by an attentiveness to form. In their approach to poetic form, rhythm, and not rhyme, was the key distinction between poetry and prose, a vision within which Tagore's even cadences worked perfectly.[61] Their understanding of gitanjali is manifest, for instance, in Xu Zhimo's 1923 poem "Tai shan richu" 泰山日出, which Gvili describes as "a song of prayer completely devoid of divine presence."[62]

Tagore's considerable print presence in China was soon enhanced by his physical arrival. Tagore went to China in 1924, giving a series of lectures on the invitation of the prominent reformer Liang Qichao

(梁啟超, 1873–1929). Tagore's talks in China, both in their original occasion of address and in their later publications, were in English, yet only in the published version did they have much chance of finding an audience who might follow every word. Tagore's lectures in China, as he repeatedly lamented, were English-language addresses to audiences who largely knew no English at all. The talks themselves might thus best be understood as a kind of site-specific performance, with the linguistic component operating in concert with other elements of Tagore's presentation. His words were anticipated by many but understood semantically by few. Those who could not understand him, however, seemed delighted simply to see him, often dressing up for the occasion in costumes that they imagined would match Tagore's Indian robes.[63]

While in China, Tagore traveled with a notable entourage: an internationalist ensemble of two Indians (the artist Kalidas Nag [1892–1966] and the Sanskrit scholar Kshitimohan Sen [1880–1960]), one British agriculturist (Leonard Elmhirst [1893–1974]), and two Chinese translators (the poets Lin Huiyin [林徽因, 1904–55] and Xu Zhimo). On their return to Bengal, Elmhirst typed, edited, and arranged the talks for publication; Tagore and Nag were heavily involved in this process of selection and revision. That collection of talks given in Japan and in China, heavily revised and shorn of any markers of their occasion of address, were published later that year as *Talks in China*.[64] The published volume was intended primarily for fluent readers of English, and they appeared with all dates and locations removed. Through this reframing, the book *Talks in China* evokes and yet does not fully represent the "talks in China" that it promises to print.

The book version of *Talks in China* opens with a title page that includes Chinese characters, followed by a page glossing those characters: and then, yet another title page, this time without any Chinese. From the first edition in 1924, *Talks in China* includes an introduction by Liang Qichao (credited as "Liang Chi Chao"), taken from "a speech of welcome" he delivered for Tagore in Peking (Beijing).[65] The 1925 edition adds a publisher's note that serves to introduce both the primary text and its introducer. Relying heavily on a long footnote from the British scholarly volume *Gems of Chinese Literature* (attributed here to Herbert A. "Iles" rather than Giles), the "Publisher's Note" describes Liang-chi-chao as "one of the most brilliant of the band of reformers who succeeded in establishing the Republic [of China]."[66]

Liang Qichao begins his introduction by disclaiming that it is "but my own impression as a historian and a Buddhist."[67] Noting that Tagore has "receive[d] a tremendous welcome" all over the world, he then explains that "the peoples of Europe and America" were motivated by "the meaningless idolatry of hero-worship."[68] By contrast, the Chinese welcome in Liang's estimation is linked to "the one great central idea, that he comes to us from the country which is our nearest and dearest brother,—India."[69] According to Liang, "In ancient times China . . . suffered from the disadvantage of being shut up in one corner of eastern Asia without any means of communicating with other great races and cultures."[70] With "savages" to the east and south and "barbarous and ferocious races" to the north and west, he explains, ancient China had but one source of assistance:[71]

> But across our south-western boundary, there was a great and cultured country, India. Both in character and geography, India and China are like twin brothers. Before most of the civilised races became active, we two brothers had already begun to study the great problems which concern the whole of mankind. . . . India was ahead of us and we, the little brother, followed behind.[72]

In contrast to the civilizations and races of the West, who "have come coveting our land and our wealth," the "two brothers" India and China were motivated by "the cause of universal truth" and "the destiny of mankind," devoid of "any motive of self-interest."[73] Liang concludes by celebrating "our Buddhistic heritage," through which "Indian thought has been entirely assimilated into our own world of experience and has become an inalienable part of our consciousness."[74]

For the readers of *Talks in China*, as for the audience at Tagore's reception in Beijing, Liang Qichao thus introduces Tagore as the spiritual fulfillment of a long-standing historical legacy: "In the personality of Rabindranath Tagore, as well as in his poetry, we find that exemplification of those principles of absolute love and absolute freedom, which form the basis of Hindu culture and civilisation."[75] Even as Liang's English-language introduction emphasizes Tagore's Hindu attributes, the cover of the book within which it appears performs Chineseness instead. The cover of the 1925 version (fig. 1) inscribes the title—the English words "Talks in China"—in a stylized font that runs top to bottom, as was conventional for writing Chinese, rather than left to right, as one would expect for writing English. The stylized letters are framed within a scroll-like rectangle, with Tagore's name in the Roman alphabet written from left to right at the bottom. Tagore's name also appears in another place on the cover, but this time it is a Chinese name, given to Tagore by Liang Qichao, presented only by its Chinese characters. To understand what these Chinese characters mean, one has to open the book and flip several pages to find an explanation, in which the publisher addresses both how that name "was translated" and how it "may be Englished." *Talks in China* is thus, once again, a global Anglophone text that disrupts the very English that it utilizes. The title is in English,

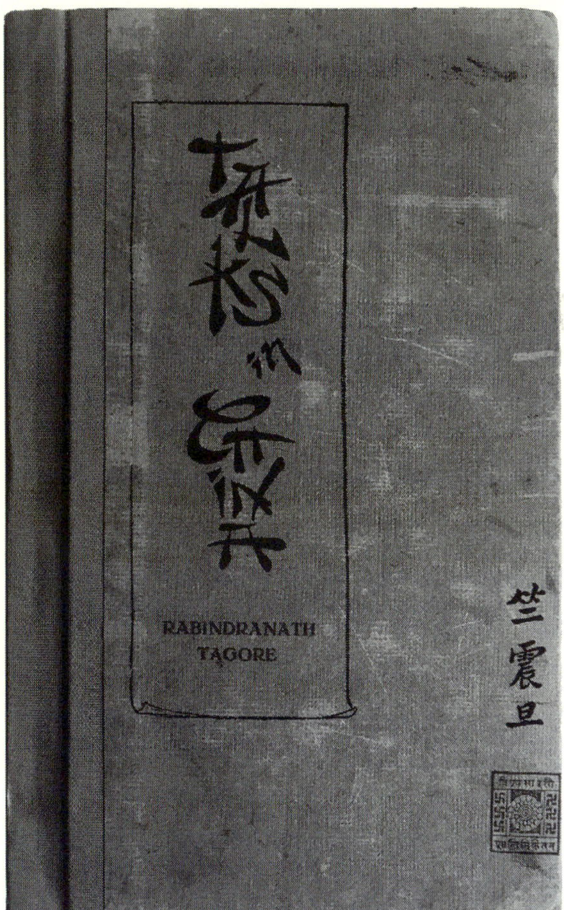

Fig. 1. The cover of Rabindranath Tagore's 1925 *Talks in China*. The title is designed to resemble Chinese characters. Along the right edge, Tagore's Chinese name appears in Chinese characters above the seal of Viswa-Bharati University. From Rabindranath Tagore, *Talks in China* (Calcutta: Viswa-Bharati, 1925).

but it is printed in letters that resemble Chinese characters; the author's name is Bengali, but on the same cover it appears only in its English-language and Chinese-language incarnations.

This volume was, in many respects, more successful than the talks from which it drew, and the first talk in the published collection explicitly stages the difficulties of internationalism that unfolds in person rather than in print. In that talk Tagore begins by discussing the coverage of his trip in an unspecified Chinese newspaper. He recounts that the paper explained that he was late to a meeting because he is out of date with "this modern age."[76] In response to this Chinese allegation of his essential anachronism, Tagore notes his

> own countrymen['s] angry remonstrances that I was too crassly modern, that I had missed all the great lessons from the past, and with it my right of entry into a venerable civilization like that of India. For your people I am obsolete, and therefore useless, and for mine, newfangled and therefore obnoxious.[77]

This opening anecdote suggests that a straightforward, linear temporality is inaccurate, or at least irrelevant. Tagore disproves this idea, however, not by asserting the value of his contrarian position, but by revealing both modernity and antiquity as seemingly universal concepts that have nonetheless been created through culturally specific interpretations.

As we see in his later correspondence, Tagore became increasingly reluctant to take on the mystical role that was inevitably demanded of him by Western readers, audiences, and interlocutors. We can only imagine his response when this demand was thrust upon him even *within* "the East" to which he proudly belonged. What distinguishes his travels within Asia, however, is that in those instances the Eastern spiritual wisdom that was desired from Tagore by his audience was similar to that which he expected to receive from them. The ancient Eastern civilizational inheritance of spirituality, which all parties agreed they shared as "Asiatics," became, in the moment of encounter, that which they earnestly sought in the Asiatic most different from themselves.

Tagore's reception in China was frequently hostile, with revolutionaries like Lu Xun (魯迅, 1881–1936) protesting him as a dangerous antimodernizing influence.[78] Yet in his published *Talks in China*, Tagore repeatedly inscribed his experience in China as one of continuity and similarity, devoid of "any undue sense of race feeling, or difference of tradition."[79] This sense of commonality, he reports, was enhanced by the natural environment yet undercut by linguistic difference, for, as he explained: "Your hills speak the same language as ours, your lake has the same smile as our lakes, . . . [but] as human beings, we have no common language through which we can come close to one another."[80] In the absence of a common language, Tagore spoke to audiences who believed he was a poet because, as he joked in one lecture, "I have a beautiful grey beard."[81] Instead of ascribing his large Chinese audiences to his worldwide celebrity, Tagore attributed it to the ancient Asian commonalities he had first discovered through Okakura and Nivedita. Tagore proclaimed:

> I know that many of you do not understand me, but something has drawn you to come and look at me. It is not because you expect any message from me, but, as I believe, because of some memory of that glorious time when India did send her messengers of love to this land.[82]

The act of "look[ing] at me" may seem trivial in most English-language texts, but here it invokes the two-way gaze known as *darshan*, crucial in South Asia as both a devotional and a political form of reciprocal vision. They come to look at him, even as he speaks in a language they cannot understand: his English words may not carry "any message" to them, but his *darshan* can nonetheless evoke "some memory" in them. The "glorious time" that is recollected, moreover, dates to the beginning of the Common Era: as with Okakura's perception of the Ajanta sculptures in *The Ideals of the East*, the visual apprehension of Tagore by his Chinese audiences can trigger recollections that are Asian rather than individual.

This notion—of linguistic incomprehension superseded by the commonality of shared Asianness—is crucial to understanding Tagore's print internationalism. In this project, English operates as the mediating language, but it does not supersede other linguistic regimes. Tagore, for instance, encourages his Chinese audience to learn the Bengali language. He warns them that they cannot truly enjoy his poetry in translation, for

> languages are jealous. They do not give up their best treasures to those who try to deal with them through an intermediary belonging to an alien rival. You have to court them

> in person and dance attendance on them. . . . You cannot receive the smiles and glances of your sweetheart through an attorney, however diligent and dutiful he may be.[83]

Though he is speaking fluently in his nonprimary language, Tagore nonetheless warns that he cannot give them the "best treasures" of his literary talents. The fault, notably, lies not in the skill of the language user, "however diligent and dutiful," but in the nature of language itself. In Tagore's eroticized vision, languages exist in a state of rivalry, but for emotional reasons, and not geopolitical ones, in keeping with his dismissal of political considerations in favor of social concerns.

Yet Tagore's disregard for courtship by attorney does not prevent him from engaging in depth with Chinese works in translated form: rather than question the intermediary language of these translations, he confidently derails conventional translations in search of the intimate connections of shared Asianness. Much as he had argued, in his English-language criticisms of Gandhi, that "swaraj" was simply "maya," here he reaches once again through English to translate Asian words, working this time between classical Chinese and Sanskrit rather than solely within Sanskrit. His "Civilisation and Progress" lecture in China uses the Sanskrit term "dharma" as "the nearest synonym in our own language" for "civilization," then explicates it using the words of "the great Chinese sage, Lao-tze" (now usually Laozi 老子).[84] English is the "diligent and dutiful" attorney who introduces him to the sixth-century B.C.E. treatise *Tao Te Ching* (*Daode Jing* 道德經), a text attributed to Laozi that Tagore read in the 1913 English translation titled *The Canon of Reason and Virtue*. Although the word *dao* 道 had served as an early Chinese translation of the Pali *dhamma* (Sanskrit *dharma*), and it was still occasionally used to translate "dharma" in the sense of "teachings," "dao" and "dharma" had long ago bifurcated from a primary association. By the time of Tagore's lecture, "dharma" in Chinese was almost always rendered as *fa* 法, which also means "law." Tagore's lecture thus revived a relatively rare and explicitly nonlegalistic usage, and in the process he created commonality across Asia.[85] This Chinese wisdom comes to Tagore through the global Anglophone, in a translation by the German American editor Paul Carus and the Japanese scholar D. T. Suzuki that was first published in the United States. He then delivers his understanding of this wisdom back to the Chinese, once again in the medium of English, but with a metonymic kernel of a shared Asianness—the Sanskrit word—now carefully connected (or, as he might insist, reconnected). Although commentators today, both scholarly and popular, frequently describe "dharma" as untranslatable, for Tagore it is anything but: for him "dharma" serves as the vehicle for associations of equivalence, in a manner similar to the desires of translation but irreducible to its laws of interchange.

This interpretive relationship to the global Anglophone would be epitomized three years later, in 1927. While aboard a ship docked in Singapore, then part of the British colony known as the Straits Settlements, Tagore wrote an introduction to a new translation by Lim Boon Keng (Lin Wenqing 林文慶, 1869–1957) of the classical Chinese poem known as the *Li Sao* 離騷. The *Li Sao*—a title sometimes translated as *Encountering Sorrow*—narrates in the first person the quest of a noble hero unjustly dismissed from the court. It is the longest and best-known of the anthology of rhymed, metrical works known as the *Chu-ci* 楚辭 (*The Lyrics of Chu*), which originated in southern China around the fourth century B.C.E. The poem is shamanistic, and it "has been traditionally read as the authentic voice of Qu Yuan" (屈原, c. 340–278 B.C.E.).[86] While the *Li Sao* had been translated into English before, it had never been translated by anyone of Chinese ancestry. Its translator in the early twentieth century was a Singaporean intellectual of Hokkien-Malay descent (sometimes called *baba* or Straits Chinese), Lim Boon Keng, who discovered ancient Chinese culture while attending medical school in Scotland.[87] His subsequent advocacy of Confucianism would alienate him from the most influential of his mainland contemporaries, and it would also result, in the later twentieth century, in his celebration as a cosmopolitan visionary. Through projects like the *Straits Chinese Magazine*, which he edited from 1897 to 1907, Lim propagated a modern identity for Southeast Asians of Chinese ancestry, then mostly living under European colonialism, and he did so by foregrounding their connections to ancient China. In the process, he rejected missionary and imperial narratives of diasporic degeneracy, for these "Straits Chinese," he argued, belonged perfectly within a larger Asian geography.

Because of this political Asianist project, Tagore's Asianist internationalism resonated with the efforts—antiracist and revivalist alike—of ethnically Chinese intellectuals living under British colonialism in Southeast Asia. The Chinese diaspora boomed after the forced opening of China to Western powers in 1842, and by the late nineteenth century Chinese emigrants, now called *huaqiao* 華僑 ("overseas Chinese"), were no longer seen as traitors to the mainland.[88] In the tumultuous decades between the fall of the Qing dynasty (1911) and the establishment of the People's Republic of China (1949), the elite among these overseas Chinese jostled to position themselves within a changing global order. Lim Boon Keng, for instance, argued that the Straits Chinese could serve as bicultural interpreters between China and the West, a position welcomed by British colonial officials. Much as Tagore at Visva-Bharati aimed to teach a shared Asian inheritance without knowing any non-Indian languages, Lim worked to restore Confucianism without ever mastering modern spoken Chinese. Linked not only by these views but also by their shared British subjecthood, Tagore and Lim met during Tagore's 1924 tour of China, when Lim Boon Keng, then the president of Amoy (now Xiamen) University in southern China, sought his guidance on creating a position in Indian culture and history.[89]

In providing his preface to Lim Boon Keng's translation of *his* cultural patrimony, Tagore paralleled W. B. Yeats's prefatory work for Tagore's translations of his own poems in *Gitanjali*. In excavating these nested connections, we unearth an alternate geography, shaped—but not defined—by British and U.S. imperialism. Ireland to Bengal, and then Bengal to Singapore: this is a literary cartography particular to the global Anglophone. In writing a preface for Lim Boon Keng's translation, Tagore intervened not only within the British Empire but also within a rapidly changing China. Lim's volume, published from Shanghai in 1929, opens with an introduction by Hugh Clifford, a British official writing from Singapore, who explains that Lim's traditionalism should be read as "in accordance with modern ideas,"[90] for Lim "inhale[s] with equal ease the atmosphere of modern China and that of the country [Singapore] of his birth."[91] Tagore's preface appears between a preface by the British sinologist H. A. Giles and another by the Chinese economic historian Chen Huan-Cheng. While Giles, praising the *Li Sao* as "a pindaric ode," proclaims that Lim's work "go[es] far to leave the British Empire precisely where it was,"[92] Chen Huan-Cheng, in keeping with his Confucian revivalism, inscribes his text within the newly devised Confucian calendar. Tagore's preface, by contrast, provides no specific historical comparisons.

Tagore's preface may be short, but his contribution plays a substantial role in establishing not only this translation but the *Li Sao* itself. As Lim Boon Keng explained in his "Translator's Preface," he "felt the need for the advice of one of the *literati*, a poet and a Sinologue of recognized authority."[93] Whereas both Western and Chinese sinologists had compared the *Li Sao* to the literature of classical Greece, Tagore situates it within contemporary poetry. He thus proves Lim's suggestion in his "Translator's Preface" that he would highlight "some aspects of Sinological studies often overlooked,"[94] and he also affirms Lim's argument that the poem registers the voice of a surprisingly modern individual, Qu Yuan. Tagore proves the literary value of the *Li Sao* and, by extension, all of Chinese literature, not through scholarly comparisons but because as "a genuine poet" Tagore can perceive true art in all of its varied manifestations. Lim explains that while "European critics . . . are inclined to follow the pioneer Sinologues . . . in disparaging not only 'The Li Sao' as a mediocre work but also the genius of the whole Chinese nation,"[95] this judgment merely reveals their misunderstanding of the Chinese approach to genre. He explains that

> the Chinese use poetry solely as the medium for the expression of the disharmony of the emotions. . . . If the Chinese are so minded, there is no obvious reason why their poets may not, like Virgil or Milton, imitate the methods of Homer. But the fact is that the Chinese prefer to relegate romance, myth, or religion either to history or fiction.[96]

The problem, Lim politely suggests, lies not in Chinese poetry but in the narrow conception of poetry prevalent in the West. Because Western critics, in his view, associate poetry with the epic tradition of Homer (c. eighth century B.C.E.), Virgil (70–19 B.C.E.), and John Milton (1608–74), they have lost the capacity to appreciate poetry properly. Their literary perception, he gently implies, has been fatally damaged by their Eurocentrism. Lim concludes his introduction by explaining how one must understand poetry: through an aesthetic sensibility for which Tagore is the exemplar.

> To appreciate the beauty of a poem, the reader must be in a position to place himself *en rapport* with the proper environment, and must fully understand the psychology of the poet and the times. We must confess that "The Li Sao" does not lend itself readily to the appreciation of its readers, but whoever will persevere in meditating over the problems involved will, sooner or later, come to appreciate its peculiar style and beauty, such as Dr. Tagore, a genuine poet, has at once done. Dr. Tagore's just and eloquent tribute shows an instinctive perception of the true character of Chinese poetry, which will be duly appreciated in the East.[97]

"Dr. Tagore" does "at once" what others will do "sooner or later": his genius is unique in its rapidity but potentially universal in its skills. Like Okakura in the Ajanta caves or the Chinese spectators at Tagore's talks, Tagore here immediately apprehends Asia's ancient treasures and thereby facilitates their transmission into the wider world. Rabindranath Tagore and Lim Boon Keng thus participate in a relationship of reciprocal recognition: Tagore recognizes "the true character of Chinese poetry," and Lim recognizes him as "a genuine poet" in return. Whereas mainland Chinese audiences had rebuked the Indian poet as both foreign and anachronistic, Lim celebrates Tagore's "instinctive perception," or what he describes as his ability "to place himself *en rapport* with the proper environment."[98]

By bestowing this ability to understand China on a Bengali subject of British India, Lim Boon Keng shores up his own claims to reliably present China to non-Chinese persons, without undermining the necessity of his intermediary role. He suggests that the *Li Sao* translation will be "of some slight use to those who desire to understand the 'Chinese mind'" through what he describes as "the wonderful language of Shakespeare and Milton destined now to be the world's language of commerce and diplomacy."[99] Tagore may have renounced his knighthood and his loyalty to the British Crown, yet in enabling this diasporic Chinese publication he allied himself once again with a politics that subsumed the needs of Asians to the ostensible wisdom of the British Empire. Much as Tagore's nominalism gitanjali indicated both a specifically Asian cultural inheritance and a devotional approach to the aesthetic that could be practiced by anyone, Lim Boon Keng here argued "that Chinese values were not only timeless but recoverable by all."[100]

The marked difference between Tagore's reading of the *Li Sao* and the contemporary scholarly consensus registers the extraordinary changes that have happened at the intersection of poetry and multiculturalism over the course of the twentieth century. Whereas the sinologist Stephen Owen argued in an academic publication in 1996 that the *Li Sao* was complicated, contested and may never be fully understood,[101] Tagore in 1927 told his nonscholarly readership that the *Li Sao* offered "transparent simplicity and directness." Tagore began his preface with an optimistic assertion:

> To-day most of the classical poets of China have passed through the narrow, tortuous passages of scholarship into the intimate assembly of living letters. They, like the ancient

> Chinese art, have won their recognition from the creative minds of the West, offering to them a new source of inspiration in their transparent simplicity and directness. Undoubtedly, the time has come when some Chinese writers, to whom the spirit of their native language readily yields her subtle secrets, should gather the best fruits of their literature, not for the pigeonholes of archaeological classification, but for the universal feast of mind.[102]

Tagore's assertion here—of the utilities of "some Chinese writers" to "gather the best fruits of their literature"—affirms Lim's racial claim to Chineseness even as he misrecognizes the powers of the "native language." The classical Chinese of the *Li Sao*, after all, was a literary language and not an everyday idiom; therefore, it was not the ordinary linguistic medium for anyone, Chinese or not. Much as Yeats, Pound, and other Anglo-American modernists exoticized the language from which Tagore had translated his *Gitanjali*, Tagore here stakes much on those who are racially Chinese possessing "the spirit of their native language," so that they can "gather the best fruits of their literature" for worldwide enjoyment. Fusing race, language, and literary inheritance, Tagore's arrangement of the "intimate assembly of living letters" and the "universal feast of mind" relies on English to make a transregional literary community appear. The "subtle secrets" that might exist in poetry are now transmuted onto the language itself, and these secrets yield "readily" to the "Chinese writer" who seeks to translate such texts. This linguistic claim, moreover, collapses "the classical poets of China" from earlier centuries with "some Chinese writers" of the current moment. By passing both groups at once "through the narrow, tortuous passages of scholarship"—including the scholarship of the very preface that Tagore is writing—he brings "Chinese literature," shorn of temporal markers and authorial identities, into this universal realm.

Whereas scholars today generally read the *Li Sao* for its exploration of individual subjectivity, Tagore positions it as a political lament with a generalizable social sentiment. As he explains, "The verses of this poem carry in them a lament, political in character, which makes vivid to us the background of a great people's mind, whose best aspiration was for building a stable basis of society founded upon the spirit of moral obligation."[103] China thus provides the past of a great civilization for this Indian intellectual, Tagore, prefacing a Chinese publication in the global Anglophone, much as India indicates an ancient greatness for the Chinese intellectual Liang Qichao, who prefaced Tagore's global Anglophone volume *Talks in China*. By describing Lim's work on the *Li Sao* in this manner, Tagore converts it into a gitanjali: a "song offering," from both Lim Boon Keng and Qu Yuan, to the "universal feast of mind." The *Li Sao* is famously unlike any other text of ancient Chinese literature in the intensity of its imagery and emotions, yet Tagore signals it as representative precisely because of this intensity, his enthusiasm perhaps enhanced by its reliance on floral symbolism. Lim Boon Keng, as a Chinese person outside mainland China and the Chinese mainstream of his time, may well have chosen the *Li Sao* because it predates the standardization of the Qin and Han dynasties; Tagore, likely unfamiliar with these subtleties of Chinese literary history, perceives the *Li Sao* solely as an exemplary work of Chinese literature. This volume thus enters global Anglophone literature through Tagore's mode of print internationalism, which laminates the text not only with spiritual and civilizational claims but also with prefaces from distant admirers, which in turn connect otherwise culturally particular texts to vastly different parts of the global Anglophone.

In this chapter, on Rabindranath Tagore's gitanjali, we have witnessed the power of the global Anglophone to facilitate a print internationalism opposed to Anglo-American hegemony. The key innovation that enabled Tagore's subversive use of the global Anglophone was not only his deployment of a beguiling neologism but also his elucidation, through that neologism, of an interpretive method for those who were desired to share his apprehension of new worldwide possibilities. By following the devotional understanding of aesthetic activities that Tagore named gitanjali, Asian internationalists who wished to utilize English without perpetuating its guiding regimes could approach other Asian cultures in their translated forms, and find in them both new insights and a reassuring commonality. Perhaps if we, following Tagore's lead, approach the global Anglophone sphere with new methods of interpretation, we too can subvert its circulations toward our destabilizing dreams.

The approach to the global Anglophone developed in this chapter will be further developed in the next, where we turn our attentions to Gandhi and his neologism "satyagraha." While Gandhi, like Tagore, finds Sanskrit useful for the global Anglophone, he diverges greatly from Tagore in emphasizing the replicability of his practices in any location, rather than enabling their divergence, as in Tagore's understanding of translation. This difference is evident, for instance, in the debates with Gandhi discussed earlier in this chapter, including in how Gandhi himself used Sanskrit for this English-language yet entirely India-related disagreement. Gandhi's rejoinders to Tagore's criticisms appeared in *Young India*, a weekly journal edited by Gandhi himself and published out of his ashram in Gujarat. Appearing in slim issues of eight pages, featuring only such spiritual and historical material as relevant to the current political agitations, with no advertisements and little visual ornamentation, Gandhi's rejoinders, like the journal in which they were published, argued for the value of a concrete political focus. Gandhi's criticisms of Tagore were frequently personal. He explains that Tagore "lives in a magnificent world of his own creation—his world of ideas" and "presents the world with new and attractive things from day to day," for "the Poet is an inventor—he creates, destroys and recreates."[104] Gandhi, by contrast, "is a slave of somebody else's creation—the spinning wheel," and he "can merely show the hidden possibilities of old and even worn out things," for "I am an explorer."[105] Declaring that "the Poet's criticism is a poetic license," Gandhi announces that Tagore had "denounced what he has imagined."[106]

Yet despite his trenchant objections to Tagore's methods, Gandhi too turned to scripture even as he dismissed, in general, the value of poems and songs: "I have found it impossible to soothe suffering patients with a song from Kabir. The hungry millions ask for one poem—invigorating food."[107] Whereas Tagore translated the iconoclastic fifteenth-century poet Kabir from Hindi to English in 1915, using poems collected from traveling mendicants and from source manuscripts,[108] Gandhi in 1921 describes those poems as irrelevant to the "hungry millions," for whom the only desired poem is "invigorating food." Yet Gandhi followed this dismissal of poetry with a long quotation from a different poem: the *Bhagavad Gita*. The Edwin Arnold translation that Gandhi read and admired had been published under the title *The Song Celestial*: it seems that for Gandhi, "a song from Kabir" is useless, but a Sanskrit song is vital. Whereas Kabir lived around the fifteenth century, the *Bhagavad Gita* was likely composed in the first century of the Common Era. It forms a central part of the long epic poem known as the *Mahabharata*, and it is a central component of Hindu theology, connecting the social emphasis of earlier texts with the interpretive individualism of modern Hinduism. Despite its nomination as a "geet" (a song or a lyric poem), it is best categorized in generic terms as a philosophical dialogue rendered in verse. Whereas the Hindi-language poems of Kabir were mystical and syncretic, outraging both the Hindu and the Muslim orthodoxies of his time, the Sanskrit verses of Gita, here untranslated and presented in Nagari script, are located firmly within doctrinal Hinduism. Moreover, whereas Kabir's poetry, much like the Upanishads quoted by Tagore, comprised mystical verses necessitating careful contemplation, the *Bhagavad Gita* is comparatively easy to read, with clearly defined characters and a strong narrative arc.

In this 1921 publication Gandhi quotes verses 8–16 from the third teaching of the *Bhagavad Gita*, "Karmayoga," which has been translated variously as "Virtue in Work" and "Discipline of Action."[109] Gandhi's long quotation celebrates necessary action as a kind of sacrifice toward the divine, and it concludes with a verse about turning a wheel:

> एवं प्रवर्तितं चक्रं नानुवर्तयतीह यः।
> अघायुरिन्द्रियारामो मोघं पार्थ स जीवति।।[110]
> (*Bhagavad Gita* 3.16)
>
> He who fails to keep turning
> the wheel here set in motion
> wastes his life in sin,
> addicted to the senses, Arjuna.[111]

The verse thus explicitly invokes the cosmic wheel (*chakra* चक्रं) that was frequently associated with the spinning wheel (*charkha* चरखा), a semantic and phonetic association that Gandhi deployed to great effect. Within Hindu and Buddhist traditions, the *chakra* was a model for understanding both time and space, indicating at once the recursivity of the universe and the path toward enlightenment. By the twentieth century the *chakra* had come to represent a continuous inheritance from Indian antiquity, even as, within Hinduism and Buddhism, it indicated an epochal temporality, not a historical one.

The wheel reference in this portion of the *Bhagavad Gita* is clearly cosmological in its implications, yet Gandhi, leaving the quotation untranslated, encouraged a confusion between the *chakra* and the *charkha*: between the cosmic wheel of the *Bhagavad Gita* and the spinning wheel of his political program. In replying to Tagore, Gandhi thus facilitated an associative form of interpretation that blurred the literal with the metaphorical. Instead of a gloss, he writes only that "in these verses is contained for me the whole truth of the spinning wheel as an indispensable sacrament for the India of to-day."[112]

Gandhi's quotation of this extended passage in Sanskrit, unexplained and untranslated within his English-language essay, seems not to have had its intended effect. In the following week's issue of *Young India*, Gandhi published an initial section titled "The Charkha in the Gita," providing therein the entire portion quoted earlier, but this time in English. He quoted, as he put it, "Edwin Arnold's rendering of the verses from his Song Celestial,"[113] and his long quotation had the following final verse:

> He that abstains
> To help the rolling wheels of this great world,
> Glutting his idle sense, lives a lost life,
> Shameful and vain.[114]

After this quotation, Gandhi provided a decidedly unconventional gloss:

> Work here undoubtedly refers to physical labour, and work by way of sacrifice can only be work to be done by all for the common benefit. Such work—such sacrifice can only be spinning. I do not wish to suggest, that the author of the Divine Song had the spinning wheel in mind. He merely laid down a fundamental principle of conduct. And reading in and applying it to India I can only think of spinning as the fittest and most acceptable sacrificial body labour.[115]

Gandhi thus literalizes the metaphorical, whereas Tagore, as we have seen in this chapter, repeatedly metaphorizes the literal, from landscapes to languages.

This was only one instance of the strong associations that the Gandhian *charkha* forged with the *chakra*, both on the page and in daily life, yet it is particularly egregious for Gandhi's central critic.[116] Tagore, after all, believed in the epochal that resided within the symbols of the literal (much as the words "dao" and "dharma" could be found, through his careful interpretation, to contain the same universal truth). In choosing instead to encourage an interpretive practice that literalized the metaphorical, Gandhi thus reified the quotidian as the universal through its widespread replication, in direct contrast to Tagore's interpretative unification of seemingly discrepant things. In dismissing Gandhi's call to the *charkha* as a magical formula, Tagore was invoking, in part, this desired collapse in Gandhi's politics between the *chakra* and the *charkha*: between the wheel as a cosmology and the wheel as an implement for spinning.

This distinction in their interpretive methods will result, as we shall see in the following chapter, in a very different trajectory for Gandhi's print internationalism. Whereas Tagore moved from a nationalist politics to an internationalist one, Gandhi began his political career in an internationalist frame from South Africa, only to turn to a purely nationalist politics later in his career. In between his disagreements with Tagore, however, Gandhi wrote the narratives of South Africa that would serve as the interpretive grid for his nationalism. As we find in the following chapter, Gandhi thereby created a print internationalism with a similar emphasis on interpretation but with a marked difference in its understanding of representation. Whereas Tagore demonstrated how the most apparently local of experiences could serve, through proper interpretation, as a form of print internationalism, Gandhi would argue that even an international experience, when properly regarded, was essentially transportable.

CHAPTER 2

People of Color

M. K. Gandhi's Satyagraha

On November 6, 1923, an imprisoned M. K. (Mahatma) Gandhi began to write about his South African protests for his Indian followers. In diaries that soon spawned both a history and an autobiography, he decided to explain the origins of the name of his increasingly effective method of protest: "satyagraha." He wrote that the term, which he coined during his time living in South Africa (1896–1915), originated in a desire to differentiate his protest politics from those of other movements. Gandhi wrote from his Indian prison cell that referring to the Indian agitation as "passive resistance" had created both confusion and shame. That shame was twofold: first, it was shameful "to permit this great struggle to be known only by an English name," and second, it was shameful to allow the Indians' struggle to be associated with that of British women agitating for the right to vote, for they had increasingly turned to the destruction of property in their protests.[1] These British women, writes Gandhi, were "weak in numbers as well as in physical force," and any association with their use of passive resistance would lead people to perceive the Indian passive resisters to be similarly weak. After all, Gandhi assures us, Indian protesters "were in a position to use [physical force] effectively," but they chose to abstain from doing so.[2]

Seeking to distance himself from the weakness of women and from the verbiage of the West, Gandhi had solicited ideas for a new term through a 1909 contest in *Indian Opinion*, his newspaper in South Africa. The winning entry was the word "sadagraha." As Gandhi explained retrospectively in his prison writings,

> I liked the word, but it did not fully represent the whole idea I wished it to connote. I therefore corrected it to "satyagraha." Truth (*satya*) implies love, and firmness (*agraha*) engenders and therefore serves as a synonym for force. I thus began to call the Indian movement "satyagraha," that is to say, the Force which is born of Truth and Love or non-violence, and gave up the use of the phrase "passive resistance" in connection with it, so much so that even in English writing we often avoided it.[3]

In explaining how he has "corrected" "sadagraha" to "satyagraha," Gandhi changes *sada*, with its connotations of constancy, to *satya*, which he glosses as "truth"—a widely accepted definition. He then deviates, however, by saying that truth "implies love," and he expands *graha*, usually defined as "holding," to mean "firmness," which he equates with "force."[4] In describing this expansive concept of linguistic "correction," Gandhi's desire for a new Indian idiom of political practice also reveals his faith in the constitutive power of linguistic description, drawing here on the word for one who offers satyagraha, a satyagrahi: "If we continue to . . . offer passive resistance, our resistance will never make us strong. . . . On the other hand if we are satyagrahis . . . we grow stronger and stronger every day."[5]

This chapter analyzes Gandhi's print internationalism as it coalesced around his transportable concept of satyagraha. His approach was very different, as we have seen, from that of his friend, compatriot, and sometime debate partner Rabindranath Tagore. Tagore developed a practice of print internationalism to enable connections across seemingly distinct cultures and peoples. Gandhi, by contrast, designed a print internationalism that championed replicability in the service of a politics that became increasingly national in its contours. Whereas Tagore celebrated an inclusive vision of Asia that dissolved national boundaries, Gandhi imagined liberation along specifically national contours, even as he moved across nations. Whether in South Africa or in the worldwide celebrity of his later time in India, however, Gandhi's nearly exclusive preoccupation with *Indians'* sufferings under imperial injustice has posed uncomfortable questions for those who would valorize him today. I argue that the emphasis in Gandhi's print internationalism on replicability facilitated his oft-deplored decision to ignore the sufferings of Africans and other colonized peoples in his political struggles. Consequently, in examining Gandhi's print internationalism, we can presage the difficulties that mark the contemporary concept "people of color."

A variety of hierarchies—for instance, between savage and civilized, or between the republican and the autocratic—have long been used, and typically in overlapping fashion, to rationalize and perpetuate imperialism. As Gandhi struggled with imperial politics in the early twentieth century, these hierarchical binaries were slowly being resolved into a single polarity: that between White people and everyone else.[6] As the twentieth century's global color line emerged, the self-nomination of one side as White required, in due course, the emergence of a name for that othered and denigrated side: "people of color." Much as that term gains its applicability through its abstracted application to many persons, so too Gandhi's "satyagraha" can travel. In each instance, however, these terms' vagueness prevents a substantial articulation of the uneven terrain within various experiences of racist oppression, whether in Gandhi's twentieth century or in our twenty-first.

While "person of color" and "colored person" appear in English-language texts as early as the eighteenth century, they were then used to refer, with no necessary political implications, to a non-White person. The term "people of color" as a collective identity seems to be a U.S. invention of the late 1980s, appearing (albeit infrequently) in the MLA bibliography from the early 1990s onward. Perhaps traceable to a translation of the French term *gens de coleur libres*, here the French use of the preposition "de" enables a new phrase that is laudatory—"people of color"—whereas "colored people," by around the 1960s, was already a derogatory and vanishing term. As early as 1988, William Safire explained in the *New York Times*: "It strikes me, then, that *people of color* is a phrase often used by nonwhites to put *nonwhite* positively. (Why should anybody want to define himself by what he is not?) Politically, it expresses solidarity with other nonwhites, and subtly reminds whites that they are a minority."[7] Much as "the global Anglophone," as we saw in the previous chapter, finds traction in literary studies as a seemingly inclusive moniker for a category primarily defined by the lack of two dominant countries (the United Kingdom and the United States), so too the term "people of color" is adapted as a positive articulation for a category again defined by the absence of the hegemonic group. But the term recognizes (albeit for antiracist purposes) a difference between White people and the rest of humanity that had first been asserted for the purposes of White supremacism. Consequently, it raises rather than resolves a fundamental conundrum: how does one recognize the common sufferings of various non-White peoples? Scholars and activists have tried to resolve this dilemma, perhaps most famously the South African leader Steve Biko, who in the 1970s proposed another possibility: separating racism's victims according to their political dispositions. Biko proposed a divide between "non-whites"—whose "aspiration is whiteness but [whose] pigmentation makes attainment of this impossible"—and "blacks"—"those who are by law or tradition politically, economically and socially discriminated against as a group in the South African society and identifying themselves as a unit in the struggle towards the realization of their aspirations."[8]

Gandhi too sought an antiracist politics that would restructure the very terms of the debate, decentering Whiteness from its primacy as an opponent and articulating antiracist identities in positive terms instead. Yet whereas Biko, writing decades later, was able to articulate an inclusive Blackness, Gandhi turned to the resources of specifically Indian civilization for a positive term, as in his eclectic coinage of the neologism "satyagraha." Gandhi's coinage of "satyagraha" in *Indian Opinion* was, crucially, neither fully traditional nor entirely falsifiable in its Sanskrit usage. As we saw earlier, he argued that: "Truth (*satya*) implies love, and firmness (*agraha*) engenders and therefore serves as a synonym for force."[9] Gandhi's retrospective explanation of the term's origin begins in a conventional fashion, by defining the first root, and then expands to associate new concepts with it. Truth, for instance, does not signal love etymologically—which would require that the word *satya* be a Sanskrit word meaning "love," which it is not—but, rather, "Truth (*satya*) implies love" because Gandhi insists, both here and elsewhere, that truth and love are intrinsically related concepts. The insertion of *satya*, within parentheses, thus operates as the occasion for a recalibration of words, forcing new linkages across the global Anglophone. The Anglophone context facilitates this process, precisely because Sanskrit roots like *sat* serve no obvious role in the English language. Gandhi thus coins new words in an old language by writing them within another linguistic medium: he writes these Sanskritisms within his English and his Gujarati, and thereby asserts modernity and tradition at the same time.

For Gandhi, an idea proceeds its linguistic articulation, and his writings frequently recount a search for the appropriate language to name one of his already existing innovations. In *The Story of My Experiments with Truth* (henceforth *My Experiments*), for instance, he wrote:

> The principle called Satyagraha came into being before that name was invented. Indeed when it was born, I myself could not say what it was. In Gujarati also we used the English phrase "passive resistance" to describe it. When in a meeting of Europeans I found that the term "passive resistance" was too narrowly construed, that it was supposed to be a weapon of the weak, that it could be characterized by hatred and that it could finally manifest itself as violence, I had to demur to all these statements and explain the real nature of the Indian movement. It was clear that a new word must be coined by the Indians to designate their struggle.[10]

The English phrase worked smoothly among Gujarati audiences, yet it failed to be clearly understood at "a meeting of Europeans." The irony here is considerable: a concept borrowed, word for word, from a European language cannot be transferred back into a European conversation without a significant loss of meaning. A specifically Indian idiom is here designed in response to a problem of comprehension that originates in the global Anglophone.

Across the body of Gandhi's texts, the presence of an untranslated word indicates both authenticity and cosmopolitanism: it both marks something culturally specific and signals the opportunity for cross-cultural creativity. Much as Gandhi abandons an English phrase for a Sanskritic one in order to speak to Anglophone European audiences, so too he coins a momentous English phrase in an entirely non-Anglophone Indian context. In 1919, Gandhi spoke to an audience in Delhi "in such broken Hindi as I could command." On that occasion, he recounted in *My Experiments*, Gandhi described his upcoming political agitation "by the word 'non co-operation,'" since he "could not hit upon a suitable Hindi or Urdu word for the new idea."[11] He launched this "non-cooperation movement" while "still busy devising suitable Hindi, Gujarati and Urdu phraseology for non-co-operation," seeking in particular words that might be appropriate for "purely Moslem audiences."[12] As his account of the need for a religiously specific terminology suggests, Gandhi's ultimate interest in language was essentially theological. For example, he described how the *Bhagavad Gita*, by far his most favored religious treatise, had served as his "dictionary of conduct," with specific words like *aparigraha* and *samabhava* that "gripped" him during his "troubles and trials."[13]

Gandhi's politics thus embraced linguistic specificity: even when addressing both Hindus and Muslims with the same message of Indian nationalism, he wished to design separate terminology for each group precisely to unite them. (For a contemporary analogy, we might contrast the itemized solidarity of the U.K. category, "Black, Asian, and minority ethnic" to the generalizing inclusivity of the U.S.'s "people of color.") The closest analogue to inclusivity, I argue, is in the nominalism "satyagraha," for becoming a satyagrahi—an agent of satyagraha—is, as I discuss later in this chapter, a transformative process: one that shapes lived experience into a liberatory political consciousness. Within British imperialism, England was explicitly positioned as a model, and an ostensible tutor, for colonies as diverse and varied as India, South Africa, and Ireland; however, the relations among these colonies, while an occasional topic of metropolitan discussion, was mostly left to the colonized themselves. In the previous chapter, we witnessed how in the explicitly literary portion of the global Anglophone, this intercolonial geography came to be charted through interconnections of translating, prefacing, and publishing: the Irish W. B. Yeats and the Chinese Liang Qichao for different volumes by the Bengali Tagore, and then Tagore in turn for the Singaporean Lim Boon Keng. In the explicitly political portion of the global Anglophone, similar dynamics applied, but with a key difference: whereas the literary conduits of Yeats, Tagore, and Lim invested in the possibilities of translation, those mapped by anticolonial activists frequently insisted on exact lexemic transfer, dramatizing untranslated words in the process.

Gandhi arrived in South Africa in 1893, when it comprised four colonies under White rule. At the time, however, White people in South Africa were bitterly divided along linguistic and national lines: between the Afrikaners (in his language, Boers)[14]—who spoke Afrikaans, a Dutch-based creole spoken in South Africa and Namibia—and the British—who, like Gandhi himself, spoke English. By the time he left, in 1915, the four colonies had been reconstituted into the Union of South Africa: a state founded in 1910 that consolidated the Boer and British colonies through an explicit enshrinement of White supremacy (and, accordingly, Whites-only governance). From the Anglo-Boer Wars of the turn of the century, in which Gandhi played a supporting role, to the Act of Union of 1910, whose racist laws he protested, Gandhi witnessed a battle along linguistic contours—English versus Afrikaans—

and national ones—the British government versus the Boer colonies. These linguistic and national divides were resolved through the unifying magic of White supremacism. Because of this concatenation of linguistic identity and racial ideology, early twentieth-century South Africa is thus particularly useful for thinking about the global Anglophone. Its politics, which were formative of Gandhi's own, provide a violent demonstration of how the dividing line of English is not identical to the divide of racial privilege. Most British colonies dramatized the global reach and ostensible superiority of English against the backdrop of languages that were disparaged as primitive, parochial, and inferior, and which also had almost exclusively non-White speakers. Early twentieth-century South Africa, however, presaged the dominance of the global Anglophone over its European rivals by placing English in competition with a White language—Afrikaans. Despite this Dutch-based creole's European origins and proudly White speakers, English colonists nonetheless disparaged Afrikaans much as they did other African tongues. Thanks to their shared European descent, British and Boer may have been cultural or racial "cousins,"[15] as Gandhi terms them in 1928, but they were nonetheless divided.

As Gandhi became the author of a new Indian nation *outside* empire, his texts began to insist on often untranslated and conspicuously Indian (because Sanskritic) terminology. Along with the neologism "satyagraha," Gandhi invested heavily in two other little-known (but already extant) Sanskrit words: "ahimsa" and "swaraj." The word "ahimsa," as Leela Gandhi has shown, became a capacious concept of nonviolence that could apply to interpersonal relations as well as epistemological ones; the word "swaraj," as Ajay Skaria has argued, came to demonstrate a rule of the self at once indicative of political autonomy and yet more expansive than its Western theorizations.[16] I focus on "satyagraha" because, unlike "ahimsa" or "swaraj," it is a neologism, a coinage created by Gandhi in South Africa that nonetheless flaunted its ancient Indic roots. The trajectory of the word "satyagraha" mimics those of his clothing choices, which became less significant for their class indications and more prominent as testaments of one's race. As Gandhi began writing, on November 26, 1923, of his experiences in South Africa, he sat in Yeravda Prison in western India—but he might have been anywhere in the British Empire. The carceral structures that shaped Gandhi's political existence, in South Africa as in India, were part of an extensively and explicitly replicated set of British institutions, intended to instill law and order within a single space. From this interchangeable place of imperial incarceration, Gandhi kept a diary that on his release would be transformed into two books—*Satyagraha in South Africa* and *My Experiments with Truth*—each of which would be serialized and then published in book form.[17]

As this chapter demonstrates, for Gandhi, it was replicability, not interchangeability, that implied true equality. Commonality was created by the replication of practices like reading and hand-spinning across both time and space, and this replication would render swaraj possible. It is this emphasis on equality without interchangeability, I suggest, that has led to our repeated problems in valorizing him ever since: this is the basic way in which Gandhi, for better and worse, is not a liberal person. In generic terms, his interest in replicability rather than interchangeability manifests in a pronounced interest in the form of the parable. A long-established and frequently didactic form, the parable genre central to Gandhi's print internationalism can be compared to the genre that is central to Anderson's theorization of print nationalism: the novel. The novel produces a sense of human interchangeability that can, via Anderson, become the national "meanwhile." The parable, by contrast, encourages emulation without asserting similarity: it is the genre that demonstrates replicability without equivalence. Consequently, the parable, as I will demonstrate, becomes particularly useful as Gandhi transports his politics from South Africa to South Asia. This point about literary form is also one, crucially, about political limitations. Gandhi's use of the parable to narrate his South African experiences to an Indian readership renders his writing about South Africans woefully inadequate through its tendentious representations. Black South Africans become, in Gandhi's writings for Indian readers, merely figures for what can be and what must be done in India, holding little autonomous significance in Gandhi's didactic narratives of South Africa.

ENGAGING *INDIAN OPINION*

Gandhi's writing career itself began in an international frame: during his legal training in England. By the time of his arrival in South Africa in 1893, he was a seasoned journalist, one whose major writings, like his higher education, had been in the English language.[18] As he transformed from lawyer to activist, he became, as well, a savvy publisher and editor. In this section I narrate Gandhi's changing approach to print internationalism, attending not only to his writings while in South Africa, which mainly took the form of periodicals and pamphlets, but also to the book-length recollections of that time he penned later from India. The early Gandhi, as many have noted, was more reformist than revolutionary. This was famously clear in his political positions, as for instance in his repeated assertion of his loyalty to the British Crown. It also manifested itself, as I demonstrate, in the strategies of his printed works, which were very different from his later writings not only in their expressed opinions but also in their uses of language and layout. Instead of mobilizing ostentatiously Indian words, the early Gandhi tried to correct and contain the parameters of existing terms in the English language; instead of writing in the parable forms of his later volumes, he wrote in the anecdotal arguments beloved of liberal realism.

Decades before coining "satyagraha," Gandhi was already emphasizing the proper use of Indian-associated terms. For example, in an 1896 pamphlet, which he framed as "an appeal to the Indian public," Gandhi complained repeatedly that the restrictions placed on the indentured Indian were being applied, along with the epithet "coolie," to wealthy Indians as well. In this early writing, titled *The Grievances of the British Indians in South Africa* (also known as the *Green Pamphlet*), Gandhi does not dispute the debasement of the Indian indentured laborer; his objection, rather, is to the expansion of a class-based category into a racial designation. In his reasoning, the word "coolie," when used for an indentured laborer, is not a slur, but "coolie trader" is.[19] Using "Indian," "Arab," and "Asiatic" interchangeably, the 1896 pamphlet emphasizes the incommensurability of race and class: "coolie," for instance, is part of a "black laboring class," even as Indians are not described as "black."[20] In a text that combines consistent English with inconsistent terminology and erratic punctuation, Gandhi bemoans that

> The Press almost unanimously refuses to call the Indian by his proper name. He is "Ramsamy." He is Mr. "Samy," "He is Mr. Coolie" "He is the black man." And these offensive epithets have become so common that they at any rate—one of them—Coolie are used even in the sacred precincts of the Courts, as if the Coolie were the legal and proper name to give to any and every Indian.[21]

Gandhi here bemoans the absence of the "proper name," and while he identifies a racial problem, he seeks an individualizing solution, in keeping with the values of liberalism. Advancement is signaled here in respectable individuation: his complaint prioritizes the problem of melding together before it even mentions the "offensive epithets." This strategy would shift, however, once he left South Africa for South Asia. In contrast to the South Africa–based Gandhi of 1896, who condemned the absence of the Indian's proper name for that of "Samy," the South Asia–based Gandhi of the 1927 first volume of *My Experiments* uses that epithet as the occasion for some subversive wordplay. Noting that the Tamil suffix *-sami* is "nothing else than the Sanskrit *Swami*, meaning a master," Gandhi explains that Indians used to rebuke the insult by invoking its etymology: "Some Englishmen would wince at this, while others would get angry, swear at the Indian and if there was a chance, would even belabor him; for '*sami*' to him was nothing better than a term of contempt. To interpret it to mean a master amounted to an insult!"[22] Here etymology has become a resource for colonial subversion: as this small but crucial shift suggests, Gandhi's politics became ever more anticolonial as he began to use Sanskrit as an anticolonial implement within the global Anglophone. Gandhi explains, early on in *My Experiments*, the difference between the word "coolie" in India, where it "means only a porter or carrier," and in South Africa, where it "has a contemptuous connotation."[23] Gandhi was called a "coolie barrister," he recollects, only because White South Africans were ignorant of "the original meaning of the word 'coolie.'"[24] Instead of the "unanimous refus[al]" of Indians' individuality that the South Africa–based Gandhi once saw in these usages, the South Asia–based Gandhi here finds not White obstinacy but White ignorance.

The shifting nature of Gandhi's statements on the "coolie" status of Indians in South Africa over this thirty-year period is further indicated in the pages of his key South African publication, the periodical *Indian Opinion*. Published weekly from 1903 onward, *Indian Opinion* was a multilingual periodical of varying length that had 3,500 subscribers at its peak; while it initially ran advertisements, Gandhi soon shifted to a subscription-only model, abstaining from paid advertising in the final product as well as from paid labor in the periodical's production. It was most popular in the British colony of the Transvaal (now the South African Province of Gauteng), reaching 3,500 subscribers at its peak. Embracing both a sensibility and a constituency, the periodical orchestrated and documented the movement that would come to be known as satyagraha.[25] Gandhi established *Indian Opinion* with sections in Gujarati, Hindi, English, and Tamil. In doing so, he carefully considered the demographics of the Indian South African populace, whose linguistic divides echoed those of class, caste, and religion. Gujarati and, to a lesser extent, Hindi were the languages of the Muslim trader elites in the Transvaal region, who were also the main source of Gandhi's early support. Tamil and, to a lesser extent, Telegu were the languages of the indentured Indian laboring classes in the Natal region, who were likely to be Christian or Hindu. The English language connected the settler colonies of the Natal and the Transvaal to a wider world of English-speaking colonies, and this connectivity was often beneficial for non-White persons, whether by connecting Black South Africans to what was then British West Africa (now Ghana, Nigeria, Sierra Leone, and the Gambia) or by connecting Indian South Africans (who did not always speak Indian languages) to the Indian subcontinent. For this early Gandhi, though, English alone did not meet his textual goals.

Gandhi's South African periodical articulated its constituency in its inaugural issue, on June 4, 1903: *Indian Opinion* is for "British Indians" residing in South Africa, who are "members of a mighty empire." We are then given a sense of its imagined readership, through the description of the advantages accruing from the journal to both "the Indian community" and "the European community," and the specification of subscription rates both inside and outside "the Colony." Writing at the start of the twentieth century as a "British Indian," Gandhi demanded not the dissolution but the improvement of the British Empire. In this 1903 issue of *Indian Opinion*, Gandhi advocates a mode of representation that considers Indians and Europeans in an equal, simultaneous, and proximate fashion, both in their cultures and in their persons. The pages of his periodical perform that agenda in content and in form, with linguistic differences serving as metonyms of cultural complementarity. Declaring that the paper would work "to bring about a proper understanding between the two communities whom Providence has brought together under one flag,"[26] the page places Indian languages next to English, but without a symmetrical logic of exact translation. In the journal's second issue, published on June 11, 1903, a full-page advertisement (fig. 2) explained its method: *Indian Opinion* is published, the advertisement declares, "in FOUR languages," and those languages then descend proudly across the page in a diagonal procession: "English, Gujarati, Tamil, and Hindi." The purpose of this multilingualism is attested at the bottom of the page: "In the interest of the Indians in South Africa." Gandhi knew no Tamil, and disavowed expertise in Hindi; nevertheless, he chose these languages as the languages of the plurality of "the Indians of South Africa." These were not the Indians who were reading

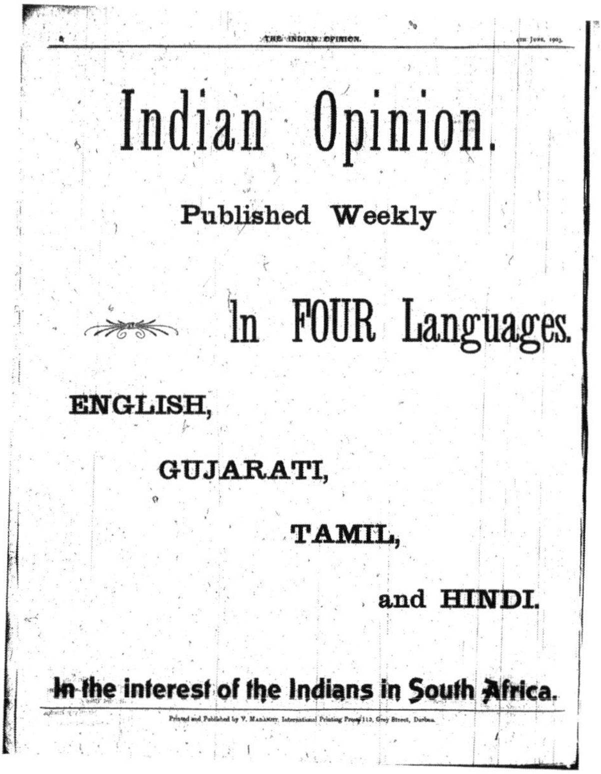

Fig. 2. A full-page advertisement in *Indian Opinion* (Durban, South Africa), June 11, 1903.

Indian Opinion, much less subscribing to it, yet by incorporating their languages Gandhi interpellated them as readers.[27]

Gandhi's seemingly minor choice of preposition—"in," not "of," South Africa—is further indicative of his early politics: he writes for the Indians *in* South Africa, not the Indians *of* South Africa. These Indians, like Indians elsewhere, are first and foremost "of" the British Empire, making their demands within the remit of what Sukanya Bannerjee has termed the "hybrid citizenship" forms of early twentieth-century Britain.[28] Because British citizenship devolved from the British Crown, the distinction between a citizen and a subject remained undefined until the British Nationality and Status of Aliens Act of 1914. In the late nineteenth and early twentieth century, consequently, Gandhi and many of his Indian contemporaries grounded their rights to reside in British-controlled Africa within their claims to British imperial citizenship. As

Indian laws, administrators, and persons moved within the imperial axis into settler colonies in Africa, Indian leaders frequently proclaimed their imperial loyalties, hoping thereby to advance their claims to land rights and trading privileges that were denied to these African colonies' African inhabitants.[29]

We can approach Gandhi's strategies of print internationalism by closely examining *Indian Opinion*'s second issue. Its first page (fig. 3) is a mélange of content and advertising (though Gandhi would soon move to an advertisement-free, exclusively subscription model). The third of six columns, and the only one to run uninterrupted down the entire length of the page, describes the services of Gandhi's International Printing Press. Each trade is articulated in terms of its human actors: the press consists of "book binders, machine rulers, and makers of rubber stamps," who offer printing in an eclectic list of eleven languages that descends diagonally: "Gujarati, Tamil, Hindi, Urdoo, Marathi, Sanscrit, French, Dutch, Zulu, &c, &c." This list was likely aspirational, for there is little evidence that the International Printing Press went substantially beyond the four languages printed in *Indian Opinion*, and even this early issue advertises for Tamil and Hindi compositors, which the press continually lacked.[30] Within a few years of its inception, *Indian Opinion* would come to be published exclusively in the languages that Gandhi knew well, English and Gujarati. By choosing multiple languages, though, *Indian Opinion* signals its desire to convene multiple communities, not a single amalgamation of those communities. This is an interpretive community whose members know how to approach the multilingual pages according to each person's individual competencies, but it is not an imagined community, whose readers imagine that others are reading the paper just as they are.

Whereas *Indian Opinion* signaled a multiplicity of readers, the replicability that is crucial to Gandhi's print internationalism is prominent in what is now the best-known of Gandhi's South African writings: a 1909 pamphlet, *Hind Swaraj*, first published in English translation under the title *Indian Home Rule* in 1910. One of many pamphlets issued by his International Printing Press, *Hind Swaraj* was the only one composed of original writing. Written after Gandhi's failed mission to London in June 1909—where he sought to secure protections for Indians in South Africa based on their status as British subjects—the story of the pamphlet's creation is the stuff of Mahatma legend. As his admirers frequently recount, Gandhi wrote continuously for ten days on the ship *Kildonan Castle*, writing with his left hand when his right grew tired. *Hind Swaraj* consists

INDIAN OPINION.

PUBLISHED IN ENGLISH. GUJARATI. TAMIL. HINDI.

Vol. 1. Durban, June 11th, 1903. No. 2.

International Printing Press, Artistic & General Printers, 113, Grey Street, Durban.

Book Binders, Machine Rulers, and Makers of Rubber Stamps.

Printing also Executed in Gujarati, Tamil, Hindi, Urdoo, Hebrew, Marathi, Sanscrit, French, Dutch, Zulu, &c. &c.

Wedding Cards, Visiting Cards, Business Cards, Memorandums, Ball Programmes, Account Forms, Menus, Letter Heads, Circulars, Billheads, Law Forms, Receipt Books, Delivery Books, Promissory Notes.

WANTED. GOOD MACHINE BOY, GOOD WAGES for suitable person. Apply to PROPRIETOR "INDIAN OPINION."

WANTED. A VERY COMPETENT MAN. WHO CAN READ AND WRITE HINDI THOROUGHLY, MUST HAVE A GOOD KNOWLEDGE OF ENGLISH. Apply to PROPRIETOR "INDIAN OPINION."

RALEIGH CYCLES. THE Rigid Rapid Reliable Kind. POPULAR PRICES: EASY RUNNING. THE PEOPLE'S FAVOURITE. 485, West Street, DURBAN.

WANTED. FIRST CLASS Tamil Compositor. Apply to PROPRIETOR, "INDIAN OPINION."

Pohoomull Brothers, 170, West Street, DURBAN, NATAL. WHOLESALE & RETAIL. Manufacturers and Direct Importers of Oriental Jewellery, High-Class Indian Art Curios and Maltese Lace Articles.

The "Indian Opinion."

This weekly newspaper is published in four languages, namley :English, Gujarati, Tamil, and Hindi, in the interests of the British Indians residing in South Africa.

THE POLICY

of the paper would be to advocate the cause of the British Indians in this sub-continent. But while it would insist upon the rights of the community, it would not be slow to point out to it its responsibilities also as members of a mighty Empire. It would persistently endeavour to bring about a proper understanding between the two communities which Providence has brought together under one flag.

THE ADVANTAGES

to the *Indian community* in subscribing to and supporting this paper would be :—

(1) It would have a newspaper that would advocate its cause as well as give to all sections of it news in their own languages.

(2) It would contain news specially affecting Indians of all parts of South Africa, besides local and general information.

(3) It would contain an epitome of events happening in India.

(4) It would give commercial intelligence.

(5) It would contain contributions from competent writers, Indian as well as European, on all subjects—Social, Moral, and Intellectual.

The advantages to the *European community* would be :—

(1) The paper would give it an idea of Indian thought and aspirations.

(2) It would acquaint it with such Indian matters as are not commonly known to it, and yet which should not be ignored by true Imperialists.

To *Europeans and Indians* alike, it would serve as the best *advertising medium* in those branches of the trade in which Indians are especially concerned.

The *rate* of annual subscription is 12s. 6d. in the Colony, and outside the Colony, 17s., payable in advance.

Single copies are sold at 3d. each.

Advertising charges can be had on application to the undersigned.

V. MADANJIT,
Proprietor, "Indian Opinion."
113, Grey Street, Durban.

Abdul Caadir, of Mahomed Cassim Camroodeen & Co.
Joosab Abdool Carim, of Messrs. Dada Abdoola & Co.
Dawad Mahomed & Co.
P. Dawjee Mahomed & Co.
Hoosen Cassim & Co.
Adamji Miankhan, of G. H. Miankhan & Co.
Parsee Rustomji.
Hajee Abdoola.
Ebrahim Hajee Cassim.
Ahmed Mahomed Parekh.
M. C. Anglia.
A. D. Munshi.

Fig. 3. The front page of *Indian Opinion* (Durban, South Africa), June 11, 1903.

of a philosophical dialogue that compares ancient and modern civilization. Once this historical comparison has been established, civilization's poles are then mapped as Eastern and Western, as Indian and English, and, finally, as the kingdom of God and the kingdom of Satan.

Hind Swaraj stages a dialogue between a "Reader" and an "Editor," modeling what Gandhi in later texts described as his desired function for a periodical: "establishing an intimate and clean bond between the editor and the readers."[31] This dialogue unfolds in an unspecified space, through an ambiguous address to a placeholder addressee. Its address has been variously read as Indian radicals in Britain or as Indian elites in South Africa, and the indecipherability of the recipient is crucial to its moral import.[32] Rather than arbitrate these divergent accounts of *Hind* Swaraj's imagined "ideal reader," I want to suggest that, in keeping with his emphasis on nonequivalence, Gandhi's text may solicit different kinds of reading across widely divergent readers: that is to say, *Hind Swaraj* envisions not one ideal readership but several. This ambiguity is built into the persona of the Reader within the dialogue. At once a character within the written text and the name for the person who interprets that text, the Reader signals the instability of the ideal reader of *Hind Swaraj*, even as it underlines the importance of reading. By this method, *Hind Swaraj* accomplishes through genre (through its version of a Socratic dialogue) what *Indian Opinion* instituted through language (by publishing in Hindi, Gujarati, Tamil, and English).

Likewise, the function of the Editor of *Hind Swaraj* is akin to that of a periodical: an instrument of expression that produces interchange, seeking both to regulate and to encourage circulation. "These views," Gandhi explains in his foreword to *Hind Swaraj*, "are mine and not mine. They are mine because I hope to act according to them. . . . But, yet, they are not mine, because I lay no claim to originality."[33] To substantiate this claim, Gandhi places a list of supplementary readings in an appendix, titled "Some Authorities," with an opening note: "The following books are recommended for perusal to follow up the study of the foregoing." The reader of *Hind Swaraj* (unlike the Reader in *Hind Swaraj*) thus reads Gandhi's "study" so that he can peruse Tolstoy, Ruskin, Thoreau, and even Plato, among others. Divorcing writing from originality, and even from authorship, Gandhi operates here much like his International Printing Press: he is not the origin of the views expressed, but the instrument of their expression.[34]

Scribbling furiously as his ship traverses the equator, Gandhi's construction of an ahistorical, unlocalizable Reader mimics his construction of a timeless, transportable East and West. In writing *Hind Swaraj* in transit for a presumably global readership, Gandhi used a different strategy than that of his 1896 pamphlet *The Grievances of the British Indians*. Whereas that pamphlet had objected to the use of a derogatory descriptor, "coolie," for all Indians and demanded that each individual's "proper name" be used instead, in *Hind Swaraj* he shifted to deploying "Indian" as itself a kind of proper name. In doing so, he reinvents

"Indian" as a civilizational and spiritual principle, rather than a racial marker, and he deploys the untranslated term "Swaraj"—a synonym for "self-rule"—to accomplish this reorganization. Gandhi writes of Indian civilization (god-fearing and virtuous) and English civilization (godless, materialistic, and immoral), but his use of these terms is more metaphorical than referential. In *Hind Swaraj* he repeatedly claims that it is not the English people, but modern civilization, that is ruling India, and he dismisses demands for Indian control of the existing state apparatus as desires for "English rule without the Englishman." Insisting on radical transformation, Gandhi articulates British rule in India as an epic battle on the boundaries of civilizations: as the locus of cultural contact and the potential locus of revitalization.

The Reader in *Hind Swaraj* bemoans India's condition in his questions, and the Editor patiently responds, frequently turning the question around on the Reader. Much as, according to Gandhi, "the community thought audibly through this correspondence" with him as the editor of *Indian Opinion*,[35] so too the readers of *Hind Swaraj*, placed alongside the Reader *in Hind Swaraj*, find themselves in a conversation with this Editor: thoughts made audible, so far as print allows. The dialogue here between their viewpoints, moreover, models that between civilizations, proving the didactive power of the initially incompatible pairing. We are not *the* Reader, but *a* reader: the person who is being addressed within the text is not a placeholder for the imagined community, but one (of many) members of the interpretive community, each of whom must learn *Hind Swaraj*'s interpretive protocols for the world.

Hind Swaraj argues that nonviolent resistance—which Gandhi at that time called soul-force or truth-force, rather than satyagraha—is the most powerful agent of historical change. When the Reader asks for evidence of soul-force's success, the Editor explains that the historical record cannot provide it. At this early stage in Gandhi's career, he defines history as the record of the interruptions of soul-force: what is understood as a historical event is precisely not the successes of soul-force but, rather, its failure. As he explains:

> Thousands, indeed tens of thousands, depend for their existence on a very active working of this force. Little quarrels of millions of families in their daily lives disappear before the exercise of this force. Hundreds of nations live in peace. History does not, and cannot, take note of this fact. History is really a record of every interruption of the even working of the force of love or of the soul. Two brothers quarrel; one

> of them repents and re-awakens the love that was lying dormant in him; the two again begin to live in peace; nobody takes note of this. But, if the two brothers, through the intervention of solicitors or some other reason, take up arms or go to law—which is another form of the exhibition of brute force—their doings would be immediately noticed in the press, they would be the talk of their neighbours, and would probably go down to history. And what is true of families and communities is true of nations. There is no reason to believe that there is one law for families and another for nations. History, then, is a record of an interruption of the course of nature. Soul-force, being natural, is not noted in history.[36]

Gandhi makes his argument for this force not only through an argument about history but also through one about scale. Jumping from thousands to millions to hundreds, all in the first three sentences, Gandhi renders individuals, families, and nations interchangeable, and all governed by "one law." Jumping then to critique the category of history, Gandhi turns to the educational possibilities of the parable. The story of the two brothers' quarrel is not factual but apocryphal, and its purported insignificance can illuminate the historical record. Gandhi makes his political argument through a rhetoric of the example—here, the apocryphal anecdote—which he asserts can be replicated in different sites and on varying scales: "What is true for families and communities is also true for nations."[37]

Whereas the liberal nation-state mimics the family by laying claim to the public and allocating it to the private, Gandhi's nations can replicate families by eliminating the distinction between the political and the domestic. This refusal of the liberal conception of the political and the public, moreover, had generic consequences for Gandhi's print practices. In his time, after all, the formal writing of history was predicated on that very distinction, relegating the stuff of mere personal recollection outside the historical field that Gandhi so memorably invoked in the above passage. Yet history-writing, in the broad sense of telling compelling stories about the past, has long been a pressing concern for marginalized peoples, Gandhi included. As a consequence, despite his disavowal of the ability of history-writing to inscribe the successes of satyagraha, Gandhi remained concerned with producing historical evidence.

Gandhi himself translated *Hind Swaraj* into English, and he initially translated the title as well: an English-language version, titled *Indian Home Rule*, appeared in 1910 from his International Printing Press. Yet after his 1915 arrival in India, the title was left untranslated for its subsequent English-language editions. Much as Tagore's *Gitanjali*, as explored in the previous chapter, only gained in the global Anglophone by deploying an untranslated title, so too the circulation of Gandhi's English-language *Hind Swaraj* under its untranslated name seems only to have added to its prestige as it traversed the global Anglophone. As he worked on his translation of *Hind Swaraj*, Gandhi seems to have wavered on the translatability of "swaraj" even within the body of the text. As Tridip Suhrud tells us, of the fifty-six uses of "swaraj" in the Gujarati text, Gandhi translated exactly half of them into "Home Rule" for his English version, leaving the remainder as simply "swaraj."[38] This variation is indicative of Gandhi's shifting views. While he was initially inspired by the Irish Home Rule movement, which would be emulated in India particularly during the First World War, Gandhi became increasingly convinced that Home Rule, an explicitly political concept, was not actually equivalent to swaraj, which he understood as emphasizing both official politics and individual conduct. This shift further reflects a larger trend in Gandhi's writings, for Gandhi increasingly wished to separate his politics from other movements, whether those with similar strategies (such as the movement for women's suffrage in Britain), or those with similar aims (such as the aspiration for Home Rule in Ireland). In this trajectory, the untranslated word became crucial: "satyagraha" announces its nonequivalence to the "passive resistance" championed by others, while "Hind Swaraj" renders Home Rule uniquely Indian. In untranslating the title, then, Gandhi moves from creating an Indian version of a still globally comprehensible politics—an Indian version of Home Rule—to declaring his politics nonequivalent to all existing agitations. Crucially, his words are "untranslated" in the sense of a reversal *after* translation. This is a reversion to the original language, not a preservation within it nor a condition of being untranslatable.

One of Gandhi's last South African publications was a special commemorative "Golden Number" of *Indian Opinion*. Already beginning to present his work in South Africa as completed, Gandhi published this special issue, titled *Souvenir of the Passive Resistance Movement in South Africa, 1906–1914*, in a cloth-bound codex format with multiple glossy photographs. This "Golden Number" of 1914 provided an overview of the movement, with thirty pages of English text, an additional twenty-four in Gujarati, and a final six-page section in Tamil. It still referred to "Passive Resistance" in its title, though less frequently in its pages: Gandhi by this point mostly avoided that term. An essay titled "The Great Central Figure," written by Gandhi's close collaborator

Henry Polak (under his pen name, A. Chessel Piquet), was accompanied by a full-page illustration. Attesting to "soul-force's success," the image presents a before-and-after narrative in visual form (fig. 4). On the left, in the medium distance, Gandhi poses as an imperial citizen, looking

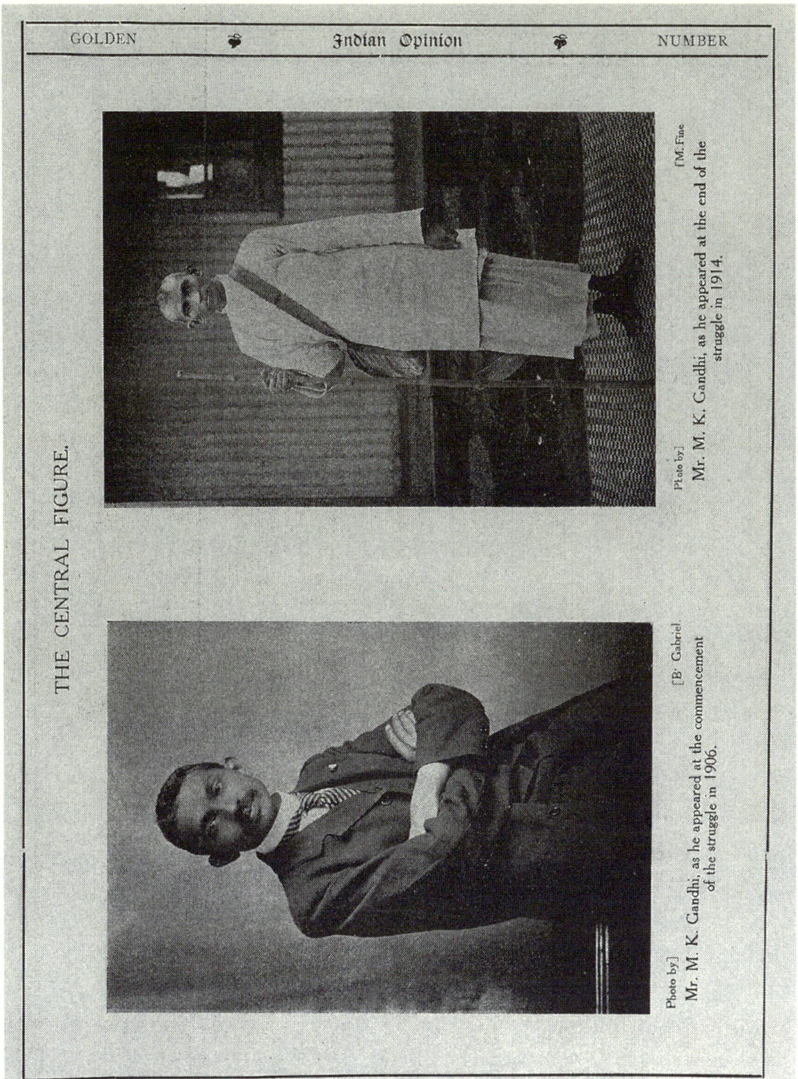

Fig. 4. Photographs of Gandhi (printed broadside) in the 1914 "Golden Number" commemorative issue of *Indian Opinion*, published separately as *Souvenir of the Passive Resistance Movement in South Africa.*

directly into the camera but with his arms crossed, in suit and tie. On the right, in a long shot, Gandhi stands looking directly at us, dressed as the most Indian of Indians, in clothing associated with indentured Indians and with traveling Hindu mendicants.[39] Despite photography's oft-noted claims to indexical representation, and its seeming ability to solidify historical detail, these images instead suggest malleability and even artifice. Here posing for the camera as an imperial citizen serves only to belie its falsity: it is a pose easily undone by the powers of satyagraha.

The backdrop of the 1906 portrait—a nondescript photography studio—has been eliminated in the 1914 portrait, which is taken outside in front of what appears to be a shed. The 1914 body, moreover, is active and open in its posture, unlike the conventionally clothed body of 1906, which leans casually on a table. As readers, moreover, we have moved farther from our "central figure": Gandhi is not only less familiar in his physical presentation but also physically farther away, and smaller, in the 1914 photograph. The narrative of transformation visualized here on the body of Gandhi is central to what becomes the Gandhian form of anticolonialism: an insistence that decolonization, like colonization, must transform not just the state but also the self. These paired photographs serve as a complete narrative, one shorn of the potential confusions of linguistic explanation. Whereas *Hind Swaraj* in 1909 insisted that soul-force could not be recorded in history, Gandhi in 1914 presents the image of his body's transformation as the evidence of soul-force's success.[40] India now seems not an abstract civilizational principle, but an embodied reality that can travel—much as Gandhi does himself.

GANDHI'S SOUTH AFRICA

Gandhi returned permanently to India in 1915, and he led the all-India satyagraha known as the noncooperation movement from 1920 to 1922, leveraging both the outrage resulting from the 1919 Jallianwala Bagh massacre and the enthusiasm generated by the pan-Islamic Khilafat movement. He was then imprisoned from 1922 to 1924, a period bookended, as we saw in the first chapter, by vociferous debates with Rabindranath Tagore. During his imprisonment, Gandhi wrote extensively of his experiences in South Africa, intending these recollections for readers in India, not in South Africa. The diaries from this period would yield two published narratives, both published initially in Gujarati (serialized in the journal *Navjivan*) and then in book form and in English translation. *Satyagraha in South Africa* appeared in English in 1928; *My Experiments* was published in two volumes in 1927 and 1928, with concurrent English serialization in his journal *Young India*. *My Experiments*, Gandhi's best-selling work, has become central to his legendary persona, and it subordinates the South African context of his political and historical "experiments" to the story of his own transformation. *My Experiments* explicitly exhorts comparative reading: by keeping *Satyagraha in South Africa* at hand, *My Experiments* explains, the reader will become capable of understanding the correspondences between the books and hence the connections across the chapters of *My Experiments* itself.[41] Yet when read together as instructed, these texts prove decidedly different.

Gandhi explains that he wrote *Satyagraha in South Africa* to demonstrate the significance of what he terms his "complete victory in South Africa," in a preface that was published in the first Gujarati serialization in 1925 but excluded from the English translation issued three years thereafter. Whereas his detractors, Gandhi writes, suggest that all his efforts "meant only that the Indians maintained their *status quo*" in South Africa, these skeptics are "ignorant" of his work's international significance.[42] Gandhi demands that his South African protests be read within a larger global geography: "Had the battle in South Africa not been fought today Indians would have been driven out not only from South Africa, but also from all other British colonies and no one would have even taken notice of it."[43] The South African "battle" is thus a victory for all British colonies, a victory evidenced through the invocation of some imagined outside observer—much like, perhaps, the geographically unspecified Reader of *Hind Swaraj*. This insistence that South Africa must be understood within an international framework forms the essential conceit of *Satyagraha in South Africa*. Just as in *Hind Swaraj* the peaceful resolution of familial conflicts can be scaled up to resolve global disputes, so here one British colony can be rescaled to suit the needs of a more populous colony, elsewhere. *My Experiments*, by contrast, is iterative but not scalable, for it is saturated with personable advice for the individual reader. Taken together, then, these texts model replicability without equivalence, for their divergent accounts of the same material nevertheless advance the same moral.

Because *My Experiments* follows Gandhi's travels, it shifts smoothly across locations, describing each incident as it occurs and emphasizing temporal, and not geographical, parameters. Whereas Gandhi started writing *Satyagraha in South Africa* to provide a record of the past for his followers, he commences writing *My Experiments*, he explains, without any "definite plan."[44] *My Experiments* is episodic, both in composition and in content: it is "written from week to week . . . just as the Spirit moves me at the time of writing."[45] The periodicity of *My Experiments* is compounded by its reliance on itemization: each protest has a victory and every peril has a moral, and their organization is meaningfully sequential, often signaled in the phrase "as we shall see later." For example, whereas political stakes are articulated in spatial terms in *Satyagraha in South Africa*, in *My Experiments* they are explained in terms of time: "Had the community [in South Africa] given up the struggle, . . . the hated impost [tax] would have continued to be levied from the indentured Indians until this day, to the eternal shame of the Indians in South Africa and of the whole of India."[46] This feared hypothetical is shaped by three commas of deferral and one practical possibility, all culminating in "the eternal shame of the Indians in South Africa and of the whole of India." The temporal emphasis of Gandhi's autobiography provides the ethical assurances for what he terms *My Experiments with Truth*: what matters is the future and the past, not the present. In the more publicly political *Satyagraha in South Africa*, by contrast, geographical comparisons in the present offer consolations for Indian followers. Writing from his prison cell, in the Gujarati preface that he originally excluded from his English translation, Gandhi confidently declares: "I see that there is nothing in our present position which I had not encountered in South Africa on a smaller scale. . . . I expect the repetition here of the experience I had of the final phase in South Africa."[47] As this passage suggests, Gandhi insists repeatedly that the difference between South Africa and India is iterative in nature, placing these regions in a primarily geographical relation to each other.

The English title of *Satyagraha in South Africa* dropped the allusion to history (*itihas*) which is present in the Gujarati title, *Dakshina Africana Satyagrahano Itihas*. Ranajit Guha has demonstrated the complex history of the term, which he glosses as "a traditional account relayed from generation to generation."[48] While *itihas* had long included the mythological corpus of Hindu epics, British officials seeking to situate Indian history within the remit of world history decreed the word "history" to be translatable as *itihas*—thereby suiting, as well, the desires of a Hindu elite that perceived, in this regime of translation, a validation of Hindu mythology.[49] Perhaps Gandhi, in his translation of *Dakshina Africana Satyagrahano Itihas* as *Satyagraha in South Africa*, felt that *itihas* simply could not be translated; or perhaps, like

Tagore in Guha's analysis, Gandhi felt that *itihas* was best understood as the *failings* of history to record the private and the personal, rather than as history itself. In his brief forward to the translation, Gandhi writes that *Satyagraha in South Africa* is not a "regular detailed history"—for which, he asserts, he had "neither the time nor the inclination"—but "a guide to any regular historian who may arise in the future" and which might be "helpful in our present struggle" to liberate India.[50] If Gandhi was not writing a history—despite the *itihas* of the Gujarati text's title—what was he writing? He provided history-specific details—like the exact years for various legislative changes—but then he also claimed that the Black inhabitants of South Africa were the descendants of escaped slaves from America—a fantastical assertion for which he provided no evidence. Between praise of Boer bravery and condemnation of British hypocrisy, Gandhi states: "The reader will note South African parallels for all our experiences in the present struggle to date. He will also see from this history that there is so far no ground whatever for despair in the fight that is going on."[51] *Satyagraha in South Africa* thus exercises what Leon de Kock has described as a key rhetorical move in missionary narratives of Africa, wherein writers claim to be merely recording facts even as they write of heroic quests, denying their authorial roles through frequent proclamations of their more serious, and nonliterary, preoccupations.[52] *Satyagraha in South Africa*'s strategic deployment of missionary modes that were already well established in the global Anglophone enables it to be both travelogue and pedagogue: a repository of African details and of Indian political hopes.

Gandhi concludes his foreword to the English translation by claiming that "those who are following the weekly chapters of *My Experiments with Truth* cannot afford to miss these chapters on satyagraha, if they would follow in all its detail the working out of the search after Truth."[53] This reference, combined with *My Experiments*' reference to *Satyagraha in South Africa*, has led some commentators to read both texts together as an extended exercise in autobiography.[54] Yet whereas *My Experiments* is deeply invested in the process of self-constitution and self-articulation, detailing Gandhi's own development in a manner which might inspire others, *Satyagraha in South Africa* forgoes the autobiographical preoccupation with the "I," using first-person narration only sporadically.

Much as *Satyagraha in South Africa* disavows its status as a history, *My Experiments* disavows the genre of autobiography, a word that today features prominently in its most common English title: *An Autobiography, or the Story of My Experiments with Truth*. In the opening pages, Gandhi ventriloquizes "a God-fearing friend" who describes the genre of autobiography as itself a Western form.[55] He clarifies that he will not "attempt a real autobiography. I simply want to tell the story of my numerous experiments with truth, and as my life consists of nothing but those experiments, it is true that the story will take the shape of an autobiography."[56] Genre here emerges as if by accident, instead of by design, and in that accidental emergence all questions of its cultural origins—and authenticity—are rendered moot. Concerned, some pages later, about "the inadequacy of all autobiography as history," Gandhi imagines "some busybody" who would "cross examine me on the chapters already written."[57] Explaining that he is writing not "to please critics" but "to provide some comfort and food for reflection for my co-workers," Gandhi declares: "Writing it [the autobiography] is itself one of the experiments with truth."[58] Genre, as explained by genre theorists, serves a communicative function, suggesting to the reader how a particular text should be read. Genre in Gandhi's account, however, is primarily a Western peril. By conceptualizing his writing in these memorializing genres—the history and the autobiography—as accidental exercises toward a spiritual goal, Gandhi directs us to interpret his print internationalism for its effects. One of these, I argue, is the unusual form of international comparativism that he develops. This comparativism serves as a rhetorical conceit that enables Gandhi to declare: "What happened in South Africa will also happen here."[59]

Gandhi's print publications frequently instructed their readers in the activity of reading: *Indian Opinion* instructs its readers to clip, share, and reread articles, while *Hind Swaraj*, as Isabel Hofmeyr has argued, "instructs readers on both the reading and the production of print culture."[60] Whereas these earlier texts achieved this instructional relation through a spare dialogism, the main portion of *Satyagraha in South Africa* consists of an account of the Indian mobilizations led by Gandhi, in a narrative that alternates between factual detail and metaphorical hyperbole. Gandhi is particularly fond of biblical analogies: speaking of the slough of despond, describing the Indian satyagrahis as pilgrims, and so forth. His text thus operates through the instructive possibilities of the parable, not only at the level of the primary narrative but also through the insertion of smaller parables for the reader's edification. The entire text, consequently, provides an exercise in proper reading. After an extended discussion of the "colour bar" (race-based restrictions), Gandhi explains that he has "deliberately discussed this question with much minuteness" so that the reader "may acquire the habit of appreciating and respecting varieties of standpoint." He explains: "I do not write this book merely for the writing of it. Nor is it my object to place one phase of the history of South Africa before the public." His objective, rather, is to make known the origins and practice of Satyagraha, so that it might be emulated by "the nation."[61] Adapting satyagraha, consequently, requires learning an art of interpretation.

Satyagraha in South Africa begins with a chapter titled "Geography," which opens on the topic of size: "Africa is one of the biggest continents in the world. India is said to be not a country but a continent, but considering area alone, four or five Indias could be carved out of Africa. Africa is a peninsula like India; South Africa is thus mainly surrounded by the sea."[62] Africa is a peninsula, and India is a continent: these partial and motivated misreadings nonetheless enable worldwide comparisons. Through schematic geography and typological characterization, *Satyagraha in South Africa* inserts Indian analogues for every South African experience. Each South African detail consequently refers, not to South Africa as such, but to a larger geographical and historical unity unfolding before us. Gandhi's text is thus allegorical, and this mode renders the personas of *Satyagraha in South Africa* typological: they are not individuated characters or human beings who seem "just like ourselves," but figures chosen from an existing vocabulary of ethical possibilities. This rhetorical choice has significant implications for today's reader of *Satyagraha in South Africa*, and particularly for our understanding of Gandhi not simply as a great man but as a great "person of color."

Satyagraha in South Africa's second chapter, which follows "Geography," is titled "History," and it undermines the earlier material in its very first sentence: "The geographical divisions briefly noticed in the first chapter are not at all ancient." According to Gandhi,

> It has not been possible definitely to ascertain who were the inhabitants of South Africa in remote times. When the Europeans settled in South Africa, they found the Negroes there. These Negroes are supposed to have been the descendants of some of the slaves in America who managed to escape from their cruel bondage and migrated to Africa.[63]

The "remote times" of the unidentifiable aboriginal inhabitants of South Africa are here pasted into a reverse migration: the "Negroes" of South Africa originated in America. In Gandhi's history, the enslaved "Negroes," fleeing "their cruel bondage," made the first settlement of South Africa before Europeans arrived in the mid-seventeenth century. White settlers had long argued that Africans were not indigenous to South Africa, using this claim—grounded in willful misunderstanding—to validate their own ownership claims.[64] These claims are often grouped under the "myth of the empty land," for they purport that Whites had encountered a vacant landscape on their arrival in South Africa, only to then face overwhelming numbers of Black migrants who encroached on these hapless settlers. Gandhi, however, makes a crucial distinction: he renders Black South Africans as present prior to European colonization, describing them as the descendants of immigrants, not as immigrants themselves.

Through this historical claim, which is set off in carefully impersonal terms—"It has not been possible," "are supposed"—Gandhi presents South Africa as having always been a place for immigrants, no matter their origins. Gandhi may have had some acquaintance with American "Negroes," from, for instance, the Fisk Jubilee Singers' tour of South Africa (1890–95) or the missionary activities of the African Methodist Episcopal Church. The American "Negro" was, by the 1920s, a figure of racial possibility for many South Africans, and we might speculate that, given the extensive presence of African American missionaries in Zululand in the late nineteenth century, Gandhi's framing of his local "Negroes" as the "descendants" of Black people escaping U.S. slavery could be a garbled interpretation of African American discourses of Providential Design.[65] More likely, however, this claim is strategic. Gandhi undermines the autochthonous claim to South Africa, even as he then provisionally acknowledges it: "These Negroes must be regarded as the original inhabitants of South Africa. But South Africa is such a vast country that it can easily support twenty or thirty times its present population of Negroes."

This assertion of South Africa's vastness and abundance is the primary objective of Gandhi's "History" chapter. Elaborating on the distances between Cape Town and Durban by rail and by sea, and the enormous area covered by the four colonies of South Africa, Gandhi provides the exactitude of numbers: 1,800 miles, 1,000 miles, and 473,000 square miles, respectively. He then supplies the Negro and European populations of South Africa in 1914 (5 million and 1.25 million, respectively).[66] The insertion of such statistical detail clashes with his long-standing arguments against positivist history, yet it testifies to his central claim. By combining historical speculation and statistical detail,

Gandhi elaborates a politics of settlement in which cultivation is more important than origins, much as in his account of South Africa's geography, good irrigation proved more important than powerful rivers. In South Africa, he suggests, the autochthonous claim is untenable—and, in any case, there is enough room for everyone.

The second paragraph of Gandhi's "History" lesson begins: "Among the Negroes, the tallest and the most handsome are the Zulus." The description he provides here, with its fulsome praise, has often been cited as evidence that Gandhi was not, in fact, racist.[67] The section itself, however, is rather more complex. After that laudatory opening sentence, Gandhi's chapter continues with an extended exegesis of the attractiveness of the Zulu people, which is also the occasion for his castigation of "our [Indian] ideal of beauty," which fixates on "a fair complexion, and a pointed nose."[68] Elaborating various body parts and specific physical attributes, Gandhi introduces these legendary Zulus and commences a sequence of syntactic operations that assert similarity between Indians and Negroes only to immediately distance the terms. For example, in his account of their accommodations, he writes:

> Like ourselves, the Negroes plaster the walls and the floor with earth and animal dung. It is said the Negroes cannot make anything square in shape. They have trained their eyes to see and make only round things. We never find nature drawing straight lines or rectilinear figures, and these innocent children of nature derive all their knowledge from their experience of her.[69]

This passage begins with the assertion of similarity but then jumps rapidly through four sentences, each with a different subject for its claim. Moving from the Negroes (who are "like ourselves") to the impersonal assertion "It is said," Gandhi becomes able to speak of a third-person plural—"they" who "have trained their eyes to see and make only round things"—and finally, and most importantly, in a first-person plural—"we," who in this sentence observe both nature and her "innocent children." Gandhi's primitivism here seems immediately offensive, yet his precise phrasing offers some subversive hints, as for instance in his curious use of the verb "trained." Recalling Gandhi's claim some pages earlier that these people had previously been enslaved in the Americas, we might wonder if they "have trained their eyes" out of angular possibilities as a chosen rebuke of White values.

Gandhi's depiction of Zulus as "innocent children of nature" diverges from the global Anglophone discourse of his day. Gandhi was directly involved in one of the last Zulu wars of resistance: the 1906 uprising against oppressive colonial taxation that came to be known as the Bambatha rebellion. Given his deep imbrication in British print culture, Gandhi would have been familiar with the trope of "the Zulus," who frequently served in British literature, as Laura Chrisman has argued, "less as metonym of blackness and more as . . . an African 'aristocracy' and indigenous structure of 'imperialism.'"[70] In contrast to this widespread Anglophone discourse, which presented the Zulu people as a premonition of what might happen to the British, Gandhi erases Zulu political and military organization entirely, instead claiming that Zulus are "so timid that a Negro is afraid at the sight even of a European child."[71] He provides, instead, several digressions on Zulu culture. The Zulu language, for example, is "very sweet," with "most words end[ing] with the sound of broad 'a' so the language sounds soft and pleasing to the ear." Gandhi writes: "I have heard and read that there is both meaning and poetry in the words," thus entertaining the possibility of a meaningless language even as he asserts its meaningfulness.[72]

To attend to Gandhi's rhetoric around Black Africans is to join a much-rehearsed and highly contentious debate about the limitations of Gandhi's antiracist politics.[73] What the debate proves, however, at either pole, is that the notion of racial solidarity across the non-White world is a remarkably recent construction. Much as the theorization of Black Consciousness by Steve Biko insisted on a fundamental conceptual distinction between "non-white"—a racial descriptor—and "Black"—a political identification—so too, in revisiting Gandhi's antiracism, we might be duly reminded that the "non-white" peoples of his era, while adversely affected by White supremacy, were not immediately conjured into the kinds of unified political orientation that are suggested in the category "people of color." On the one hand, to name Gandhi "The Stretcher-Bearer of Empire," as Ashwin Desai and Goolam Vahed do, is to misrecognize the intraimperial dynamics of the time: not only Indians but also Black and Coloured South Africans enthusiastically supported the British cause during the First World War, hoping thereby to improve their negotiating positions with the British administration.[74] On the other hand, to say that he is a man of his historical context and therefore, by implication, unable to imagine a politics that exceeds that moment's historical contours creates different problems. Such historical determinism rationalizes Gandhi's racist rhetoric only by simultaneously rendering inexplicable his radical innovations in race-based politics. Gandhi worked for the rights of migrants (who happened to be Indian); groups like the South African Natives' National Conference (which later became the African National Congress) and the African People's Organization, by contrast, worked for the rights of natives (who happened to be Black and Coloured). Neither side saw the concerns of migrants and of natives as equivalent. Gandhi's relative disinterest in solidarity with Africans indicates not the failures of his time but the questions to which he was replying: in the twentieth century, the Native Question, after all, is not equivalent to the Indian Question, much as in our own twenty-first century context indigenous rights are not identical to migrants' rights. To look back at Gandhi's rhetoric with surprise is to apply the anachronistic category of "people of color": a category brought into being well after Gandhi's time, precisely to emphasize the common concerns of non-White peoples that Gandhi himself could only vaguely apprehend. Gandhi was initially a proud imperial citizen and then a proud Indian, but he was never, in our current understanding, a proud "person of color."

Gandhi was a sophisticated journalist, memoirist, and politician: his writings, with their repeated insistence on the implications of specific words and particular genres, are not solely intended as direct reflections of his personal opinions. Whether Gandhi's rhetoric accurately reflects his views of Black people, thus, is not an easy issue to resolve. I do not know if Gandhi was or was not racist, but I am confident that if he had wished to emphasize his antiracist credentials, he certainly possessed the rhetorical dexterity to do so. That he wrote of Africans in the way that he did, therefore, is of interest not to evaluate the Mahatma but to understand what those writings accomplished in his route to Mahatmahood. Accordingly, rhetorical effects, and not righteous insights, are foregrounded in this chapter.

In attending to rhetorical effects rather than latent opinions, I am deploying a reading method that is in keeping with Gandhi's own early protestations of the necessary failures of any historical record: what we might term its constitutive gaps. For instance, Gandhi's infantilizing description of Africans in *Satyagraha in South Africa* is, I would argue, ambivalent in its effects, especially in his historical moment. By erasing the martial modernity of the Zulus, he erased a past that many southern Africans, then and now, proudly claim. In doing so, however, he also disputed the mythos of African aggression persistently used by the British and by other Europeans to justify their brutal rule in Africa. Given his familiarity with the use of that racist allegation to justify the violent suppression of Zulu protest in 1906, Gandhi's depiction of the Zulus as childlike and innocent is likely a political provocation. We might, for instance, read these comments on African naïveté—cringe-inducing to the twenty-first-century liberal reader—as the less personal corollary of his remarks about the 1906 uprising in his autobiography. In *My Experiments*, Gandhi recalls that "there was no [Zulu] resistance that one could see" for it "was no war but a man hunt."[75] In *Satyagraha in South Africa*, he makes the same point by providing ethnographic description rather than personal observations: his ersatz ethnography is troubling, but in the early twentieth century it was anti-imperial and anti-Black at once.

Moreover, thanks to Gandhi's strange and unlikely history of American Negroes' migration in *Satyagraha in South Africa*, these alleged descendants of Black settlers cannot be equated with the noble savages of European typology. From Jean-Jacques Rousseau onward, the noble savage trope was used to describe the peaceful simplicity of those untouched by the rapacity of modern civilization, thus replacing the Hobbesian state of nature with a more Edenic vision. Gandhi's figures of African simplicity, by contrast, exist well after Europeans' depredations: they are not the unchanging descendants of a culture inviolate but, rather, the cultivated offspring of those who escaped White civilization, which had enslaved them, and who then successfully established a different and harmonious settlement. These figures in Gandhi's text betoken not an anterior form of utopia, as does the European trope of the noble savage, but a laudable future possibility for all of us, no matter how ensnared in the evils of modernity we may currently be. In this respect, the "Zulus" of *Satyagraha in South Africa* serve a purpose analogous to the "India" of *Hind Swaraj*: described in mythical and laudatory terms, both attest that there are better ways to run human civilization than those preferred and propagated by the West.

Gandhi moved between different strategies of racial comparison in support of his struggles against White domination of Indians. Initially, he seems to have used Black-Indian comparisons to expose the White supremacism within Britain's ostensibly liberal imperial regime. For instance, in the 1896 pamphlet *The Grievances of the British Indians*, he wrote:

> There is a very good reason for requiring the registration of a native in that he is yet being taught the dignity and

> necessity of labour. The Indian knows it and he is imported because he knows it. Yet to have the pleasure of classifying him with the natives he too is required to be registered.[76]

The twenty-first-century reader will likely focus on the first sentence of the above quotation, horrified and perhaps surprised by Gandhi's denigration of "the natives." For Gandhi's contemporaries in the nineteenth and twentieth centuries, I argue, the subversive nature of the concluding sentence was likely more remarkable. Gandhi here mocks the "pleasure" of White chauvinism, even as he repeats the Victorian rhetoric that justifies coercing Africans into wage labor. In connecting the treatment of the Indian and the "native" and then declaring the connection absurd, Gandhi performed the connective analysis of the concept of "people of color," for "people of color" makes White supremacism evident as a deep-rooted system by showing its diverse effects. He did so, however, without then enunciating a shared struggle against that system of oppression. Whereas the category "people of color" enables us not only to recognize the subjection of the "native" and the Indian as indicative of a shared experience of White supremacism and, consequently, a shared antiracist struggle, Gandhi in the nineteenth century could only register that White supremacism was at work. He could not, through that recognition, group the (African) "native" and the "Indian" (migrant) together in common cause. Such linkage, after all, would have required him to discard of the civilizational claims that he then championed, which positioned Indians as the inheritors of Aryan civilization and Africans, by contrast, as "the children of blank heathendom and outer darkness."[77]

In the twentieth century Gandhi would move away from this dependence on the Indo-Aryan hypothesis, and his depiction of Africans would shift in the process. The 1909 *Hind Swaraj*, for instance, recounts the glories of Indian civilization without invoking the grandeur of an Aryan past, instead describing India in spiritual terms. In Gandhi's writings Africans continue to be differentiated from Indians, but they are no longer phobic figures. They are, rather, the supposed children of Nature, and Nature, for the twentieth-century Gandhi, is a repository of virtue. By 1928, in the quest narrative *Satyagraha in South Africa*, the ostensibly natural Negro helps to demonstrate that there are two civilizations, Western and Indian—which stand in contrast to the Negro's alleged lack of civilization. In this rhetorical framework, certain kinds of Black suffering are crucial to Gandhi's writings, if not always to his public mobilizations. *Satyagraha in South Africa*, for instance, emphasizes the disastrous effects of Western civilization on Negroes, and he narrates in scrupulous detail the introduction of mining in South Africa. He begins with the introduction of the poll tax and the hut tax, which were extortionate measures imposed on Africans to compel them to seek wage employment and abandon their earlier, sustainable modes of production. Rather than extolling these measures as pedagogical, as he had in the nineteenth century, Gandhi now recognizes them as yet another instance of European rapacity. The consequences of mining, Gandhi explains, have been disastrous for Negroes: "miner's phthsis," a form of tuberculosis; venereal disease, from the all-male labor compounds; and alcohol-induced criminality. He is concerned here for the suffering of Black people, because their predicaments could be replicated on the bodies of others, including Indians—not because, as we might wish from a "person of color," their sufferings under White supremacy are systemically connected to those of Indians.

Pairing the 1928 text of *Satyagraha in South Africa* with the 1927 and 1929 volumes of *My Experiments*, moreover, demonstrates an even more striking shift in Gandhi's rhetoric around African and Afro-diasporic persons. From an early anecdote in which "an American Negro" saves Gandhi from a crisis, *My Experiments* provides a far more sensitive and sympathetic portrayal of persons of African descent.[78] This is, I suggest, partly because in *My Experiments* Gandhi develops a vein of comparativism absent in *Satyagraha in South Africa*, which focuses not on geography but on persons. The Gandhi of *My Experiments* analogizes the treatment of Indians in South Africa to that of low-caste groups (Dalit in today's terms; "untouchable," "pariah," or "Harijan," in Gandhi's language) in India itself. Racial discrimination thus becomes "the punishment for our own sins," because "coolie" in South Africa, Gandhi explains, "means what a pariah or an untouchable means to us."[79] In a sustained and remarkable analogy in the second volume, Gandhi declares that "today we have become the untouchables of South Africa," much as "in Christian Europe the Jews were once its 'untouchables.'"[80] Maintaining his contention that racism against Indians is retribution for Indians' own caste prejudices, Gandhi analogizes anti-Indian racism to what he terms "a strange and even unjust retribution" on contemporary Jews because of the ancient Jews' belief that they are "the chosen people of God, to the exclusion of all others."[81] In this seeming aside, Gandhi's earlier remarks become not simply a symptom of his own racist marginalization—a good example of our contemporary concept of "internalized racism"—but also its cause within a larger spiritual history.

Satyagraha in South Africa was translated into English by Valji Desai, with input from four other Gandhi disciples, and then edited for its final version by Gandhi himself. In his 1928 foreword to the translation, Gandhi assures the reader that the text retains "the spirit of the original in Gujarati"—and, in addition, that Desai "has not hesitated to make the necessary corrections."[82] There is, in the Historical Papers at the University of the Witwatersrand, an undated manuscript of *Satyagraha in South Africa*, typewritten with copious handwritten corrections. The substitutions in this typescript are numerous and unsystematic, with terms such as "bantu" that are absent in the published English version. As my analysis has demonstrated, however, seeking to parse the lexical differences between Gandhi's use of "African" versus that of "Negro," or even his "bantu," would likely prove a futile endeavor. In a world where writing and editing, translation and correction, are rendered nearly interchangeable, a reading practice of looking for Gandhi—of hunting, endlessly, for intentions and originals—may miss the overriding intentions of his print internationalism. Gandhi was not, after all, simply translating Africans, as concept or community, to his imagined Indian readership. He was, rather, conjuring into being a category of persons, as much mythical as referential, for an ignorant readership and for his own purposes. As Gandhi moved from South Africa to South Asia, his representations of the native South African shifted decisively, from the indolent "Kafir" of his 1890s writings to the natural "Negro" of his 1920s texts. In all instances, however, they were indicative of the satyagraha-facilitating logics of Gandhi's print internationalism, and not, for better and for worse, about Africans at all.

A WHITE SECRETARY FOR PEOPLE OF COLOR

Gandhi's depictions of Africans as the children of nature in his accounts of satyagraha can help us to apprehend his analogous connection of satyagraha to the noble suffering he found natural to women. Having expressed his conception of a new mode of ethical and political protest—satyagraha—Gandhi further worked to articulate the agent of that protest form—the satyagrahi. While the prominent actors in the main text of *Satyagraha in South Africa* are Indian men, the first story of satyagraha in South Africa in that text features satyagrahis who are neither Indian nor male. This crucial early anecdote tells of the thousands of "Boer" (Afrikaner) women who were interned by the British during the Anglo-Boer War. Outnumbered and with fewer resources than the British, the Afrikaner troops nonetheless resisted British conquest for several years.[83] They were vanquished only when the British undertook scorched-earth campaigns and invented the forcible internment structures we know as concentration camps.[84] Because of their impressive (if unsuccessful) demonstration of military prowess, the British ceased to regard the Afrikaners primarily as yet another despised people of Africa, and began to consider the Afrikaners as fellow Whites who could be useful in upcoming White men's wars—wars, that is, with other European countries.[85] Consequently, their joining with the British in the Act of Union in 1910 was celebrated by the mainstream British press as a moment of triumph for British liberal imperialism.[86]

Even though the Afrikaners' postwar recognition by the British was ultimately disadvantageous to Gandhi's purposes, he nonetheless finds in the Afrikaners' war experience a demonstration of his satyagraha principle. He does so by sidelining their fabled military might—much as he did, as we saw, in describing the Zulu people. He provides the masculine history of the war in a single paragraph, writing that the English and the Dutch, who "were of course cousins," clashed as they sought to conquer the African continent. While he calls Afrikaners "brave soldiers" and declares that "every Boer is a good fighter," Gandhi attributes their success to women's suffering rather than men's valor.[87] Described as brave, simple, and inspirational, these Afrikaner women underwent what Gandhi terms "indescribable sufferings"—which he then details nonetheless:

> They starved, they suffered biting cold and scorching heat. Sometimes a soldier . . . might even assault these unprotected women. Still the brave Boer women did not flinch. And at last King Edward wrote . . . that he could not tolerate it, . . . bring[ing] the war to a speedy end.[88]

Gandhi concludes this eccentric history from a spectatorial position, describing their ordeal as "a wonderful sight": it was evidence, he writes, that "real suffering bravely borne melts even a heart of stone."[89] Gandhi's hyperbolic account of the ending of the Anglo-Boer War is provided not to tell us anything about that war but because the women's ordeal demonstrates "the potency of suffering" as such, a potency which might be deployed as well by other persons in other places.[90]

The replicability of these women's actions is demonstrated several chapters later in *Satyagraha in South Africa*, when Gandhi writes of Indian women protesting the 1913 Searle judgment, which deemed marriages conducted under Hindu or Muslim rites invalid in South Africa. Gandhi describes the satyagraha of Indian women through a substitutive rhetoric: replacing the concentration camp with the prison; King Edward with the Indian political leader Sir Pherozeshah; brave simplicity with innocent faith; and "indescribable sufferings" with "bravery [that] was beyond words." Effecting political transformation through their patient suffering, Indian women in South African prisons served much as Boer women had in British concentration camps a decade earlier: "These events stirred the heart of the Indians not only in South Africa but also in the motherland to its very depths."[91] Much as King Edward "could not bear it" when the Afrikaner women were interned in concentration camps, so the incarceration of Indian women "pleaded with [Sir Pherozeshah] as nothing else could. . . . His blood boiled at the thought of these women lying in jails herded with ordinary criminals and India could not sleep over the matter any longer."[92] Much as the Boer women's "indescribable sufferings" were nonetheless described, we are told that "the [Indian] women's bravery was beyond words"[93] just before we read all about it:

> It was an absolutely pure sacrifice that was offered by these sisters, who were innocent of legal technicalities, and many of whom had no idea of their country, their patriotism being based only upon faith. Some of them were illiterate and could not read the papers. But they knew that a mortal blow was being aimed at the Indians' honour, and their going to jail was a cry of agony and prayer offered from the bottom of their heart, was in fact the purest of all sacrifices.[94]

This account of Indian women's participation in satyagraha thus replicates the account given earlier of Boer women's suffering, signaling a replicability that is decisively gendered even as it crosses cultural divides. Women, whether Indian or Boer, seem to be the repository of the principle of satyagraha, which Gandhi in *Hind Swaraj* had situated in the resolution of a quarrel between brothers. In narrating the political work of women in South Africa, Gandhi shifts satyagraha out of the familial space and into the public sphere. The body of the traditional woman, Boer or Indian, becomes the vehicle of satyagraha's entry into the wider world as these women leave the confined space of the home for the confined spaces of the camp or the prison.

Operating out of religious and marital compulsion, these women are able to transform politics, but they do not themselves undergo the transformation experienced by the male satyagrahi, as we saw for instance in the before-and-after pictures of Gandhi in the 1914 souvenir booklet. Instead, in an article in the same booklet titled "Women and the Struggle," written by Millie Polak (née Millie Graham Downs), a close comrade and sometime housemate of Gandhi's, we are told that the women protesters were entirely unchanged through their experience as satyagrahis.[95] In that article, Polak emphasized that these women managed to undertake satyagraha "without any training for public life, accustomed to the retirement of women of India, not versed or read in the science of sociology, just patient, dutiful wives, mothers, and daughters of a struggling class of workers."[96] They were not motivated by reason, Polak argued, because "woman follows a surer path than any dictated by reason," and they were certainly not motivated by "the pride of heroism."[97] The 1914 Polak attested that "To-day, all these women are back in their homes and are busy in the usual routine of an Indian woman's life. . . . They are the same, patient, dutiful women that India has produced for centuries."[98]

Yet if in 1914 Polak repeated Gandhi's understanding of women's instinctive satyagraha grounded in their placid domesticity, in 1931 she published a book of her recollections, under the title *Mr. Gandhi: The Man*. In that later volume she subverts Gandhi's claims about women's nature rather than repeating them. In a chapter on her establishment of the Transvaal Indian Women's Association, Polak also recounts her conversations with Gandhi on women as satyagraha participants. In these recounted conversations, Gandhi reassures her that women's political involvement will not damage their domesticity, because he has "learned more of passive resistance, as a weapon of power, from Indian women than from anyone else."[99] Gandhi, as presented by Polak, proclaims that women

> must rouse themselves to do their share in the work of reform. It is for them to set the standard of life. . . . men will have to listen when women refuse to obey. . . . They can die . . . and what man can prevail against a dead woman?[100]

Polak's account renders Gandhi's position absurd: dead women, after all, are rarely dynamic agents in "the work of reform." Her text encourages us to wonder: what happens when a woman publicly "refuse[s] to obey" but no men listen—and no women die either? We can find such an example of women's autonomous (and unsuccessful) satyagraha in Gandhi's comrade Sonja Schlesin (1888–1956), who had courted arrest in her protests of the racist segregation of railway travel. Schlesin in 1912 repeatedly sat in the "reserved" compartment—that is, in one reserved for non-White travelers—during her train journeys. As a White woman, she knew this action was illegal—and she hoped, in doing so, to draw attention to the proliferation of segregation in South Africa, by being arrested and publicly prosecuted.[101] After each removal from the "reserved" car she would write a letter of protest to the railroad company. She published these exchanges in *Indian Opinion* in 1912, becoming one of the few White voices protesting the increasingly aggressive segregation of transportation.[102]

Schlesin is best remembered as Gandhi's secretary during his time in South Africa, a job she held from 1905 to 1915. Consequently, she inscribed and imprinted much of Gandhi's South African politics, whether through the ostensibly mechanical task of typing up his scribbled writings or the obviously complex machinations of coordinating events and managing people. She was the first woman in South Africa to attempt to register as an attorney's clerk—an application that was summarily denied on account of her gender—and she occasionally participated directly in protests.[103] In 1908, for instance, she wrote a speech against the Asiatic Restriction Ordinance, which Gandhi read aloud at a crucial protest rally and then published in *Indian Opinion*, printing it both in English and in Gujarati translation. In Gandhi's framing of Schlesin's words, her gender and nationality were paramount: the English-language section titles the relevant article "An Englishwoman's Sympathy" and terms her a "Colonial-born European," while the Gujarati pages describe her as "an unmarried girl of twenty" who "had obtained her parents' permission" for her writing.[104] The Moscow-born child of Lithuanian Jews who migrated to the Cape when she was four, Schlesin was British by naturalization. Despite Gandhi's published claims, however, she was neither "an Englishwoman" nor a "Colonial-born European."[105] In that speech as published, Schlesin deployed her gender as a rallying cry: she motivated the would-be satyagrahis, almost exclusively male and Indian, through the invocation of gendered shame:

> Let me remind you of a similar crusade now being waged by my sisters in England. I refer to the suffragettes. For the sake of a principle, they are prepared to lose their all, to brave in-

> numerable trials. Many have already suffered imprisonment, more are ready, nay eager, to do so. If delicately-nurtured women can do this, will hardy men, inured to toil, do less?[106]

In her own writings as published a few years later in *Indian Opinion*, Schlesin articulates herself first and foremost as a professional European woman. On the front page of *Indian Opinion*'s August 31, 1912, issue, we read Schlesin's letter to the South African Railways, protesting that she was asked to leave the compartment "'reserved for coloured people'" when she was "travel[ing] with an Indian lady friend."[107] Schlesin concludes her brief letter by arguing "that it is the coloured people, and they only, who can object to the presence of a European in a compartment reserved for their use."[108] The railway responded nearly a month later, in a letter addressed to "Mr. Sonja Schlesin" and rejecting Schlesin's claims "in terms of the regulations duly gazetted."[109] The railway's subdued procedural response reflects the regulatory transformations then underway. Trains in South Africa were initially only loosely segregated: prioritizing revenues over racists, the railways had allowed non-White persons who purchased the more expensive fares, always minuscule in number, to ride in those carriages provided that they were "respectably dressed."[110] However, White passengers and staff frequently attacked and ejected these non-White travelers, and in the early twentieth century explicit railway segregation quickly became South African law.[111] This changing regulatory context rendered Schlesin's nonviolent protests all the more urgent.[112] However, as we see in the pages of *Indian Opinion*, Schlesin continued to protest and to disobey, but she was never arrested, imprisoned, or charged. This impunity was likely gendered, and it rendered her protest less effective.

She did, however, manage to trouble the railway authorities and to record her actions in the publicity of the printed page. Schlesin's first published reply, for instance, began with an abrupt clarification: "May I, first of all, draw your attention to the fact that I belong not to the male, but to the female, sex?"[113] Schlesin then argued that "compartments [were] marked 'Reserved' . . . with a view not to wound the feelings of non-European passengers."[114] Consequently, she reiterates, only "non-European passengers" can demand a European's removal from these cars: non-Whites, but not Whites, can enforce this racial homogeneity according to Schlesin. She invokes her "comparatively helpless" companion, a "lady," thereby invoking female frailty and British chivalry even as she asserts both her authority and her womanhood.[115] The railway replied quickly, ignoring her gendered appeal and adding an ominous prediction: "If Europeans are permitted to travel in 'reserved' compartments, it will cause dissatisfaction amongst the non-European section of the community."[116]

Schlesin's published letters exposed the falsity of a racist claim: throughout the first half of the twentieth century, South Africa's White leaders insisted that Black, Indian, and Coloured passengers disliked traveling with White passengers, and that women in particular found racially integrated travel offensive, unpleasant, and dangerous.[117] Strict segregation, it was argued, could be beneficial for the public peace; it could even be the harbinger of racial equality.[118] Schlesin's published letters, however, insistently testified to the contrary: "Had I noticed the slightest trace of dissatisfaction among the non-European passengers, I should myself have undoubtedly withdrawn."[119] Her situation, she emphasizes, is constrained by her professional obligations: "My work throws me greatly with non-European people."[120] In the next published letter, Schlesin writes of traveling with two men, Indian and German, in the "reserved" car. She was asked to move, and she refused:

> The Conductor thereupon took my name and address, which, I dare say, are before you at this time. I do not know whether you propose to take any action in this matter, but it seems to me that it would be better for all concerned if my right to travel with non-European friends were tested in a Court of Law.[121]

Schlesin invokes "my right to travel with non-European friends" and emphasizes "my work," noting that she is "the Honorary Secretary of the Indian Women's Association."[122] We receive one last installment of Schlesin's railway dispute in the following week's issue of *Indian Opinion*. The temporal break, crucially, has no correlation to the dates on the letters: it indicates, instead, an editorial decision made to leave *Indian Opinion*'s readers in suspense. Will Schlesin be charged, arrested, or even imprisoned? Turn to the issue of September 7, 1912, to find out.

Despite this cliffhanger ending, however, the next week's issue offered bureaucratic repetition rather than political drama. The assistant general manager of the railway, addressing her now as "Dear Madam," reiterates much of the same regulatory detail—"as already intimated to you in a previous correspondence," "I would remind you of the fact."[123] Schlesin responds with a brief letter which "reiterate[s] . . . that, should

I be unreasonably asked to move . . . , I shall have to reluctantly decline . . . , and take the risk of a prosecution, which, indeed, I should welcome."[124] Schlesin was never sued: to do so would have embarrassed the state. Her letter campaign, when published, makes her an activist woman without invoking women's honor: it frames her as a worker, choosing in accordance with her professional responsibilities, rather than a victim. Schlesin is, moreover, quite literally in transit: she may not be transported to jail or to court, as she had wished, but she is an unmarried woman traveling around South Africa (mostly) as she pleases. According to Polak, Gandhi had claimed that women's disobedience might lead to their death, but not to men's continued misbehavior; Schlesin's nonviolent protest, despite satisfying the rules of satyagraha, fails to elicit the repressive response that would make her a satyagrahi.

Schlesin's railway segregation protest thus offers a compelling and mostly overlooked contrast to Gandhi's accounts of women's participation in satyagraha protests. The stories of women's satyagraha in the text of *Satyagraha in South Africa* are racially distinct, but they are united in their framing of women as wives and victims—and not, as in Schlesin's case, as traveling professionals. These two modes of women's nonviolent resistance to racism, moreover, are directly incompatible, as Schlesin's experience makes evident. Whereas in 1912 her secretarial position within the Transvaal Indian Women's Association facilitated her determined protest of railway segregation, with the advent of Indian women's protests in 1913, Schlesin's professional position in became an impediment to women's satyagraha, rather than its enabling function, because this professional woman was not authentically Indian.

Once the Indian members of the Transvaal Indian Women's Association became directly involved in passive resistance, *Indian Opinion*'s coverage of women's activism acquired a new racial politics. Announcing the advent of women's satyagraha activities on May 10, 1913, for instance, Gandhi ran a front-page article titled "Indian Women as Passive Resisters": as the title indicates, the contributions of White women like Schlesin were now to be obscured. The article reprinted a telegram sent to the government by the Transvaal Indian Women's Association, which warned that the affected women "would offer passive resistance and . . . suffer imprisonment."[125] This telegram, however, was signed "Sonja Schlesin, Honorary Secretary": a woman, certainly, but one neither Hindu nor Muslim; never married; and not even Indian. To explain this anomalous signature, Gandhi appended a bracketed note, in which he wrote that Schlesin would much rather "an Indian woman" occupy her position," but "her Indian sisters have not that knowledge of the English language and of South African politics which is required."[126] Women's participation thus became more prominent within satyagraha even as its interracial (and, thanks to the immigrant status of White and Indian members, international) nature came to be obscured. The expansion of women's participation entailed the contraction of racial boundaries, and the valorization of women's suffering in satyagraha meant that women's constancy, rather than their political transformation, defined the woman satyagrahi's role.

In this chapter, we have explored the print internationalism of M. K. "Mahatma" Gandhi, using his neologism "satyagraha" as an entry point into his extensive corpus. Gandhi is well known for his methods of protest and for their proven transportability into varying contexts of oppression. Responding to the significant scholarship on the translatability of Gandhian nonviolence into different cultures, I approached his print internationalism to consider that which he decides to render untranslated. In the deployment of his Sanskritic coinage "satyagraha," I found a neologism that, like Tagore's "gitanjali," signaled both a new word and a new set of practices. Yet in tracking that term's untranslated migration from South Africa to India, I demonstrated how Gandhi's powerful work against racism paradoxically relied on existing racial tropologies. Because the transportability of satyagraha required, as we saw, the conversion of past experiences into easily comprehensible allegories, Gandhi created a mode of antiracist protest that could be replicated by various peoples of color but that could not, in his practice, be inclusive of the entire category. These limits to his antiracist method became apparent not only within his well-known failure to substantively involve Black South Africans in his protests but also in the racial narrowing of women's participation in his movement. As such, Gandhi's print internationalism can assist us in thinking carefully about our choices in forging internationalism's interpretive community.

The term "satyagraha" is mentioned in what may be the most famous essay in all of postcolonial studies: Gayatri Spivak's 1988 "Can the Subaltern Speak?" In the midst of a discussion of sati, the upper-caste Hindu practice of widow immolation, Spivak suggests that sati could, and perhaps should, have been understood as a form of political violence. She ends the paragraph by jumping to Gandhi:

> The only related transformation was Mahatma Gandhi's reinscription of the notion of *satyagraha*, or hunger strike, as resistance. But this is not the place to discuss the details of that sea change. I would merely invite the reader to compare the auras of widow sacrifice and Gandhian resistance. The root in the first part of *satyagraha* and *sati* are the same.[127]

Satyagraha, as we have seen, can hardly be translated as "hunger strike," but Spivak's comma-offset phrase translates it thus nonetheless. According to Spivak, Gandhi "reinscribed" satyagraha as resistance, which was the "only related transformation" of existing ideas of female self-sacrifice to that which she proposes for widow immolation. Denying her ability to discuss "the details" of this "sea change," Spivak speaks of "auras" and "roots." She then extends an invitation to the reader, and she accompanies this invitation with a bit of Sanskrit: the shared first syllable, *sat*, in the two words of which she speaks. As Spivak's essay demonstrates, Gandhi succeeded in his indigenizing aspirations, for in seeking to articulate passive resistance in an emphatically Indian idiom, Gandhi generated a Sanskrit neologism that sounds far older than its twentieth-century origins. Eighty years later, Spivak follows the Sanskrit and, in doing so, argues that Gandhi's concept relates to widow immolation.

Spivak's sati-satyagraha connection was trenchantly criticized in a 2011 article by Harish Trivedi. Quoting the passage just mentioned, Trivedi writes:

> The misrepresentation here is matched only by the confidence of assertion. As every schoolchild in India knows, *satyagraha* does not mean "hunger strike," for which Gandhi's word was *anashan* or *upavas*. . . . As for the display of insider Sanskrit erudition here, though it is technically correct to say that the root *sat* (carrying the broad primary meaning of "being, existing," etc.) is common to both *sati* and *satyagraha*, to yoke the two words together in this manner is irrelevant and misleading, and therefore may work only with readers who have never come across either of these words before. For the same root is also common to a whole host of other words, including *satkarma*, *satkavi*, *satkara*, *satkirti*, *satpatra*, *satsanga* and *satchidananda*, which it may tax the ingenuity of even such a brilliantly resourceful critic as Spivak to configure in any coherent pattern of common semantic signification.[128]

Trivedi here performs that for which he condemns Spivak: seeking to correct Spivak's "display of insider erudition," he resorts to his own display, generating a paragraph full of Sanskritic words. As this contentious exchange between two distinguished literary scholars suggests, philology in the postcolonial world is often a confusing affair. In South Asia, there is no canonical method for discussing the philology of secular texts, and there is no *Oxford English Dictionary* to arbitrate disputes. In the absence of such institutional authorities, understandings of etymology become highly idiosyncratic. Spivak simply notes the shared root, whereas Trivedi invokes the authority of what "every schoolchild in India knows." Both roots and children, however, are highly variable.

Much like Spivak and Trivedi's presentations, Gandhi's coinage of "satyagraha," as we saw, was neither traditional nor falsifiable. In postcolonial contexts without hegemonic linguistic institutions, the moment of providing a gloss becomes both informative and transformative. Drawing on the romance, and the indisputable reality, of other languages, elsewhere, the author who writes untranslated words can summon other worlds into being. This is not, as we have seen, what Emily Apter calls an Untranslatable, whose linguistic particularity resists our repeated attempts at translation.[129] The term "satyagraha" signals novelty rather than singularity: its axis of signification is as much temporal as cultural. Even as its linguistic divergence from its global Anglophone context seems to signal geographic interruption, satyagraha seeks, through such international interconnection, to create changes within the global Anglophone, and not primarily to mark its limits.

This chapter has approached the South Africa–focused portions of Gandhi's writings through readings that sustain and engage the brief mentions of Africans in Gandhi's writings. In doing so, I hope to ameliorate what is often perceived as the damage caused by Black marginalization in both the politics and the celebration of Gandhi, which has contributed considerably to the difficulties of Indian-African relations. For Indians in India, or even in the United States, engaging allegations of Gandhi's racism can serve as an invitation to consider their own allegiances and prejudices. Within Africa, in contrast, such allegations have often served as an alibi for racially motivated violence against people of Indian descent. To ask whether Gandhi was racist in his *writing* on Africans is to ignore the most salient racial aspect of his political practices in South Africa: namely, his failure to directly incorporate the grievances of the Black and Coloured inhabitants of South Africa in his antiracist campaigns. Given this notable omission from his political mobilizations, I suggest that his writings' references to Africans are unlikely to yield some key truth about his racial views. Much as Black people in Gandhi's South African struggles served primarily as context and not as concern, so too, I suggest, Black people in Gandhi's rhetoric and writings serve as symbols and not as referents. They are rhetorical flourishes in his larger depiction of South Africa, not referential descriptions that we can mine for his personal views.

This insight does not resolve the debate, either exculpating him for his lack of intent or incriminating him for his lack of care. Instead, my contribution dramatizes the phenomenon of discrepant and simultaneous readings, each proceeding from a specific position, whether in racial or geographical terms. For readers familiar with the discipline of literary studies, I am suggesting that the question of Gandhi's racism in his writings resembles the debates around the appropriate reading of Joseph Conrad's *Heart of Darkness* (1899). Conrad's most famous novel has been both celebrated for its critique of imperialism and castigated for its racism, the latter most famously in Chinua Achebe's scathing critique. Since Achebe's intervention, first published in 1977, admirers of *Heart of Darkness* (and of Conrad) have frequently mobilized a defensive claim that Natalie Melas has termed "an imperial contradiction": "the notion that the text could be a critique of imperialism in Africa and therefore, in a fundamental sense, documentary, and have nothing to do with Africa."[130] I build on Melas's insight, expanding its purview to include Gandhi. Like *Heart of Darkness*, Gandhi's texts enable two different readers: the text is not, I would say, racist *despite* being anti-imperialist but, rather, racist and anti-imperialist *at the same time*, that is, during the time of reading, depending on the reader's self-assumed task. To read Gandhi's writings *about* South Africa *for* India appropriately, I argue, we have to read at once "from" India—his intended readership—and "from" Africa—his site of allegorization. This process facilitates a kind of split postcolonial subjectivity, but not one that resides in the split between the (post)colony and the (former) metropole. Instead, this split postcolonial subject lies between regions once linked through explicitly defined circuits of imperial subjugation and now connected primarily through the linkages that we choose or decline to recognize. We will revisit this split in more detail in the following chapter, which considers, via the work of W. E. B. Du Bois, the cleavage between the African diaspora and the Indian one.

In this respect, reading Gandhi's writings on Africans is emblematic of the problems of postcolonial reading as theorized by Melas, in which parts of the world that have long been subordinated can (and should) read and respond to texts with "a distinctly local positionality as well as a partial and an almost intimate mode of identification."[131] To read "from" Africa—that is, to read with an attentiveness to that part of the world that Gandhi's text, like Conrad's, prefers to "deploy as metaphor"—is to read *from* the metaphor rather than to read with it or through it.[132] Whether or not Gandhi's writings are racist is thus a question of reading that cannot be resolved into the methodological debates of close versus distant, paranoid versus reparative, surface versus symptomatic. The kind of reading that will resolve this debate requires not an adjectival modifier but a prepositional phrase. One reads Gandhi's (alleged) racism, not with or against the grain, but *from* somewhere—or, ideally, from two places at once. The postcolonial reading that I propose, accordingly, is split not between the metropole and the colony but between two former colonies at once. This is a dialectical mode of reading that seizes on the "imperial contradiction"—the allowance that one could write about a place and yet not write about a place, at the same time—and interrogates its enabling logic. Reading in this manner precipitates, then, to the simplest of interpretive classroom tasks: to attend simultaneously to the literal and the figurative. This practice of simultaneous and discrepant reading, moreover, echoes the simultaneous and discrepant analysis that our contemporary category "people of color" ethically demands. U.S. advocates for "people of color," for instance, may champion "Black Lives Matter" at the same time, even though the first phrase emphasizes the shared experience of racism across diverse racial categories and the latter emphasizes the unique precarity of a single racial group. As this example suggests, embracing "people of color," like approaching Gandhi's anti-racism, demands a split subjectivity: the insistence that recognizing the shared nature of racism can enable an antiracist agenda that prioritizes its particular forms.

CHAPTER 3

The Global South

W. E. B. Du Bois's Brownies

In 1919, as racist violence raged with particular ferocity across the United States, W. E. B. Du Bois became concerned that the antiracist periodical he edited, *The Crisis: A Record of the Darker Races*, might be harming the children he most wished to help. *The Crisis* itself was in excellent condition. The monthly publication of the National Association for the Advancement of Colored People (NAACP), it had grown in both length and influence since its founding in 1910, expanding from just twenty pages to fifty pages by April 1912 and reaching its peak circulation of over a hundred thousand in 1919. Du Bois, too, was experiencing considerable success: already acclaimed for book-length works like the sociological study *The Philadelphia Negro* (1899) and the polyphonic masterpiece *The Souls of Black Folk* (hereafter *Souls*, 1903), he was beginning to gain recognition for his editorial work as well. Leading *The Crisis* from its inception until 1934, Du Bois pioneered an editorial strategy that interwove stories of Black achievement with those of racist injustice, using a variety of genres: reportage as well as fiction and poetry; photography and illustrations; and even children's literature. In keeping with his concern for the well-being of the youngest African Americans, Du Bois published two specifically youth-oriented issues of *The Crisis* each year. Every August, the "Education Number" would feature the beaming portraits of recent graduates; every October, the "Children's Number" would include writing for children alongside photographs of children.

Yet in the October 1919 issue of *The Crisis*, Du Bois declared that "in the problem of our children we black folk are sorely puzzled."[1] In a column titled "The True Brownies," he began by mentioning the overwhelming popularity of the "Children's Number," which—despite its thematic focus—invariably included the news of "some horror," usually a lynching. As he explained: "This was inevitable in our role as newspaper—but what effect must it have on our children? To educate them in human hatred is more disastrous to them than to the hated; to seek to raise them in ignorance of their racial identity and peculiar situation is inadvisable—impossible."[2] In response to this problem, Du Bois laid out a mission for a new magazine, which he called the *Brownies' Book*. This new publication, he declared, would "be a thing of Joy and Beauty, dealing in Happiness, Laughter and Emulation" and would "teach Universal Love and Brotherhood for all little folk—black and brown and yellow and white."[3] Two months later, in January 1921, the first issue of the *Brownies' Book* appeared, selling for $0.15 an issue or $1.50 for a year's subscription: the same pricing as that for *The Crisis*.

But who were the brownies—or, as his title put it, "the true brownies"? In the twenty-four issues published over the next two years, the *Brownies' Book* would refer to its imagined readers as "our children" or "the children of the sun," yet without exception the central term—"brownies"—remained undefined. Unlike *The Crisis*, which explicitly announced in its subtitle that it was "A Record of the Darker Races," the *Brownies' Book* kept its community of readers opaque: the first issue explained simply that it was "for all children, but especially *Ours*."

As several Du Bois scholars have documented, Du Bois's internationalism was extensively manifest in his personal travels and correspondence, as well as his organizational work with the Pan-African Congresses and his attendance at the Universal Races Congress.[4] Unlike Gandhi, who began his activism within an imperial frame and then transposed it to a nationalist agenda, or Tagore, who articulated a British Indian subjectivity only to reject both imperialism and nationalism in favor of an internationalist universalism, Du Bois consistently calibrated his national political agenda within an internationalist framework, shifting his emphasis as occasion demanded. Moreover, while Du Bois was prosperous compared to most of his African American contemporaries, he did not command the substantial resources common among his White compatriots, or even among the Indian elite. Consequently, his travels were initially far less extensive than those of the better-resourced lives discussed in the preceding chapters. As early as the 1920s, for instance, Du Bois had been approached for a lecture tour in East Africa and South Asia, but he could not afford to do it at the compensation offered.[5] As a consequence of these limitations, the *print* of print internationalism assumes particular importance in assessing Du Bois's work. As he repeatedly insists, whether in reportage or in fiction, one need not travel to work on the entire world. He argued that print can make such transformations possible, and in accordance with what I call print internationalism Du Bois sent his publications all over the world. The *Brownies' Book*, as we will see, had subscribers in western and southern Africa, and *The Crisis*, in its far longer existence, had subscribers and readers all over the world, even appearing on foreign newsstands.[6]

In keeping with the connective powers of print internationalism, even Du Bois's most distant readers felt that they too could contribute to his creative works. Thus, for instance, "an old reader of *The Crisis* and your other literary works" writes from "10,000 miles distant from you and after an absence of more than a quarter of a century from America," suggesting from the Philippines that Du Bois write a libretto.[7] Another reader identifies himself as an Indian from the modest city of Pietermaritzburg, South Africa: he wonders if he too might publish something in *The Crisis* "on the improvement of Coloured people and other matters pertaining to [their] welfare."[8] Within India, Du Bois's texts circulated through the global Anglophone to influence even those who worked primarily in other languages. Prominent Hindi litterateurs like Ramrakh Singh Sahgal (1896–1952) and Banarsidas Chaturvedi (1892–1985), for instance, were readers and admirers of Du Bois's work, and they even wished to publish Du Bois's writing in their Indian publications.[9] Even a seemingly U.S.-centered text like *Souls* circulated well beyond North American shores: Gandhi's Sabarmati Ashram in western India, for instance, possessed a copy of *Souls*, and it was eagerly read and admired by prominent Indian leaders.[10]

In sending his writings out across the world, Du Bois won influence and acclaim, but he also attracted criticism. Print internationalism, after all, is not simply an extended vision for a print nationalist agenda, but one that disrupts nationalism through its insistence on larger connections. Thus, for instance, one subscriber was delighted to read *The Crisis* in his New York City home but horrified when he encountered it abroad. Writing to "discontinue my subscription," Du Bois's compatriot explained:

> When I was in London last summer I was much shocked to see sandwich men walking along the Strand carrying large posters referring to the lynchings in the United States. . . . There can be no question that this lynching situation is a serious blemish on civilization in the United States, but no matter how seriously anyone is affected, this is no excuse for spreading it broadcast in other countries.[11]

In objecting to Du Bois's print internationalism, this disgruntled subscriber objected to its motivating claim: Du Bois undertook print internationalism, after all, because he believed that racism was never simply a national concern.

Du Bois famously posited the color line as a global problem, yet articulating this globality presented daunting rhetorical challenges. In this chapter I examine the *Brownies' Book* (1920–21); *The Crisis* under Du Bois's editorship (1910–34); and Du Bois's novel *Dark Princess: a Romance* (1928), and I demonstrate how, in each instance, print internationalism is articulated both through explicit content and strategic absences. By including many details about non-U.S. contexts but rarely explaining them in a predictable fashion, Du Bois compelled his readers to weave this unity across "the darker races of the world" as they read. The readers of these Du Bois works thus encounter the unity of a printed text that nonetheless lacks clearly articulated connections.

In leading us through these works, I will focus on the strange neologism mentioned earlier: the brownie. At first sight, "brownies" seems like a racial-chromatic deployment: it describes, we might assume, those with brown skin. This apparent simplicity, however, is belied by the modifier "true" in Du Bois's first column on the topic. He implies a distinction between his "true" brownies and some other brownies, who are not explained in this column but can be easily found in the archival record. These brownies first appear in the early sixteenth century, in the annals of British folklore: according to the *Oxford English Dictionary*, a brownie is "a benevolent spirit or goblin, of shaggy appearance, supposed to haunt old houses, esp. farmhouses, in Scotland, and sometimes to perform useful household work while the family were asleep." This folkloric creature entered British print culture in the mid-nineteenth century, where it was rapidly put to political use. The Scottish author James Hogg used the brownie to inscribe local culture in his 1818 *The Brownie of Hoggsbeck*, while the English author Juliana Horatia Ewing used her 1865 story "The Brownies" to emphasize the gendered drudgery of domestic work. At the turn of the twentieth century, brownies became pervasive in North American children's culture as well, through the phenomenally popular works of the Quebecois author Palmer Cox. From the publication of his first brownie story in 1883 to his death in 1924, Cox's masculine and mobile brownies saturated the worlds of both children's print culture and everyday consumer goods, advertising everything from Kodak cameras to Ivory soap.[12] They became North America's first mass market brand, comparable only to Disney's later successes in their saturation of the children's market in their time. Cox published several books of brownie stories, and each book included a prefatory note: "BROWNIES, like fairies and goblins, are imaginary little sprites, who are supposed to delight in harmless pranks and helpful deeds. They work and sport while weary households sleep, and never allow themselves to be seen by mortal eyes."[13] Cox himself believed that the nomenclature "brownies" was "because of their brown hair and weather-beaten countenances": he always depicted them as small, squat, and White.[14] His brownies expanded into a collection of distinctive characters, differentiated along lines of costume, profession, and nationality: included among their ranks were a dandy, a policeman, a soldier, a sailor, a cowboy, and a clown. Their entourage eventually came to include ten different named nationalities, but their adventures always promoted U.S. imperialism. For instance, in the 1904 bestseller *The Brownies in the Philippines*, Cox's brownies re-created the U.S. military's conquest of the Philippine people through their victories over tigers and flying fish. Whereas the brownies of British folklore were solitary, always confined to the home or the field, Cox's brownies were gregarious and adventurous. They were, in twenty-first-century terms, "early adopters"—his brownies explored the bicycle, the airplane, and the automobile soon after each was invented.[15]

Humans and brownies are never simultaneously present in Cox's world, and the brownies thus substitute a familiar world at a child-friendly scale. Yet in figuring this seemingly friendly world, Cox's brownies reproduced the exclusions of U.S. racism. In *The Brownies around the World* (1894), for instance, a group of proudly American brownies visited "the native land of each member," which ranged across Europe, the Middle East, East Asia, and "the Polar regions."[16] Canada was included, but not Mexico; Egypt was included, but no other part of Africa. The Americanness celebrated by Cox's brownies, and by millions of U.S. children and their families, was thus incapable of accommodating the groups we now know as Black and Latino (or, to use the gender-inclusive neologism, Latinx): groups that, then as now, formed a significant portion of the U.S. population. Racist exclusion thus formed a constitutive exception in North America's first mass market children's brand.[17] On reading Cox's brownie stories, the children with whom Du Bois was most concerned would have found themselves entirely and emphatically absent.

While Cox's brownies championed U.S. imperial expansion, another group of Brownies propagated the values of the British Empire through scouting groups for girls. The global scouting movement began with the 1908 publication of the British army officer Robert Baden-Powell's *Scouting for Boys*. Drawing on his military experience in South Africa, Baden-Powell transformed a hierarchical vision of imperial camaraderie into a horizontal game of imperial brotherhood. His book appropriated imperialism's subjugated cultures—for instance, by teaching purportedly Native American tracking skills and supposedly Zulu exercises. Children in scouting groups learned these skills to help them serve the British Empire, and in doing so they acquired both the weapons of imperial conquest and its spoils.[18] To distinguish girls' scouting groups from those of the boys, the girl scouts came to be called Brownies.[19]

Before 1920, then, "brownies" existed in two culturally dominant sources: North American popular culture and British folklore revivals, and in both cases those brownies explicitly supported White supremacy and Anglo-American imperialism. In discussing "the true brownies" in 1919 and naming the "children of the sun" as "brownies," Du Bois did much more than recast the chromatic condition of racially subordinated children in magical terms: he claimed a term familiar from the dominant culture of Anglo-American childhood. A variety of names, both respectful and offensive, have long been used for persons of African descent in the United States, yet the use of "brownie" for U.S. children of African descent arguably offered more imaginative possibilities than any other name could. What distinguishes Du Bois's usage of brownie is its creativity: its ability to use a false cognate (brown skin) to enable a resonant match (the brownies of popular culture), thereby spawning a new category of persons—"the children of the sun"—for a better and less racist world yet to come. Du Bois foregrounded his challenge—in the figure of the raced child—to both U.S. and British imperialism.

As this history indicates, the *Brownies' Book* signals a decisive restructuring of the propaganda of U.S. childhood, shifting the term "brownie" from nationalist imperialism to antiracist internationalism. Whereas Cox's brownies were exclusively male and the scouting Brownies exclusively female, the *Brownies' Book* never addressed female and male children separately. Remarkably for its historical moment, and perhaps even for ours, the *Brownies' Book* never spelled out gender-specific behavioral norms for its young readers, emphatically rebutting the constitutive gendering of the brownies of imperialism. In addition, whereas both Baden-Powell's and Cox's texts invoked foreign knowledge to affirm readers' cosmopolitan expertise, the *Brownies' Book* printed foreign material in a manner that encouraged further inquiry, often highlighting how much was left to be learned. The *Brownies Book*, finally, extensively published the work of amateur writers, 98 percent of whom were non-White and the majority of whom were women.[20] The brownies of White publications were written *about*; the brownies of the *Brownies' Book* participated in their inscription, with many of its child readers submitting their writing for publication. Intermixed with puzzles, photographs, and illustrations, each issue of the *Brownies' Book* is typical of the editorial and curatorial practices of Du Bois and his collaborators at *The Crisis*, though it reflects most clearly the vision of one particular collaborator, the African American author Jessie Redmon Fauset, who served as both its managing editor and its main writer, with Du Bois in a supporting role.

The *Brownies' Book* under Fauset's leadership further developed the print internationalism already evident in *The Crisis*, rendering it child-friendly while retaining an ambitious remit. The result is a periodical attuned, not only to the affective variations of accomplishment and suffering that characterized *The Crisis*, but also to vast variations in literacy, maturity, and experience among its readers and writers. In addressing Fauset's print internationalism in the *Brownies' Book*, I build on the growing body of scholarship that has highlighted her commitment to extranational allegiances, whether in *The Crisis* or in her fiction. Much as Du Bois in *Dark Princess* would champion the liberatory powers of romance and fantasy, arguing that these could enliven minds otherwise constrained by racist oppression, so too Fauset would embrace the freedoms of romantic and fantastical writing, whether in her literary reviews, her nonfiction reportage, her novels, or her editorial work, as part of her print internationalism.[21] Much as Fauset's fiction situated these worldwide solidarities within the solidity of the domestic sphere,[22] so too did the print internationalism of the *Brownies' Book* bring the world home to its young readers and their families.

An investment in writing for and about children permeates Du Bois's work; that insistence has proven deeply unsatisfying to most of his progressive critics, whether for its escapism or its normative heterosexual conservatism. Some commentators have read Du Bois's recourse to the child as the failure of a more substantial political proposal; others have found in that child figure a normative, regulatory script for African American sexual practice.[23] In Du Bois's texts, as these critics demonstrate, the child functions as a particularly unsatisfying narrative resolution, and this insufficiency reflects, I argue, what Du Bois and Fauset saw as the constitutive conundrum of caring for colored children: the desire to preserve their innocence while preparing them for a racist and often hostile world. The children figured in such publications, consequently, are at once innocent and mature: they are both the wide-eyed and playful kids in the photographs and drawings in the very same issues, and the sophisticated political agents of the text.

The children who preoccupied Du Bois, crucially, are both actually existing, as in the enthusiastic readers of the *Brownies' Book* and the "Children's Numbers" of *The Crisis*, as well as imagined, as in the infant-savior born at the very end of Du Bois's novel *Dark Princess*. By foregrounding the child, both as a political figure and as an imagined reader, these texts challenged the racist infantilization of Black culture in general, by asserting the developmental significance of a Black person's life cycle. In material terms, moreover, Black people had long been excluded from literacy in the United States, which meant that the adults in most early twentieth-century Black families were not better readers than their children, who were often granted educational opportunities that had been denied to their elders. Consequently, the Black child envisioned by Du Bois was not necessarily opposed to the masterful adult, as was usually the case with literature aimed at White children.

The normative child of U.S. culture is defined, as Kathryn Bond Stockton has argued, as "a creature of *gradual growth* and *managed delay*," demarcated sharply from adults by its constitutive innocence.[24] In contrast, the child figured as a brownie is differentiated from adults, and from the rest of the ordinary world, by its magical indeterminacy. Consequently, much as the *Brownies' Book* produced emotionally and politically savvy Black children from existing child readers, the production of a transformative child within the narrative of *Dark Princess* served a specific role for adults. Despite that novel's explicit invocation of the genre of romance and the fairy tale, the novel was emphatically adults-only, not only because of its length and complexity but also because of then-scandalous passages depicting extramarital sex. Whereas the topics of racism and inequality render the child's reading of the *Brownies' Book* more serious, and less frivolous, than most children's literature, the childish world of fantasy saturating *Dark Princess* restores imaginative function to the adult's reading experience. The child in Du Bois's writings is best read both textually and paratextually, as the brownie that Du Bois wished to produce: at once serious, thoughtful, and internationally informed as well as imaginative, playful, and astonishingly creative. This is not the child without history: rather, this is the child *of* history.

By foregrounding children, and then rendering them mysterious brownies, Du Bois emphasizes the acquisition of multiple literacies: linguistic, cultural, and political. In highlighting both the importance of individual maturation and its unpredictable correlation to one's biological age, Du Bois is able to advance a powerful moral: it is one's political maturity, and not simply chronological advancement, through time that most matters. When we consider reading as a skill that changes over one's lifetime, we can envisage reading as a process of study rather than a practice of mastery. Consequently, when brownies are central, the imaginative possibilities of the text are rendered as important as its informative properties, a key emphasis in Du Bois's print internationalism. This brownie-centered print internationalism thus presents ignorance as opportunity, and literacy as transformation, and it transmutes our limited knowledge of other regions into yet another precious chance for education.

The strategies of Du Bois's print internationalism were first laid out in the pages of *The Crisis*. In addition to using the strategic pairing of image and text for sophisticated political effects,[25] Du Bois also manipulated the layout and format of words themselves to convey his radical goals. In an editorial from 1915 titled "That Capital 'N,'" for instance, Du Bois reported on an exchange in the U.S. children's magazine the *Youth's Companion*, which refused to capitalize the word "Negro" on the grounds that they would not capitalize "*white* men or *red* men when referring to Anglo-Saxons or Indians."[26] To rebut this argument, Du Bois invoked what he terms "the smiling gods of logic." Instead of providing an ideological or grammatical refutation, Du Bois published a minimalist diagram:

black	*white*	*red*
negro	*Anglo-Saxon*	*Indian*[27]

In simply looking at this pattern of words, and perhaps even without full reading comprehension, anyone might immediately recognize the glaring inconsistency in the pattern. As this example suggests, on Du Bois's pages, formal details frequently produced substantive arguments.

Du Bois's production of these carefully staged textual encounters make it particularly difficult to evaluate his internationalist sentiments on the basis of selective quotation. Whether through the pairing of incongruous visuals and texts, or through the sequencing of different kinds of writing, the collage and montage effects of Du Bois's editing, as Anne Carroll argues, produced "composite texts" that required active, and often uncomfortable, readerly engagement.[28] This formal sophistication was, in part, born of necessity: by using these methods of presentation and narration, *The Crisis* relayed a strong antiracist critique without the explicit statements that would have attracted state persecution. His texts operate as wholes, not as parts: what is said is only as important as what has been implied through the relations, usually unexplained, among the various components of the text as a whole. This interpretive gap, I suggest, introduces an effect into a single-language text akin to that of the untranslated word. It provides a space for projection, fantasy, and imagination, in a text that might otherwise be amenable to closure.

The importance of these gaps, moreover, means that the role of the neologism is less prominent here than in previous chapters. Whereas satyagraha and gitanjali served Gandhi and Tagore as explicit guiding practices, the brownie of Du Bois surfaces as prominently in what is unsaid as what is said. Consequently, in illuminating the role of the brownie in enabling Du Bois's print internationalism, this chapter will attend to an aspect of his construction of solidarity across what we call the Global South through the reliance on a seemingly unrelated rubric: that of caste. Du Bois's invocation of caste converts race into class by rendering class inequality inheritable. In an age when racial difference was often seen as biologically determinate, Du Bois used the brownie to imagine a child who would inherit darker skin but not the disadvantages that had accrued to its darker-skinned parents: that is, it would inherit its parents' color, but not their caste. The differentiation, both national and conceptual, between these two descent-based forms of discrimination becomes crucial for Du Bois's politics. He is not against class per se, but he objects to the inheritance of class privilege along strictly racial lines.

CONSUMMATING THE GLOBAL SOUTH

In a long article titled "Gandhi and India," published in the March 1922 issue of *The Crisis*, Du Bois spent several pages explaining Indian politics, and Gandhi in particular, to his readers. He also explained what he had omitted:

> India was the contemporary of great Egypt, ancient Assyria and Persia, but unlike her contemporaries of antiquity she lives. They are dead. Through a continuous period running back to most archaic times, she has come with her literature, her religions, her customs—in short—with all that makes her justly proud today. . . . We cannot consider here the interesting facts of her kingdoms and empires, her wars and warriors, of which the Mahabharata so gloriously sings; nor of the coming of Islam and the great empires of the Moguls. It is certainly not possible to write here of Indian society—of caste; of poverty widespread and dazzling wealth; of the depth of illiteracy which grips the country octopus-like and a culture and education as noted for their literary and scholarly achievements as for their far reach back into the haze of unhistorical days; of marriage, home, and family.[29]

India lives on, while her "contemporaries of antiquity" are "dead," and in that strange phrase, which unites contemporaneity with antiquity, is signaled the centrality of India for Du Bois's worldwide vision: India signals both what once was and what could be. Du Bois as journalist is here the voice of the present: writing in the lockstep of newspaper time, he finds that these "interesting facts" cannot be narrated. Four years later, when he began writing *Dark Princess* in 1926, Du Bois would reach back "into the haze of unhistorical days," pushing the explicit politics to the background.[30]

Dark Princess works with the material of Indian anticolonial nationalism to invigorate the creative energies of what is finally a U.S.-focused antiracist effort. The protagonist is Matthew Townes, a talented African American man who, following a few hundred pages of disillusionment with both the liberal and the radical strains of Black American activism, partners, both romantically and politically, with the title's "dark princess": Princess Kautilya of Bwodpur, India. He participates, through her acquaintance, in a Berlin Conference of the Darker Peoples of the World, and they ultimately dismiss both Indian anticolonialism and U.S. democracy in favor of an intimately coordinated project of worldwide liberation. At the end of the novel's passionate plot, these problems are resolved through the birth of Matthew and Kautilya's messianic, mixed-race, Brahminically blessed baby.

Du Bois deployed print internationalism to forge connections across the Global South, even in situations of disagreement, incomprehension, and divergence. Whereas events like the 1911 United Races Congress could bring diverse peoples together temporarily in a single location, only the printed text could produce a portable solidarity, one whose materiality would keep it from changing dramatically in differently racialized places. In *Dark Princess*, internationalism comes into the United States through the presence of Kautilya; nonetheless, she explains that one need not travel to change the world:

> "The black belt of the Congo, the Nile, and the Ganges reaches up by way of Guiana, Haiti, and Jamaica, like a red arrow up into the heart of white America. Thus I see a mighty synthesis: you can work in Africa and Asia right here in America if you work in the Black Belt."[31]

Detouring through three countries marked by both African slavery and Indian indenture, the "black belt" transforms, via simile, into a weapon directed against "white America." The "black belt" of Du Bois's thought usually references the high density of Black people in a geographical region. In Kautilya's words, however, the belt commences as riverine and unspecified, appearing as metaphor through its lack of capitalization. At once "black belt" and "red arrow," both river system and land mass, Du Bois's internationalism maps multiple territories onto one another. These unpredictable correspondences between locations ultimately enable multiple, and simultaneous, political agendas. This geographical vision for antiracist activism is, as I demonstrate in this chapter, essentially identical to our contemporary concept of the Global South.

The term "Global South" originated in the late 1960s, when the axis of global conflict was rearticulated in latitude rather than longitude. No longer were developmental organizations most concerned with the conflict between East and West; instead, they proclaimed that the most significant tension was a "north-south gap" in economic development. This spawned, at first, a quite literal concern with geographical divergence—an influential 1980 report, titled *North-South: A Programme for Survival*, drew a line at 30 degrees north of the equator, with a slight detour to exclude Australia. In time, this cartography generated two metaphorical regions, "the North"—which was prosperous and industrialized—and "the South"—which was not. This geographical metaphor became vastly more popular after 1991, with the dissolution of the Soviet Union and the concomitant decline of the "Three Worlds Theory." The category of the "Third World," long used to designate poorer and previously colonized countries, seemed no longer relevant when the "Second World," that of socialism, seemed to have collapsed—and one could hardly call them "developing countries" when it was evident that many of these poor regions were not "developing" at all.

The term "Global South" flourished in that post–Cold War context, quickly gaining a following among those who wished to be less "Western-centric, economistic," and nation-centric in their intellectual and political work.[32] The addition of a modifier to form the phrase "Global South" served to distinguish it from nationally specific usages of "the South" and to emphasize its metaphorical remit. Thus, for instance, by the twenty-first century, medical scholars could use the elasticity of the Global South to argue that the city of Detroit should be included, despite being in the United States—the global North nation par excellence.[33]

Du Bois's representations of Indian elites in *Dark Princess* sought precisely to form this metaphorical geography. His novel emerged within the shifting landscape of immigration and naturalization law in the early twentieth-century United States, which often singled out those of Asian descent for exclusionary treatment. U.S. citizenship was officially extended to those of African ancestry in the late nineteenth century, yet that period also saw the introduction of anti-Asian restrictions that would not abate for almost a hundred years.[34] Whereas many restrictions focused on nonracial categories—banning polygamists and those with contagious diseases in 1891, and anarchists, beggars, and pimps in 1903—restrictions against Asian immigration historically constituted the only U.S. immigration prohibition on a racial or ethnic basis.

Du Bois thus wrote about an Asian character in the United States at a time when U.S. citizens could be Black or White but could almost never be Asian. As a consequence, I argue, *Dark Princess* can be read as a troubling of U.S. race politics because of, not in spite of, the titular character's elite Indian origins. Existing scholarship on *Dark Princess* has frequently resorted to one of two options: either Kautilya is simply an evasion of U.S. race categories, in which case her Indianness is insignificant, or Kautilya is merely a referent for India, in which case the novel's U.S.-centrism seems problematic. Du Bois's contemporaries were so struck by the figure of Kautilya that they searched for her among his acquaintances: Herbert Aptheker, for instance, conjectured that there was such a woman at Fisk University, while Mary White Ovington claimed that Kautilya was based on an Indian princess whom

Du Bois had met at the First Universal Races Congress in London in 1911. My reading of *Dark Princess* approaches Kautilya as an entirely fictional character with no specific historical or biographical referent, in keeping with the archival evidence of Du Bois's research queries, which I discuss later in this chapter. Much as my sustained engagement in the previous chapter with Gandhi's brief mentions of Black South Africans argued for reading from, rather than through, those textual details, so here my elaborate engagement with the fictional Kautilya's Indianness advances Du Bois's Indian references as more than mere accessories to his better-known U.S. goals. I thereby continue the dialectical reading method discussed at the end of the previous chapter, which seizes on a text that is about the Global South by writing about India, yet hopes to be read as not principally about India at all: to read, that is, from the metaphor of the "dark princess," not merely with it or through it. In this instance, this reading requires a kind of literalism that renders the text's tropes unfamiliar: I will focus on the surface of the text before I discuss its symbolic depths.[35]

For instance, applying the legal realities of the United States in the 1920s to the world depicted in *Dark Princess* has immediate ramifications: Princess Kautilya would have been settled illegally in the United States—in today's terms, as an undocumented person (or, as some would say, an illegal alien). Her child would be a U.S. citizen because of his birth on U.S. soil and—crucially—his African ancestry. (Children born in the United States to foreigners were entitled to U.S. citizenship after the 1898 judgment in *United States v. Wong Kim Ark*, but that judgment excluded those born to foreign rulers like Kautilya—and, in any case, the judgment would not be seen as conclusive until the 1940s.) Even after marrying Matthew, however, Kautilya would have remained ineligible for naturalization, no matter that she was the wife of one citizen and the mother of another (a key contrast with our current immigration regime). The characters of novels are not the people of historical record, yet the symbolic implications are worth noting. Much as Du Bois worked across his oeuvre to center the "black all-mother" as a motor for world belonging,[36] by choosing an Indian mother at a time of U.S. exclusions against Asians, Du Bois once again demonstrated that the U.S. government sinned against maternity, and against children. By constructing a fictional narrative in which the mother of a U.S. citizen would be barred from U.S. citizenship or even residency, Du Bois suggested that the regimes of familial belonging and national belonging in the United States remained fundamentally at odds. Instead, then, of depicting children as but one component of a proper and respectable bourgeois family, *Dark Princess* reveals the non-White child as a brownie: a magical creature who is both politically and socially disruptive.

In choosing a "dark princess" who was not only Asian but a high-caste Hindu, moreover, Du Bois invoked the confused categorizations of race and caste in his time. The dominant ethnology of the early twentieth-century United States usually divided humanity into four categories: "Caucasoid," "Mongoloid," "Negroid," and "Amerind," correlating roughly to our contemporary categories of White, Asian, Black, and Native American. Debates surrounding Indian immigration, however, frequently pondered whether a racial distinction should be drawn *among* Hindus, and not simply against them. In such discussions, prevalent in the late nineteenth and early twentieth centuries, high-caste Hindus were argued to be Aryan, and therefore White, while lower-caste Indians were consistently understood as not Aryan, and therefore not White either. These claims were persistent and widespread. In 1916, even Du Bois's friend Lala Lajpat Rai (1865–1928) emphasized that Hindus and Europeans came from the same racial stock; as late as 1927, the ill-fated Hindu Citizenship Bill argued that Indians had a right to U.S. citizenship because of their Aryan ancestry.[37]

Whereas other claims to Whiteness were often resolved on cultural grounds, the Indian claim to Whiteness in the early twentieth-century United States was invariably figured in ethnological terms. These grounds, however, could shift as needed. As the governments of North America's Pacific Coast moved from the exclusion of specific nationalities—Chinese, Japanese, Korean, Indian—to the exclusion of a generalized category of "the Asiatic," the racial contours of these prohibitions became increasingly evident.[38] In 1922, the U.S. Supreme Court invoked ethnology to eliminate Japanese claims to citizenship, but a year later it eviscerated ethnology to eradicate Indian claims as well.[39] The racial status of upper-caste Indians would be legally resolved in the 1923 case of *United States v. Bhagat Singh Thind*, in which the U.S. Supreme Court pondered: "Is a high-caste Hindu, of full Indian blood, . . . a white person?" Describing "white persons" as "words of common speech, and not of scientific origin," the Court argued that, despite the scientific truth that "the blond Scandinavian and the brown Hindu" were of shared Aryan ancestry, "the average man knows perfectly well that there are unmistakable and profound differences between them today."[40] Precistely because of these partial and inconsistent privileges, the problem of *Asian* racial difference makes racism evident in a manner that Blackness could not. The Japanese were considered "civilized" after the Meiji Restoration (1868), and Indians were recognized as ancestral kin (as "Aryan"), but neither was given full access to the privileges of Whiteness. U.S. racism may be famously centered along a Black/White binary, but as early twentieth-century U.S. citizenship law demonstrates, the U.S. articulation of anti-Asian racism was singularly effective in making White supremacism baldly evident.

As always, the concerns of racism also centered on those of reproduction. In the *Thind* judgment, Indians' lack of Whiteness was conclusively demonstrated by the inassimilability of their future children: whereas children of "European parentage quickly merge into the mass of our population," the Court argued that "the children born in this country of Hindu parents would retain indefinitely the clear evidence of their ancestry."[41] The discursive possibility of upper-caste Hindus' Whiteness becomes an enabling condition for Du Bois's *Dark Princess*, which he began writing in 1926, shortly after the *Thind* judgment. Matthew and Kautilya are characterized as racially distinct, and Du Bois thereby renders the novel's conclusion recognizably a scene of racial intermixture. Yet because U.S. miscegenation law had only targeted the interracial marriages of Whites, this moment of emphatic miscegenation also highlights the possibly White status of an elite Indian person like the fictional Kautilya. In a context wherein the dominant science decried racial mixture as degeneration, the possibilities of joyful sexual intermingling were synonymous with those of democracy.[42]

Du Bois engaged the Aryan argument for Indian origins in his nonfiction to reclaim elite ancestry for persons not White. In 1915, in "The Coming of Black Men," Du Bois described the subcontinent as evolving through contact between Dravidian aborigines and Aryan immigrants. He thereby echoed the race theories of the early twentieth century, yet he changed the debate by defining Dravidians as "Negroes with some mixture of Mongoloid and later of Caucasoid stocks."[43] He wrote that the Rig Veda, a Sanskrit text composed in the second millennium B.C.E., recounted "the fierce struggles between these whites and blacks for the mastery of India," featuring Hindu deities both White (Indra) and Black (Krishna).[44] This original conflict soon gave way, in Du Bois's narrative, to multiracial harmony: "The whites long held the conquered blacks in caste servitude, but eventually the color line disappeared. . . . The whites enlisted in the service of the blacks and fought under Negro chiefs. . . . One of the leading Aryan chiefs was a Negro."[45] Du Bois's key intervention here lies not in undermining the Aryan migration thesis but, rather, in claiming Aryans as Black. Whereas White commentators depicted an ongoing battle in India between White Brahmins and Black Dravidians, Du Bois revealed a subcontinent peopled by Black Brahmins. *Dark Princess*'s central romance, the illegitimate affair between Matthew and Kautilya, explicitly references the Hindu narrative of Radha-Krishna,[46] and in doing so it prefigures Du Bois's claim of Krishna's racial (and not just chromatic) Blackness in his 1947 essay "Asia in Africa."[47] Like the Matthew-as-Krishna tropes of the 1928 novel, the Krishna of that later nonfictional analysis is a Negro. At a time when the caste system was often invoked to justify British colonial rule, Du Bois's depiction of a country cohered by caste, not ruptured by the color line, was a dramatic rebuke to those who would keep India under Western rule. In contrast to our contemporary understandings of caste and race as intertwined evils, Du Bois used caste to combat race without problematizing the former term, in keeping with the elitist sympathies of his early career. From our vantage point, then, we find a profound political and moral failure: Du Bois was antiracist, but he was not exactly anticaste.

In an attempt to build solidarity among the "colored peoples of the world," Du Bois worked with the figural language of color—red, black, yellow, brown—on a problem that he nevertheless saw in materialist terms. For example, Du Bois's contribution to *The New Negro*, the 1924 anthology edited by Alain Locke that became a landmark collection of the Harlem Renaissance, was published under a distinct section "Worlds of Color," which contained only his essay, titled "The Negro Mind Reaches Out." Always attentive to both the material and the figural, Du Bois there discusses racism and colonialism as constitutive effects of capitalism and modernity, and yet on the same page he wrote of the "vast gulf between the red-black South and the yellow-brown East."[48] Neither the South nor the East is literally red-black or yellow-brown, but they are, quite literally, "all victims of white colonialism," which forms the first clause of that same sentence. By the time of *Dark Princess*, in which the Indian love-interest is literally darkened by her difficult experiences of employment, Du Bois's understanding of race was definitively tied to the exploitation of the working class. I have demonstrated elsewhere that *Dark Princess* reflects a serious engagement with Indian politics;[49] here I build on that work to explore the implications of Du Bois's reliance on the prejudices of caste.

The rhetoric of caste was central to U.S. debates on race and equality in the nineteenth century,[50] and Du Bois refined these claims as both an activist and a social scientist. A distinguished sociologist, Du Bois possessed a sophisticated understanding of India's caste system, and the category of caste surfaces repeatedly in his writings. Whether in lectures with titles like "Caste in America" (1903) and "Profit and Caste" (1925), or in the caste-framed analysis that opens and closes *Black Reconstruction in America* (1935), Du Bois recoded Black Americans' problems as problems for the entire United States, arguing that their treatment suggested the incursion on U.S. soil of the Indian affliction of caste, which has "ruined lives, overturned governments and buried civilizations."[51] Class, he accepted, was "perfectly natural and necessary" in "any great and growing nation"; an unchanging and inherited sense of class, however, was profoundly un-American.[52] While this exotic danger chiefly manifested itself, Du Bois explained, in a "color caste" system directed against Black Americans, he warned that it was spreading into the United States as a whole, "growing [into] a feeling that White children of certain social classes do not need high schools, that social standing ought to bestow certain privileges by a sort of divine right and that the man who wrote the declaration of independence was a fool."[53] Du Bois further argued that restrictions on intermarriage, place of residence, occupation, and educational access along racial lines provide "a true picture of the caste situation in the United States today."[54] Americans are thus becoming, he implies, akin to the long-colonized inhabitants of the Indian subcontinent. For this rhetoric to work, however, Du Bois cannot simply criticize caste: he must also criticize India itself, associating caste, as many Euro-American writers long had, with the downfall of once-great civilizations.

In his work before his 1935 *Black Reconstruction*, caste provides a rhetoric that renders American racism un-American: through his conception of "color caste," Du Bois reframes the difficulty of being "both a Negro and an American" as a problem with Indian resonances.[55] To emphasize this frightful possibility, Du Bois needs to depict an India that is heavily overwrought by caste and hierarchy, not an India that is moving toward egalitarianism or meritocracy. This necessary emphasis perhaps explains his choice, in *Dark Princess*, of a royal figure with a retinue of servants and minders. In a novel where the Pullman porters and factory workers of the United States receive careful and sympathetic elaboration, the lower-caste figures who attend Princess Kautilya appear without any characterization, serving only to evidence the unyielding dehumanization caused by India's distinctive stratification.

Du Bois's print internationalism thus drew on the common Western claim that Indian society, due to caste, was fundamentally inimical to egalitarianism, even as he foregrounded Indian news in his political reportage. By retaining this fundamentally civilizational distinction, Du Bois was able to use caste as a phobic object in his struggle against American racism—a racism that, when simply named as such, frequently failed to concern many of his fellow Americans. *Dark Princess* thus demonstrates the complex pleasures of imagined national difference: not only as fantasy, in the delights of Kautilya's royal existence, but also as phobia, in the nameless drudgery of those born into her servitude. Rendering Indian civilization directly useful to his vision for the Global South necessitated recoding essential incompatibility—casteism versus egalitarianism—as essential complementarity. By centering *Dark Princess* on a romance between a man who happens to be Black American and a woman who happens to be Indian, Du Bois recoded civilizational difference as sexual difference. Much as sexual difference is then represented as that which, because of the dissimilarity, can combine two individuals to produce yet another, Du Bois depicted a caste-ridden society that could nonetheless help the United States, coded as essentially democratic, produce a better world.

The Indian iconography invoked in *Dark Princess* is mostly Hindu, with occasional touches of a Buddhism entirely compatible with Hinduism. The appearance of a Muslim "priest" in the final scene of the novel is the only notable reference to Islam, and it participates in that scene's vision of interreligious union. Du Bois's novel constructs easy religious parallels: Hindu mythology for Kautilya's civilization, and Christian songs for Matthew's. Du Bois further uses tropes of the guru and of renunciation to develop the politics of his romance, explicitly citing the Gandhian model. Kautilya tells Matthew:

> "And when I saw that old mother of yours . . . I knew that I was looking upon one of the ancient prophets of India and that she was to lead me out of the depths in which I found myself and up to the atonement for which I yearned. So I started with her upon that path of seven years. . . .
>
> "You had stepped down into menial service at my request. . . . It was now my turn to step down to the bottom of the world and see it for myself. So I put aside my silken garments and cut my hair, and, selling my jewels, I started out on the long path which should lead to you."[56]

Du Bois valorizes Matthew's African American mother by invoking Brahminical notions of renunciation. In seeking "atonement," Kautilya "step[s] down to the bottom of the world" and into "menial service." She thereby diverges from the story of the Buddha, who never undertook manual labor, and instead impersonates a person of a lower caste, becoming darker skinned in the process.

Du Bois's willingness to value caste in India (but not in the United States) is further reflected in a distinctly hierarchical vision for India's liberation in *Dark Princess*. Kautilya's position on religion, for instance, is explicitly Brahminical. She desires to "go back to the ancient simplicity of Brahma" and to "clean the slate" of popular religious practices in favor of the Brahminical texts of the Vedas.[57] Whereas Matthew's program for U.S. uplift requires "distributing wealth more evenly" and "democratic control of industry," Kautilya's plan for India requires that "we must first emancipate ourselves. . . . Then we must learn to rule ourselves politically and to organize our old industry on new modern lines," in search of "our own social uplift" rather than democracy or equality.[58] The romance narrative sutures this unlikely coalition, for Du Bois's novel is heterosexual not only in its plot but in its very temperament. The romance unfolds between two fantastically attractive characters, who are fundamentally differentiated not only by nationality but also by gender. That attraction—the familiar story of a man loving a woman, and vice versa—is then laminated with the attraction of differences that might be accorded to their variance in race and nation, so that the accomplishment of international solidarity becomes inextricable from their seemingly natural unification, wherein they are different from each other exactly as reproduction intended. Heterosexuality, and the desire across difference espoused within it, thus provides the necessary template for an internationalism rife with essential differences.

Dark Princess culminates with Madhu Chandragupta Singh, the messianic brownie of the novel's triumphal ending, whose "gurgling, golden self" might generate an antiracist world. The reproductive plot of Kautilya and Matthew's pairing includes Matthew's mother, and it is contingent on the child's recognition not only by the father, Matthew, but also by a panoply of international visitors. It thus figures a reciprocal reproduction through which not just an infant but also a preacher, an ancient woman, and a variety of religious brown men are created. *Dark Princess*'s wedding scene is too belated to serve the social roles usually accorded to the institution of marriage, for the couple are married only after their union has been sexually consummated. Their child is born out of wedlock, but wedlock follows nonetheless, shifting the emphasis from the act of union to its products. The lyrical narration soon breaks into disjointed dialogue, without speaker attribution; we then witness "the ancient woman," presumably Matthew's mother, perform a speech of ecstatic prayer, which suddenly devolves into a dialogue reported as "The Woman" and "The Man." Finally, a "pageant" of men "in white with shining swords" emerges from the woods, from which three old men step forward and invoke Krishna, Buddha, and Allah. After all this prayer and ritual, we are shown "a thrill of delight; its little feet, curled petals; its mouth a kiss; its hands like waving prayers."[59] This child, described in nonhuman terms, is a figure we have seen elsewhere in Du Bois's print internationalism: the magical child figured in the mixed-race brownie.

CRAFTING THE *BROWNIES' BOOK*

Du Bois's 1919 editorial on "the true brownies" suggests that *The Crisis*, and particularly the October "Children's Numbers," were rarely consumed in private or read exclusively by adult readers. They were, rather, part of the family library, and the object of the attentions of people of varying age and maturity, an aspect that surfaces repeatedly in archives and memoirs.[60] The *Brownies' Book* was thus created to intentionally address a readership—children and younger persons—that *The Crisis* had interpellated mostly by happenstance. Perhaps as a consequence, we find a two-way traffic between the publications. The *Brownies' Book*, for instance, modeled its "Little People of the Month" page, which portrayed exemplary community members, on *The Crisis*'s recurring "Men of the Month" feature, while *The Crisis* later adopted the "As the Crow Flies" column that originated in the *Brownies' Book*. Both publications share a preoccupation with internationalism, yet the one explicitly intended for children carries its internationalism differently—in many respects, I would argue, more effectively. In *The Crisis*, internationalism was most often presented as current events and political information, with cursory historical background offered by the writers as needed: its reader was interpellated as a fully literate adult, even if the reality of readers' skills was likely more varied. The *Brownies' Book*, by contrast, explicitly anticipates that it will be read by families, and by readers at different stages of development. As a consequence, it often excludes the most recent newsworthy details, providing instead broad and memorable sweeps of world history and culture. *The Crisis*, with its urgent title—and its subtitle "A Record of the Darker Races"—

committed to the periodical inscription of the contemporary even as it was often preserved as long as possible by its committed readers. Proclaiming its status as a book, by contrast, the *Brownies' Book* declared its permanence and specifically encouraged long-term inclusion in the family library. This periodical's consequential nomination as a "book" is underscored by the "Dedication" limerick, written by Fauset, that concludes its very first issue:

> To Children, who with eager look
> Scanned vainly library shelf and nook,
> For History or Song or Story
> That told of Colored Peoples' glory,—
> We dedicate THE BROWNIES' BOOK.[61]

Fauset's limerick is transepochal and nonnational, and its content challenges the strictures of genre: the children seek the codex format, regardless of the literary forms inside it.

By positioning itself as a periodical for children, the *Brownies' Book* was able to engage fundamental concerns that were otherwise seen as unworthy of explicit instruction. It could, for instance, decree the very rules of reading. In June 1920, Fauset's recurring column "The Judge" responded to "the question of questions, the question in comparison with which all other kiddie matters fade into insignificance, and that is WHAT SHALL I READ?"[62] Whereas Fauset's regular column in *The Crisis* had instructed its readers, as its title explained, in "What to Read," her commentary in the *Brownies' Book* explained the *how* of reading instead.[63] Before providing a long list of suggested texts, Fauset's "Judge" persona explained that reading had rules much like those for any game:

> 1. Don't skip;
> 2. Read straight through;
> 3. Finish.
>
> These are the rules of the game just like the base in "I spy" and the ring in marbles. You cannot have a game unless you follow the rules. Skipping is not reading; it is worse than nothing. Reading the end of a story before you have read the beginning is unfair; it is cheating. And in reading, as in other things, when you start a job finish it—get the habit.[64]

In developing this parallel between reading and play, Fauset implies the sociability of reading: to read here is to follow the rules, so as to "have a game" with the other readers, writers, and editors of this printed world. The three rules she offers may be short and simple, articulated as yet another game requiring fair play. The actual application of these rules of reading to the *Brownies' Book*, however, could prove staggeringly complex. The issues are full of gaps—geographical, historical, and generic—and even the photos range widely in their subject matter. To read the *Brownies' Book* "straight through"—to "finish," without "skipping"—is to be tasked with cognitive syntheses of enormous proportions.

The *Brownies' Book* pairs fanciful lessons like this one with prose features devoted to explicit didacticism, with the most meaningful instruction generally situated within the space of the family. Through these lessons, the *Brownies' Book* insists that "the children of the sun" see themselves within a larger global geography, one both practical and fanciful. This is accomplished, in the nonfiction, through the juxtaposition of various places within successive pages; in the fiction, it often demands a kind of imaginary alignment, as in the "Folk Tales" section of the second issue:

> The only thing that is nicer than telling a story is to listen to it. Did you ever stop to think that just as you sit very still in the twilight and listen to Father or Mother telling stories, just so children are listening all over the world,—in Sweden, in India, in Georgia, and in Uganda?[65]

As with Gandhi's conception of the audible conversation between the Editor and the Reader that we discussed in chapter 2, here too the print periodical can make conversations audible between parents and children all over the world.

The managing editor of the *Brownies' Book* was Jessie Redmon Fauset. Born to an established and respectable, though not wealthy, African American family, Fauset was raised primarily in Philadelphia—a city that, despite its relatively tolerant racial hierarchies, would repeatedly bar her from its educational institutions, first as a student and later as a teacher. Acutely aware of the complex intersections of race and class, she was part of a Black middle class that would form the central topic of her fictional works. She began contributing to *The Crisis* in 1912 and served as its literary editor from 1919 to 1926, rapidly transforming it into the most distinguished venue for Black literature in the

United States. When Du Bois traveled, which he did frequently, Fauset also served as its managing editor, as for instance from December 1918 to June 1919.[66] Despite her degrees from Cornell University and the University of Pennsylvania, her influential interlude at *The Crisis*, and her fiction and nonfiction publications, she was never able to attain the kinds of full-time leadership positions open to Black men in the U.S. who held similar credentials. Instead, Fauset spent most of her life in the most intellectual career then open to African American women: as a schoolteacher. This particular combination of experiences, nevertheless, made her a perfect editor and lead writer for the *Brownies' Book*.

Fauset's writings for *The Crisis*, as well as her work in the *Brownies' Book*, reflect her commitment to print internationalism: she authored, for instance, a series of profiles on great men of African ancestry all over the world, and a report on the Pan-African Congress of 1921.[67] Much as the *Brownies' Book* would reflect an openness to other languages in its publication of African folklore, so too Fauset in *The Crisis* would conduct French-language writing into the global Anglophone, reviewing and translating works from African and Caribbean writers and showering particular praise on Haitian poetry.[68]

Whereas *The Crisis*'s "Children's Number" paired adorable photos of readers' children with appalling stories of racial persecution, the *Brownies' Book* traffics in less obvious contrasts, subordinating its collage effects to the sensitivities of a presumably younger readership. In choosing to understate atrocities, however, it does not abandon complexity, including a rich variety of materials that provoke further inquiry. The inaugural issue opens with a full-page photograph of Zaouditou, the Empress of Ethiopia; the next page, all text, transports us "in the Land of Sure Enough, away down South, in a most wonderful land named Georgia."[69] The connection between the items is not explained, leaving the reader to envision their commonality: their shared location in what we now call "the Global South." In putting these two next to each other, moreover, Fauset subverts the usual definitions of the familiar and the exotic: Ethiopia is introduced through the modern medium of photography, in a portrait whose elite subject makes direct eye contact, while Georgia, although in the United States, is presented as a quasi-magical location in a story of "a most wonderful land." A few pages later, a "dialect poem" (that is, one written in nonstandard English) promises to tell us "the origin of White folks";[70] a full-page poem in standard U.S. English, titled "Kindergarten Song," teaches racial unity through four stanzas. Much as the "Origin of White

Folks" poem uses dialect and irony to rich effect, the "Kindergarten Song" that follows subverts the associations of standard English even as it scrupulously follows its rules. Written by the activist and poet Carrie W. Clifford, whose 1911 *Race Rhymes* collection was explicit in its engagement of U.S. racism, this poem places all of the races together, without copula or explanation. It is patterned simply—it is, after all, a "kindergarten song"—in four verses of four lines, each with an AABB rhyme scheme. Each of the first three verses uses the third line to itemize: "No hair, crinkled hair, straight hair, curls—"; "Red child, yellow child, black child, white—"; "Zulu, Esquimaux, Saxon, Jew." A similar function is performed in the final stanza, but this time in the fourth line, thus making "White man, red man, black man, tall" the final line of the poem as well.[71] The tight rhyme scheme of the poem renders each term irreplaceable in form much as each is claimed to be in content, even as no effort is made to resolve the relations between them: "tall," for instance, ends an otherwise chromatic list of white, red, and black. As this example demonstrates, that which aids the novice reader—in this instance, the deployment of a tight rhyme scheme—can also assist the novice internationalist.

Fauset's choice of fiction reflected a worldwide frame, as she published, and when necessary translated, fiction, poetry, and folktales from across what we now call the global South.[72] Her print internationalism was further reflected in her reportage, for instance, in a continuing interest in Southeast Asian politics. Although Fauset generally delivered international news through a fictional character named "Uncle Jim," this did not restrain her from providing an impressive amount of detail. For example, a few pages into the inaugural issue, we find ourselves "over the ocean wave." In the story of that title, likely written by Fauset, the recurring child characters Betty and Philip saw "a picture of two young colored girls" at the movies and recognized them as "some colored folks just like us." These were the Filipina students Parhata Miran and Carmen Aguinaldo, who were, as the facticity of the included photograph indicates, actually existing persons (unlike Philip and Betty, whose fictionality renders them placeholders for the reader). Uncle Jim explains that "they are colored,—that is their skin is not white; but they belong to a different division of people from what we do." He then explains Philippine politics, noting that Emilio Aguinaldo (father of the photographed Carmen), though seen as "a bandit, or outlaw" by the United States, was regarded as "a patriot" by his compatriots. The article ends in masquerade: playing at being Filipinos, one child declares: "I am going to be the bandit!"[73] A few months later we receive another lesson on Southeast Asia, this time regarding the then-disputed island of Yap. Betty and Philip recall Uncle Jim's previous lesson, listing the islands of the Philippine archipelago; Uncle Jim teaches them the history of Yap's repeated colonization, explaining that its inhabitants "belong to the Colored Peoples of the world."

As this early example indicates, the dialogue format used here enables Fauset to give us all the newsworth details—the U.S. military interest, the earlier political upheaval—as well as trivia about clothing, money, and culture. The result is a combination of frivolous and serious information that was likely engaging for readers of all ages. Many larger features in the *Brownies' Book* assert a transnational genealogy, with pride of place given to "ancient Africa and mysterious Asia": as the author of one piece exclaims: "The world is really very small and East and West are always meeting!"[74] It is likely that the lived world of the *Brownies' Book*'s readers was indeed quite small, given the constraints on Black mobility in the early twentieth century, but in the *Brownies' Book* East and West are always meeting in a world easily available for Black engagement.

The print internationalism developed through poetry and story was further propagated through Du Bois's reportage in the *Brownies' Book*, which appeared in a recurring feature titled "As the Crow Flies." Du Bois invented this Crow persona specifically for the *Brownies' Book*, and it would become his narrative structure for periodicals like *The Crisis* and the *Amsterdam News* as well. In those later pages, which were explicitly designed for adult readers, Du Bois's Crow was strictly metaphorical, its line of flight literally surpassing established boundaries and trade routes. Suggestive of the idiom used to describe the shortest distance between two points, this Crow always flew homeward, sharing the relevant news of distant lands before (re)turning his gaze to the United States. His dispatches mapped the distance between other places and Black America, connecting them, the idiom implies, with superlative proximity. In reading this narrative structure, scholars have often criticized Du Bois's tendency to move from international concerns to national ones, arguing that this indicates his fundamental provincialism. I propose, however, that—as the expression suggests—the transformative connection among places, and *not* the particular regions covered, is the moral of this narrative structure. Through the Crow persona, Du Bois suggests, that the "darker races" are at a surpassable distance from one another, if only "as the crow flies."

Several scholars have remarked on the black coloring of the Crow as central to its figural role, yet I submit that its trajectory is more significant than its color. The title, after all, is an established idiom, likely suggesting its conventional meaning (that of distance) to most readers rather than its central creature's appearance. Consequently, the Crow is not a metaphor for African American readers, but a symbol of the unprecedented connections that can be forged through print internationalism. This nonmetaphorical aspect of "As the Crow Flies" is reflected in the format's origins. In his initial iteration of the column in the first issue of the *Brownies' Book*, Du Bois's Crow was literal and, as a consequence, magical. In that first appearance, a first-person narrator named the Crow is accompanied by a child interlocutor, described both as the "Little Boy with the Big Voice" and the "Little Voice with the Big Boy."[75] In later issues, the Crow speaks to his crowlings: like "brownies," "crowlings" is a nonce word that nonetheless seems in context both chromatic and self-evident. As the Crow confides: "Don't you think that Human Folks are just the funniest ever? Sometimes I just quit flying and hold my sides and laugh. 'Haw, haw—caw, caw!' I gurgle with delight, because the Earth Folks are so passing queer."[76] The Crow's cawing and hawing gifts the children with a "delighted" distance from the often-terrible world of "Earth Folks" and "Human Folks," enabling them to both observe and avoid the bitter realities inevitably reflected in the news that the Crow nonetheless reports. Much as the animals of fables and folktales reflect truths about common people, the Crow finds connections across nations, races, and places. The Crow's aerial distance enables an international perspective and, to use his terms, a "passing queer" point of view. Du Bois and Fauset may not have queered the child, but they have queered "Human Folks." After a summary of world news, which is mostly war, strikes, and other difficulties, the Crow concludes:

> What I cannot see, is why these Human Folk do not watch us Crow Folk more, and learn how to be happy and free, high up in these wide spaces. Seems to me that the World People live too much cooped up in little dark holes. That's enough to make anybody act funny.[77]

Soaring above the earth with the Crow, *Brownies' Book* readers learn about politics in summary form, always progressing from the worldwide back to the national. This first issue, published in the midst of horrendous racist violence in the U.S., shifts readers' focus abroad, starting with pronunciation guidance for Irish politics and demographic details about India and Egypt.[78] We then read of "many race riots and lynchings" in the United States, but only for four lines of a three-page spread.

The role of the *Brownies' Book* in the appropriate raising of children is explicitly addressed in its third issue. In this early iteration of "The Judge," Fauset writes separate sections "To Father" and "To Mother." Whereas she tells Father to avoid excessive corporal punishment—informing him that "the sorrows of your children, although they may seem trivial to you, are just as tragic as any of your own"—she advises Mothers to be more strict, for

> the mothers . . . know how hard their lives and their parents' lives were; they know how many rebuffs and difficulties their children are going to meet; and they try and make this up to them by giving them all the candy they want, by letting them be just as saucy as they will, and by letting them run around wherever they want to.
>
> Now of all the ways of training children's characters to meet difficulties which they are going to find in the present world of the color-line, these are the very worst.[79]

Fauset's counsel to Father responds to the racist stereotype of the Black child as impervious to pain; that addressed to Mother hints at the stereotyping of Black children as indolent and extravagant. What unites Fauset's disparate advice is her consistent emphasis on the deadly seriousness, always suggested but never explicitly written, of the singular vulnerability of Black children in the United States. Fauset concludes: "What you want to do is to strengthen, not weaken, your children. Make them serious, not frivolous; make them thoughtful, not rattle-brained."[80]

Creating a serious child, however, requires a sensitive approach. The fantasy worlds of children's literature here operate as sites wherein the inequalities of the real world are revealed and ridiculed, not as spaces of reassurance where morality is always simple. The antiracist critique in the *Brownies' Book* is always delivered indirectly, as for instance in a poem by the celebrated poet and playwright Georgia Douglas Johnson. Her contribution, titled "The Ancestor," reads:

> They boasted of their ancestry, and flaunted in his face
> The glory of their royal line, the valor of their race;
> A moment Tom was clothed in thought,—he was no orator,—
> Then shouted,—"Boys, I say, by Jove, I'll be an ANCESTOR!"[81]

Johnson's poem pairs the realities of racial chauvinism with the absurdity of its claims. Print internationalism can provide ethical lessons for any age group, but the children's version, unlike the adult one, carries a generous dose of subversive humor.

The *Brownies' Book* operated as a key locus of women's participation in print culture, not least because of its explicit solicitation of familial reading. It was mostly written by women, as the names on the pieces attest, and so were the letters to the editor, making the *Brownies' Book* a space within which women write and read and learn from one another. In the first issue, letters to the periodical were printed with salutations such as "Dear Sir" and "Dear Dr. Du Bois" and even "Dear *Crisis*," reflecting its launch as a spinoff from a periodical nearly synonymous with Du Bois himself. Later issues, however, printed these letters without salutations whatsoever, in an implicit recognition of the journal's guiding editor: not Du Bois, nor any other man, but Jessie Redmon Fauset.[82]

The letter writers to the *Brownies' Book* frequently note the particular significance of print. For instance, in a letter in the second issue, Bella Seymour of New York City reports that her daughter asks, "Didn't colored folks do anything?" Presenting an exchange that Fauset would restage nearly verbatim in her 1924 novel, *There Is Confusion*,[83] Bella Seymour laments:

> When I tell her as much as I know about our folks, she says: "Well, that's just stories. Didn't they ever do anything in a book?" I have not had much schooling, and I am a busy woman with my sewing and my housekeeping, so I don't get much time to read and I can't tell my little girl where to find these things. But I am sure you know and that now you will tell her.[84]

For Bella Seymour's "little girl," spoken knowledge and "stories" will not do: accomplishments only signify once they have been memorialized through publication—a problem the *Brownies' Book* is singularly poised to assuage. We do not hear from Bella Seymour again, but we do encounter, a few months later, a letter from Hattie Porter. Much as Bella wrote of her daughter from New York City, Hattie writes of her mother from the city of San Francisco:

> My mother likes me to sit and tell her stories while she sews. I used to tell her all the fairy tales I ever read. But now I tell her the stories out of *The Brownies' Book*. She is so busy, she never gets a chance to look at it. I am trying very hard to write a story nice enough for you to accept, dear Mr. Editor. I work very slowly, but some day I'll have it finished and will send it to you. If you would just print it! I'd take the book to my mother and say "See what I did!" I know she'd look at it then.[85]

Hattie's letter appears in "The Jury"; Bella's appeared in "The Grown-Ups' Corner," and across these issues they respond to each other poignantly. In this world, books are accomplishments, far more than "just stories" told by mothers and daughters to one another. The effect of these cascading names, each of which rarely appears in more than one issue, is that of a dispersed community across what we would now term the Global South. The abundance of these names—woman after woman after woman—is startling to encounter in the archives. We know nothing about these letter writers, yet I mention some of their names here because the volume, and continuity, of their presence across each issue is itself an example of print internationalism at work. Women from a vast variety of locations, who did not directly know one another and may have had no other connection to publishing or activism, were able to congregate through the printed pages of the *Brownies' Book*.

This print community of women readers and writers spanned large parts of the world, with several contributions from women in southern and western Africa. These women wrote for children: both for their reading and on their behalf. Yet through their named participation, they both claimed their assigned roles as caretakers of children and exceeded those social bounds, becoming themselves the authors of an eclectic print internationalism. This narrative strategy could be particularly effective in cases of marked cultural difference. For instance, the Liberian activist Kathleen Easmon opens her essay "A Little Talk about West Africa"[86] by positioning herself within networks of child-to-child exchange:

> Many of you who read *The Brownies' Book* have already heard stories from many parts of Africa. I am bringing you a greeting from the Brownies on the west coast. If they knew how, they would write you a letter, but as very few of them have an opportunity of going to school, it is customary when they want to tell any one of what is happening in their particular village for them to send a greeting by someone who is travelling.[87]

The adult here carries the message, and she enables connections across children—and countries—in the process. By the second year, moreover, Fauset was explicitly advising her readers how to behave toward other races. In a staged conversation typical of "The Judge" column, Fauset's Judge admonishes one of the fictional children for teasing the equally fictional Hong Loo, a "Chinaman."[88] Hong Loo's right not to be teased is predicated not on his Americanness or even his fundamental humanity but on how Americans might be treated on going to China. The brownie of this story is an actor for world peace, or for world war, depending on how he treats the "laundryman" down the street. The column's moral, crucially, is at once charmingly exaggerated and utterly accurate, in an age when immigration rights were usually negotiated through arrangements of national reciprocity.[89]

The internationalism of the *Brownies' Book* included the publication of material that was challenging in its explicit foreignness. Much as Tagore, as we saw in chapter 1, used unorthodox approaches to translation to bend the global Anglophone to his Asianist purposes, so too did Fauset publish contributions whose use of non-English words enabled the English-language *Brownies' Book* to unsettle the global Anglophone. In February 1921, for example, Fauset published a short story by the Mozambican intellectual C. Kamba Simango, under the English subtitle "The Lion and the Hare," but with an untranslated title—"Mphontholo Ne Shulo"—written boldly across the page.[90] The story retains many Ndau words and expressions: we learn how to say "Look at this one—he is very fat" (*Lingiloup ih zinthinya*) and, for the plural, that several people are very fat (*manthikinya*).[91] We also learn how to discuss holding or dropping a rock, and the dangers thereof. These phrases may not easily apply to many situations, but they form the narrative crux of this Ndau story of the lion and the hare. Whereas other features in the *Brownies' Book* encouraged a global sentiment based on interdependence and commonality, this story builds internationalism through difference: not by domesticating the lion and the hare to the traditions of folklore that American readers might already know but by allowing Simango's *mponthobo* and *shulo* to retain their original names.[92] Much as Gandhi, as we saw in the previous chapter, untranslated the title of the translated English text of *Hind Swaraj* and thereby enabled its circulation within the global Anglophone, so Fauset and Simango, by retaining Ndau words within these English pages, signaled through the global Anglophone the persistence of the Global South.

Much as *The Crisis*'s "Children's Numbers" published an array of photographs of readers' children, the *Brownies' Book* published such photos in every issue alongside descriptions of their accomplishments. In the second issue, the periodical requests photos of high school graduates and adds: "In fact, whenever you hear of anything that a colored child has done well, hasten to tell us. But, of course, tell the exact truth—don't exaggerate or over-state."[93] In the third issue, the editors repeat the request, and add: "And letters! Do have your children write and tell us about their schools, their ambitions, their views of life, in general. A great deal of wisdom comes from the mouth of babes."[94] By the second year, "The Jury" section was being promoted as a correspondence page, with children encouraged to reply to each other directly through its publishing mechanism.[95]

At that stage, moreover, the collaborative constitution of the *Brownies' Book* was asserted as proof of its value:

> Did you know that 98% of the articles appearing in THE BROWNIES' BOOK have been written by *colored* men, women and children? You see we are really creating modern Negro literature. And all of the original drawings—*but one*—have come from the pen of colored artists. . . . This is a stimulus to the expression of modern Negro art.[96]

The readers of the *Brownies' Book* co-constituted that periodical in their exchanges and contributions, and they also mimicked it through what Ellen Gruber Garvey has termed "writing with scissors":[97] these readers would cut, paste, and collate various materials to create composite volumes (the nineteenth-century scrapbook) that emulated what they appreciated about the *Brownies' Book*.[98] At the one-year mark, "The Grown-Ups' Corner" explicitly requested assistance from its readers, asking for manuscripts and pictures, and encouraging them to recruit new subscribers. While financial pressures were certainly a consideration, the insistence on inclusion suggests that the editors were soliciting ideas as much as they were hoping to increase funds. Seeking "new and interesting stories about colored children, their interests, their difficulties, the way they live and the places they live in," the editors were "especially eager" to educate different regions of the U.S. about each other and to have information from "people who have friends in foreign countries where there are dark people."[99]

The *Brownies' Book* was part of the 1920s flourishing of African American literature and culture that came to be known as the Harlem Renaissance. The writers of that period placed particular emphasis on the child, both real and figural, whether through writings aimed at raising the right kind of children or at encouraging respectable, bourgeois domesticity. This focus was, after all, the logical extension of the celebration of novelty attendant in that celebrated moment of the "New Negro," whose very naming as a "Renaissance" evoked the language of birth.[100]

The focus on the child that emerged in the works of Du Bois, Fauset, and their contemporaries consequently works very differently from the discourse of the child as it is taken up in today's queer theoretical critiques.[101] The child figured in those scholarly discussions is idealized because that child is viewed as pure and free from the contradictions of actually lived democratic life, and of the burden of history. The child figured in the *Brownies' Book*, by contrast, approaches citizenship through its denial; adulthood and childhood coexist in the absence of safety and security. The positioning of a mature, sophisticated Black child, as I have shown, has a melancholic tinge: the Black child is sophisticated through the prohibition of youthful pleasures, necessarily knowledgeable due to the omnipresent dangers of racism. Neither bemoaning this maturity nor celebrating it, the *Brownies' Book* developed a politically responsive vision for the child marginalized by racism.[102]

The internationalism of the *Brownies' Book*, moreover, can teach us much about Du Bois's print internationalism more broadly. In a country where Black children worry that they cannot, in fact, become architects or musicians, stories of "Brownies" and of childhoods in faraway places proffer a larger world that would, at the least, offer different challenges and prohibitions. In lived contexts that frequently belittle Black children, the *Brownies' Book* encourages them to think big: to inculcate an expansive geography and, thereby, an expansive sense of possibility. Internationalism here is more imagination than information—and as such it relies heavily on the correspondence across disparate pages and places.

DU BOIS'S INDIA

Whereas Du Bois's internationalism has generally attracted admiration, his Indian engagements in *Dark Princess* have, for many commentators, proved both a lure and a frustration. If, as the record shows, Du Bois knew so much about Indian history and even corresponded with Indian contemporaries, why did he not yoke his novel more firmly to the actual and the historical? Where intentions cannot be ascertained, archival records can. The research trail for *Dark Princess* evidences a beguiling combination of attention to both the fantastical and the literal.

Initially titled "The Princess and the Porter," the novel gained its published title through conversation with the publisher, Harcourt, Brace, and Company, which suggested either "Dark Princess" or "Dark Alliance" as a title.[103] The title that Du Bois had intended suggests a fairy tale, an impression reinforced by the novel's opening and closing epigraphs. The titles proposed by the publishing house, by contrast, emphasized its racial politics. On October 11, 1927, Du Bois sent two matter-of-fact query letters regarding the American portions of the novel: the first, to an Illinois senator with a numbered list of questions about local hotels that his protagonist might visit, and the second, to a New York doctor with three questions, and the relevant passages, regarding the protagonist's medical career.[104] His Indian inquiries, however, were far more elaborate. Du Bois sent his manuscript to Lajpat Rai in an exchange that has received some critical attention.[105] Already prominent in the Indian nationalist movement, Lajpat Rai wrote to Du Bois on October 6, 1927, seeking material for his rejoinder (*Unhappy India*, 1928) to the American journalist Katherine Mayo's controversial *Mother India* (1926). He accordingly requested from Du Bois both written details and "some telling pictures of the cruelties inflicted on your people by the whites of America."[106] Du Bois replied a month later, enclosing the last six issues of *The Crisis*, "one picture of a lynching," and his own request as well. He invited Rai's "criticism" on a novel that "touches India incidentally in the person of an Indian Princess. I am sending enclosed the pages about her."[107]

Whereas Lajpat Rai's correspondence with Du Bois suggests an easy reciprocity, Du Bois also sought out assistance from another Indian, Dhan Gopal Mukerji, in a much more ambiguous fashion. Scholarship on the novel has often noted Lajpat Rai's input but not Dhan Gopal Mukerji's, with the unfortunate consequence of obscuring Du Bois's unreciprocated aspirations for collaborative authorship, if only for the novel's Indian portions.[108] I highlight this seemingly minor exchange because it demonstrates the creativity and unevenness that characterizes Du Bois's approach to the Global South. Whereas his exchange with Lala Lajpat Rai contains the symmetry of two national problems, the one with Dhan Gopal Mukerji has intentionally porous boundaries, perhaps because Mukerji, unlike Lajpat Rai, was not only Indian but Indian American.

On October 29, 1927, eleven days before he would share his manuscript with Lajpat Rai, Du Bois solicited editorial "service" from the Indian American writer Dhan Gopal Mukerji. Du Bois explained in his letter that he had written a novel that "touches slightly upon India":

> I want very much to have someone who knows India and its customs to read three or four pages of the manuscript and criticize any errors or inconsistencies in which I may have fallen. I have never had the pleasure of visiting India and my knowledge is solely from reading and my acquaintanceship with Indians.[109]

Du Bois here sought criticism of his "errors and inconsistencies" about an unseen country whose news he followed (and reported) in considerable detail. Mukerji quickly confirmed his desire to read the manuscript, and he sent his comments on November 4, explaining that he had "made slight changes in your narration" so as to "tell the facts that I know accurately."[110] Mukerji in that letter explicitly disclaimed any further ability to "criticize" or "alter" Du Bois's manuscript, yet within three days Du Bois sent him a numbered list of queries—a list striking enough to merit quoting at length:

> 1. With regard to the Maharanee, I am, of course, making her do the unconventional thing. She has been twice married yet not married at all. Her boy husband being killed before the marriage was consummated, and her second husband being eighty years of age and died very soon after. Moreover, by her English education she is thoroughly emancipated and has an object in life so great that everything is subordinated to that. Under the circumstances might she not had [*sic*] chosen this unconventional way to assure the royal succession in Bwodpur?
> 2. I have called my Indian country Bwodpur, modeling the name after Jodpur, and yet naming in reality Nepal. Is the name Bwodpur sufficiently Indian?

3. In the case of her wedding the American, what representatives of her religion would be present? I want to indicate in her marriage a union of Hinduism, Mohammedism, and Christianity. According to my story she is first married by an American Protestant minister and then comes the pageant of her Indian marriage, and I have indicated three "priests," two Hindus and a Mohammedan. Would it be wrong to call these men priests? Is my description of the ceremony and the pageant reasonable? And finally, is what she says when she raises the child up, a reasonably possible invocation?
4. Assuming the father of the child was named Matthew Townes and that the Maharanee Royal Family of Bwodpur had the name Chandragupta Singh, would he be christened Matthew Chandragupta Singh?

Du Bois concludes this list with thanks, enclosing "again the last two pages to refresh your memory."[111]

The questions that Du Bois poses are decidedly unusual, for they are far more speculative than his usual research queries. The first asks for plausibility within the acknowledged confines of "the unconventional thing"; the second asks whether a made-up word is a "sufficiently Indian" name for what is "in reality Nepal"; the third worries about the procedures for a nearly unimaginable multifaith wedding. The fourth question is the easiest one: Du Bois wonders how genealogical naming conventions might collude in this instance, to provide the patronymic as given name (resonant in light of slavery's disruption of African American genealogy) and the family name as the sign of royal lineage. The plausibility concern here lies in what Du Bois terms the "reasonable" and the "reasonably possible." These questions, with their imaginative demands, interpolate Mukerji as both foreign informant and fellow fiction writer, rendering him a cocreator of the novel's concluding scenes. Focusing on the intermarriage plot, Du Bois asks Mukerji to commingle his authorial energies with his own—as though inviting him to join in creating the book's mixed-race brownie.

As this research trail suggests, Du Bois's romance novel is built on a complex network of correspondence. The final text is a masterwork of startling relations, pairing a self-made African American with a mysterious Indian royal, in rapid jumps between styles and locales. By corresponding with Indians about his novel in this fashion, Du Bois germinated a print internationalism that was more collaborative than transactional. The exchange with Lajpat Rai is clearly reciprocal; that with Mukerji, by contrast, goes well beyond the norms of simple factual queries. Much like the crucial correspondence sections that Fauset developed in the print internationalism of the *Brownies' Book*, which rendered that volume a dynamic collaboration, so too the complex correspondence of this *Dark Princess* research trail reflects the interest in collaboration that is formative to Du Bois's print internationalism. This collaborative approach manifests not only in his private correspondence but also in his publication and annotation of messages from Indian leaders in *The Crisis*.

On February 19, 1929, Du Bois wrote to Gandhi, requesting an article for publication in *The Crisis*.[112] Replying to Du Bois, whom he addressed as "Friend," on May 1, 1929, Gandhi wrote: "It is useless for me even to attempt to send you an article for your magazine. I therefore send you herewith a little love message."[113] Having requested an article, and received a "little love message" instead, Du Bois proceeded to transform that message into a feature suitable for publication. In the July 1929 issue, Du Bois published Gandhi's note under the title "To the American Negro," reproducing a facsimile of Gandhi's typed message (fig. 5):

> Let not the 12 million Negroes be ashamed of the fact that they are the grand children of slaves. There is no dishonour in being slaves. There is dishonour in being slave-owners. But let us not think of honor and dishonor in connection with the past. Let us realize that the future is with those who would be truthful, pure and loving. For as the old wise men have said, truth ever is, untruth never was. Love alone binds and truth and love accrue only to the truly humble.
>
> Sabarmati,
> May 1, 1929
> M. K. Gandhi[114]

Gandhi's note here scrambles past, present, and future, invoking shame and dishonor only to disavow their relevance. Du Bois, in commenting on this note, configured a meaning for *The Crisis* that cannot be understood as a simple translation of Gandhi's words. His note, in much smaller, italicized print to the left of Gandhi's large-font words, functions as both biography and pedagogy. It begins with "Mohandas Karamchand Gandhi, the greatest colored man in the world, and perhaps the greatest man in the world." Du Bois then provides some details about Gandhi's education in England and his public life in South Africa. On arriving in South Africa, Du Bois writes, Gandhi "gave up the law and devoted himself

To the American Negro

A Message from Mahatma Gandhi

Mahandas Karamchand Gandhi, the greatest colored man in the world, and perhaps the greatest man in the world, was born October 2, 1869 in India. He finished High School and then studied for three years in England at London University, and at the Law School of the Inner Temple. Returning, he began to practice law in Bombay, but not being successful, he went to South Africa in 1893, and there his public life began. He gave up the law and devoted himself to the Indian people who were being persecuted along with the natives in that land. He served with the Red Cross during the Boer War, attending friend and foe alike. For twenty years he toiled in South Africa to remove race prejudice. He led his people; he went to jail; he agitated; and finally triumphed by gaining for the Indians of South Africa a large measure of freedom. At the outbreak of the Great War, he returned to India, and although a Pacifist, aided the great war. But when after the war there came repression, the massacre of Amritsar, and the infamous Rowlatt bills, Gandhi was disillusioned. He came out for Home Rule and announced his great Gospel of conquest through peace. Agitation, non-violence, refusal to cooperate with the oppressor, became his watchword and with it he is leading all India to freedom. Here and today, he stretches out his hand in fellowship to his colored friends of the West.

Let not the 12 million Negroes be ashamed of the fact that they are the grand children of the slaves. There is no dishonour in being slaves. There is dishonour in being slave-owners. But let us not think of honour or dishonour in connection with the past. Let us realise that the future is with those who would be truthful, pure and loving. For, as the old wise men have said, truth ever is, untruth never was. Love alone binds and truth and love accrue only to the truly humble.

Sabarmati,
1st May, 1929.

South African Native Conference for the Elliot Farm School (Page 240)

July, 1929 225

Fig. 5. “To the American Negro: A Message from Mahatma Gandhi,” *The Crisis*, July 1929, 225. At right is a facsimile of a note from Gandhi, with annotations by W. E. B. Du Bois to its left. At bottom is a posed photograph of several men, seated and standing, with the caption “South African Native Conference for the Elliot Farm School.”

to the Indian people who were being persecuted along with the natives in the land." During the Boer War, Gandhi served with the Red Cross, "attending friend and foe alike. . . . For twenty years he toiled in South Africa to remove race prejudice."[115] As Du Bois most certainly knew, this presentation of Gandhi's behavior in South Africa carefully elided his political relationships with Black and Coloured South Africans, relationships which were, as we saw in the previous chapter, broadly sympathetic but mostly inconsequential. The ambiguous placement of a nested subordinate clause—"devoted himself to the Indian people who were being persecuted along with the natives in the land"—permits the reader to imagine that the "along with" modifies not only the persecution but also the devotion of Gandhi's work. Similarly, Gandhi's work with an ambulance corps in support of the British military is presented here as treating "friend and foe alike," with neither friend nor foe specified.

Du Bois further encourages generous interpretation by juxtaposing the text with a photograph of the South African Natives' Conference. Gandhi never attended this conference, and we do not see him (or any other Indian-looking person, for that matter) in this image. The reader nonetheless senses, in this juxtaposition of text and image, that Gandhi must have made common cause with his African neighbors. On returning to India, Du Bois's text explains, Gandhi was disillusioned by "the massacre of Amritsar, and the infamous Rowlatt bills,"[116] at which point

> he came out for Home Rule and announced his great Gospel of conquest through peace. Agitation, non-violence, refusal to cooperate with the oppressor, became his watchword and with it he is leading all India to freedom. Here and today, he stretches out his hand in fellowship to his colored friends of the West.[117]

Du Bois here acts as both interlocutor and translator: he defines Gandhi for his readership in a specifically Christian idiom, as a colored man preaching a "great Gospel." Through these strategic additions to Gandhi's note, both visual and rhetorical, Du Bois renders Gandhi's particularly Indian politics relevant to his primarily African American readers.

Whereas additive juxtaposition was sufficient for Du Bois's publication of Gandhi in *The Crisis*, his engagement with Rabindranath Tagore required both transcription and facsimile reproduction. In 1929 Du Bois also solicited a note from Tagore, which he included in the October "Children's Number" of *The Crisis* (fig. 6). Tagore's note was inscribed,

A Message to the American Negro from Rabindranath Tagore

RABINDRANATH TAGORE was born in 1861 and educated privately. From the age of 24 to 40 he had charge of his father's estate and did much of his writing. At the age of 40, he founded a school at Santi-Niketan, Bengal, which developed into an international institution and has been his life's work. He has visited Europe several times and also Asia and North and South America. He received the Nobel Prize for Literature in 1913. He has published about thirty poetical works and numerous books, essays and dramas. He has also set to music over three thousand songs. In 1915, he was created a Knight by the Engilsh Government, but after the massacre of Amritsar, he refused the designation.

Some time ago through the good offices of Mr. C. F. Andrews, the Editor wrote to Mr. Tagore. His Secretary replies as follows:

Visva-Bharati
Santi-Niketan, Bengal

July 12th, 1929

Dear Sir:

Dr. Tagore has just returned from Canada to Santiniketan where he finds your letter awaiting him. He is extremely sorry that he could not send you a message earlier, but he hopes that the few lines which he offers to you now may still be some use to you and your friends.

The writing I may add is in the Poet's own hand.

With regards,

Yours truly,

(Signed) AMIYA C. CHAKRAVARTZ
(Private Secretary to
Dr. R. N. Tagore)

The Message, which is reproduced in Mr. Tagore's handwriting on this page, is as follows:

"What is the great fact of this age? It is that the Messenger has knocked at our gate and all the bars have given way. Our doors have burst open. The human races have come out of their enclosures. They have gathered together.

"We have been engaged in cultivating each his own individual life, and within the forced seclusion of our racial tradition. We had neither the wisdom nor the opportunity to harmonize our growth with world tendencies. But there are no longer walls to hide us. We have at length to prove our worth to the whole world, not merely to admiring groups of our own people. We must justify our own existence. We must show, each in our own civilization, that which is universal in the heart of the unique.

"RABINDRANATH TAGORE."

What is the great fact of this age? It is that the messenger has knocked at our gate and all the bars have given way. Our doors have burst open. The human races have come out of their enclosures. They have gathered together.

We have been engaged in cultivating each his own individual life, within the forced seclusion of our racial tradition. We had neither the wisdom nor the opportunity to harmonize

October, 1929 333

Fig. 6. "A Message to the American Negro from Rabindranath Tagore," *The Crisis*, October 1929, 333–34. At top left, Tagore looks directly at the camera; his handwritten note is reproduced at the bottom right of this page and the bottom left of the following page. Du Bois's typed commentary runs alongside and above Tagore's note.

Many of our readers will peruse these words with a certain puzzlement. Here is a man who is colored, who writes with practically nothing of what we are learning to call "race consciousness." His Message is universal. He has risen to something quite above the artificial limitations of race, color and nation. He recognizes the Messenger of Human Culture as bursting racial bonds. He sees racial and national development as hindrances rather than helps to universal culture. We are all of us black, red, white or yellow. Out under the blazing sun of world news and knowledge, our great duty is to prove our worth to the world and not merely to ourselves. White civilization and white people must justify their worth to the world. Black people and yellow people must do the same. There is no question of domination, of rule, of superiority and inferiority. The Universal which in the heart of the Individual must show itself in every civilization.

This is Tagore's message in a language which neither white or black Americans can easily understand. White America is provincial and material to the last degree. To its little narrow mind nothing in earth, sky or sea is as big and rich and efficient as America. But we who criticize white America, have also by our very criticism been forced into provincialism. We are narrow by our own grievances and hates. This is natural, and today perhaps and in this generation, almost inescapable.

Even Tagore himself when he came to America found his environment so narrow and discourteous that he cancelled his engagements and went home. He said in Tokio, June 16th, that he had cancelled his tour of American universities because he was oppressed by the air of suspicion and incivility toward Asiatics.

"I had promised many people in the United States to come there.

"I came to the United States. The immigration officials asked me to come into the office to present my documents. I entered the office and waited a half-hour. I could hear the official talking and laughing with a lady in the next room. He came to the door, saw me waiting and saw another gentleman. He talked to him for some time.

"Then he beckoned me into his office, without a word, a nod or any sort of civility. He pointed to a chair and began to question me. Did I know the restrictions of time within which I could remain in the country? How long did I expect to remain? Was I prepared to deposit the required amount as guarantee that I would leave? Did I know the penalties for staying longer?

"His insulting questions and attitude were deeply humiliating. I was not used to such treatment. I had been universally and most cordially welcomed in Europe. Never had I had such an experience. Perhaps it is due to new regulations. Certainly it was an attitude I had never encountered. I hesitated about entering the country at all, but I had my tickets, had taken leave of my friends and had no desire to cause a row.

"I came into the country, but my mind was not at ease. I went to Los Angeles, stayed there and lectured. But all the time I was impressed by the spirit in the air. The people seemed cultivating an attitude of suspicion and incivility toward Asiatics. I did not at all like it. I could not stay on sufferance, suffer indignities for being an Asiatic. It was not a personal grievance, but as a representative of all Asiatic peoples I could not remain under the shadow of such an insult. I took passage without delay.

"I have many friends in America, genuine idealists for whom I have the highest regard. I have read books by their great men which have attracted my heart. I hope they have a great future in carrying on the mission of civilization as it has been begun in the West. I have real respect for the people, but also respect for my own people, 'colored' people. If they must meet such treatment in that country it is best for any self-respecting Asiatic not to thrust himself upon its hospitality.

"I was silent when reporters came to me in Los Angeles. I wanted to go away quietly and not create a sensation. I am not used to airing my grievances, it is undignified. But I had an American companion, who felt the insult more keenly than I. He reviled the officer, using strong and picturesque American expressions which I had never heard before. Otherwise, it would never have come out.

"Let me emphasize once more that I bear no antipathy to the American people. I have been received with kindness in the Eastern States, overrun with kindness. People have listened to me with respect and received my message sincerely. That is why it has hurt so much this time. Why does such a country treat the peoples of Asia, colored peoples, all strangers who come within her gates with open minds, in such a manner that they get such an impression as I received?"

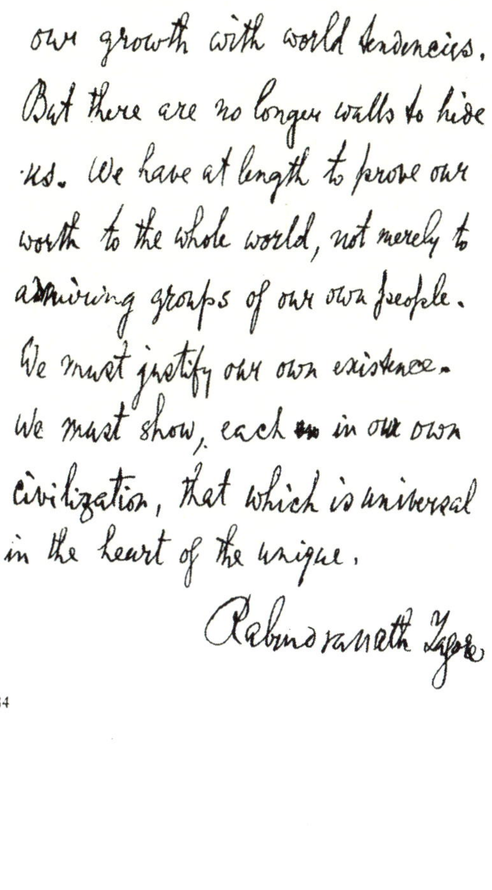

as Du Bois's text declares, "in the Poet's own hand," and the facsimile reproduction of that message reads:

> What is the greatest fact of this age? It is that the messenger has knocked at our gate and all the bars have given way. Our doors have burst open. The human races have come out of their enclosures. They have gathered together.
>
> We have been engaged in cultivating each his own individual life, within the fenced seclusion of our racial tradition. We had neither the wisdom nor the opportunity to harmonize our growth with world tendencies. But there are no longer walls to hide us. We have at length to prove our worth to the whole world, not merely to admiring groups of our own people. We must justify our own existence. We must show, each in our own civilization, that which is universal in the heart of the unique.
>
> Rabindranath Tagore[118]

Tagore's note evokes both spirituality and imprisonment, producing a universalist encouragement of the intermingling and "gathering together" of the various "human races," through "burst open" doors and bars that "have given way." His message is published in *The Crisis* in a facsimile version of his handwriting, across two pages and framed by Du Bois's commentary. Du Bois's gloss begins, as usual, with biographical material, then reproduces the text of a missive from Tagore's secretary, "Amiya C. Chakravartz [Chakravarty]," that accompanied the note itself. Du Bois further provides a typeset version of the note, printing it within the body of his lengthy commentary, even as Tagore's handwriting, containing only two illegible scribbles, looms large across both pages. Tagore's message, in its anti-imperial and antiracist universalism, says Du Bois, "is in a language which neither white nor black Americans can easily understand."[119] It is as though the reader of *The Crisis* might not be able to read, much less understand, Tagore's message unless Du Bois types it out for him.

In the typed transcription, Du Bois writes of "the forced seclusion of our racial tradition"; the handwritten note, in keeping with Tagore's imagery elsewhere, mentions "the *fenced* seclusion of our racial tradition" (my italics). In this moment of print internationalism, "fenced" becomes "forced," and it bridges two very different contexts in the process. In late colonial India, the fencing off of an essentialized tradition produces an exclusionary nationalism; in the United States of the same period, ideologies of racial hierarchy find their invidious institutionalization in state-sanctioned racial segregation. Whereas India's fenced seclusions enable the assertions of anticolonial nationalism, the forced seclusions of the U.S. elevate White citizens above their compatriots.

Even after typing out and delicately editing Tagore's language, Du Bois worries that his cherished message may still be incomprehensible to the readers of *The Crisis*:

> Many of our readers will peruse these words with a certain puzzlement. Here is a man who is colored, who writes practically nothing of what we are learning to call "race consciousness." His Message is universal. He has risen to something quite above the artificial limitations of race, color and nation. He recognizes the Messenger of Human Culture as bursting racial bonds. . . . The Universal which [is] in the heart of the Individual must show itself in every civilization.
>
> This is Tagore's message in a language which neither white nor black Americans can easily understand. White America is provincial and material to the last degree. To its little narrow mind nothing in earth, sky or sea is as big and rich and ancient as America. But we who criticize white America have also by our very criticism been forced into provincialism.[120]

Du Bois celebrates his foreign contributor as "quite above the artificial limitations of race, color and nation." Tagore's failure to express "what we are learning to call 'race consciousness'" is rearticulated by Du Bois as a position that comes after, and not before, the development of an antiracist sensibility. Tagore's message is "in a language which neither white nor black Americans can easily understand," but not because it is in Tagore's primary language of Bengali. Instead, the language problem resides inside the American mind: White America's "provincial and material" nature has "forced" even its Black critics "into provincialism." Du Bois ends the gloss—and the two-page feature more generally—by reprinting, in quotes, a lengthy account of how "even Tagore himself when he came to America found his environment so narrow and discourteous that he cancelled his engagements and went home."[121]

Du Bois had reported on Tagore's ill-fated U.S. visit for the African American weekly the *Pittsburgh Courier* only a few months earlier, in an article titled "Indian Philosopher Hits Race Prejudice: Hindu Poet and British Knight Declare America Has Contemptuous Attitude to All with Skins Not White."[122] In that article, Du Bois faithfully reported that Tagore said his "poor health prompted his departure": in keeping with his reticence on the topic to the U.S. press, Tagore described his immigration experience as "very trivial, though unpleasant" and added that he "do[es] not judge American people by that one incident." Yet in the commentary he provides for Tagore's note in *The Crisis*, Du Bois proves Tagore's antiracist anger by including seven paragraphs of quotation from Tagore's account to the Japanese journal the *Trans-Pacific*:

> The people [in the western United States] seemed to be cultivating an attitude of suspicion and incivility toward Asiatics. I did not at all like it. I could not stay on sufferance, suffer indignities for being an Asiatic. It was not a personal grievance, but as a representative of all Asiatic peoples I could not remain under the shadow of such an insult. I took passage without delay.[123]

This report, which Du Bois obtained by reading an English-language journal published from Tokyo, echoes Japanese protests of the 1924 Immigration Act, which extended the logic of 1882 Chinese Exclusion Act to exclude all Asian persons. It thus marked, in legislative terms, the extension of "suspicion and incivility" to all "Asiatics." As Tagore ruefully wrote, in a quotation reproduced by Du Bois:

> I have real respect for the [American] people, but also respect for my own people, 'colored' people. . . . Why does such a country treat the peoples of Asia, colored peoples, all strangers who come within her gates with open minds, in such a manner that they get such an impression as I received?[124]

This question is aimed at some universal thinker: it is unanswerable, by Americans as by America's "strangers." It is also the question, in Tagore's quoted voice, with which Du Bois ends his commentary in *The Crisis*.[125]

Much as Du Bois reshaped his Indian correspondents' notes for his U.S. publication into collaborative pages through his strategic annotation, so too Du Bois's own work would be reframed when it was published in an Indian periodical. We now turn to an essay that has been anthologized often and has been quoted frequently for its beautiful demonstration of Du Bois's prescient articulation of the Global South. However, the context of its publication has rarely been discussed, and this context, as I demonstrate, shows both the pitfalls and the potential of this now-familiar concept, whether in Du Bois's time or in our own.

In March 1936 Du Bois's writing was published in the *Aryan Path*, a Theosophical journal based in Bombay (now renamed Mumbai). Du Bois had been invited to contribute on any topic, and he had replied suggesting that he write on religious divergences and economic cooperation between Indians and American Negroes.[126] The editors in New York, however, suggested "some special features of Negro culture," and Du Bois agreed.[127] Some weeks later, however, the Bombay office requested an article on one of Du Bois's original suggestions, "the methods of increasing the interest and knowledge between Indians and American Negroes."[128]

This ongoing editorial exchange reflects the constitutive uncertainty among the editors about the relevance of Du Bois's expertise to Indian concerns. Even as the early twentieth-century syncretism of Theosophy developed its own narrative of racial intermingling and universal brotherhood, it was broadly uninterested in the kinds of racial struggle that preoccupied Du Bois, which inevitably required recognizing racist oppression and racial conflict.[129] Thus, when the *Aryan Path* published Du Bois's essay on "Indians and American Negroes," as it was titled in his manuscript version, they did so within a tripartite essay whose title announced a message of racial synthesis: "The World Is One." In an opening note, titled "East and West," the editors introduce Du Bois as the "world-famous leader of the Negroes of the U.S.A."[130] They caution readers that his "very thought provoking article . . . needs to be considered from the Indian standpoint," and they promise to publish a response "from a well-known Indian authority."[131] Du Bois's contribution, finally titled "The Clash of Colour," appeared between a meditative opening called "The Clash of Ideals," by the Frenchman Luc Durtain, and an optimistic conclusion titled "The Emergence of Harmony," by the Scotsman Miller Watson.[132] The first essay described the mystical Orient and the mechanical Occident, while the second positioned Brazil as a postracial utopia. Neither of those articles was provincialized, and neither was promised an Indian response.

Through this framing for publication, Du Bois's message of solidarity among the colored peoples of the world was subsumed to a narrative of a postracial future, even as the essay itself was not altered: the words printed under Du Bois's name are, with the exception of the title, consistent with his manuscript version. Whereas the adjacent essays enthusiastically addressed an assumed White reader, Du Bois's essay assumes an Indian reader and warns that

> India . . . has long wished to regard herself as "Aryan" rather than "colored" and to think of herself as much nearer physically and spiritually to Germany and England than to Africa, China, or the South Seas. And yet the history of the modern world shows the futility of this thought. European exploitation desires the black slave, the Chinese coolie, and the Indian laborer for the same ends and the same purposes, and calls them all "niggers." (All quotation marks in the original)[133]

Much as Gandhi, writing in 1896, was willing to group the African "native" and the Indian "coolie" within the same "black laboring class," Du Bois in 1936 too understands the laboring class as constituted by racial hierarchies.[134] He adds emotional significance through his pointed use of slurs: Black, Chinese, and Indian are all united undeer a single pejorative epithet, as "niggers," in a modern world structured by White exploitation. He acknowledges the Indo-Aryan thesis yet suggests that its claims are "futile." The murky truths of ancestry, he emphasizes, cannot compete with the modern realities of capitalism.

Du Bois explains that the "great difficulty" between Indians and American Negroes lies in their "almost utter lack of knowledge" about each other.[135] This educational problem is only exacerbated by the media, for

> to the editors of the great news agencies, Indians and Negroes are not news. They distribute, therefore, and emphasise only such things as are bizarre and uncommon: lynchings and mobs in the Southern States of the United States, dialect and funny stories; and from India, stories of religious frenzy, fights between Hindus and Mohammedans, the deeds of masters of magic and the wealth of Indian princes.[136]

Much as Gandhi had claimed in 1909 that only conflict was seen as notable in the annals of history, Du Bois in 1936 builds implicitly on this thesis, arguing that only peculiarity and violence will be reported when it comes to non-White people. Whereas contemporary desires for multicultural understanding frequently emphasize the importance of interpersonal exchange, Du Bois's internationalist project placed particular emphasis, instead, on literature and print, rather than on direct contact. As Du Bois explains, when Indians come to the United States

> they meet a peculiar variation of the Colour Line. An Indian may be dark in colour, but if he dons his turban and travels in the South, he does not have to be subjected to the separate-car laws and other discriminations against Negroes in that part of the country where the mass of Negroes live. This public recognition of the fact that he is not a Negro may, and often does, flatter his vanity so that he rather rejoices that in this country at least he is not as other dark men are, but is classified with the Whites.[137]

Just as the robes of the wealthy in Gandhi's 1896 pamphlet might have exempted them from the racial restrictions of South Africa, the turban of the traveling Indian can remove him from the oppressed side of the U.S. color line. Perhaps informed by Tagore's experience of racism on the west coast of the U.S., Du Bois notes that this applies only in the South. Moreover, he warns, if looking "for employment or for citizenship or any economic status," Indians would "find the tables quite turned."[138] Instead of personal experience, then, we need "literature directed toward the masses of these two peoples."[139] He suggests that Indians write for Negro papers, and vice versa, so that we recognize "the fact that these people have common aims."[140] Through this print internationalism, he advocates "the union of the darker races," which might create "a new and beautiful world, not simply for themselves, but for all men."[141]

Following Du Bois's faith in the powers of print internationalism, I have traced in this section Indians—Gandhi and Tagore—writing for a "Negro" paper, and an "American Negro"—Du Bois—writing for an Indian journal. Yet the Bombay-based *Aryan Path* finally has little space for the Negro, nor for any criticism of White supremacy, as is demonstrated in the response to Du Bois's article. Published under the headline "The Union of Colour," the Kannada leader Subba Rao in the next issue praises Du Bois's writing but fundamentally disagrees: Indians, he asserts, are not racist, nor do they have anything in common with those of African descent. Rather than the "Union of Color" that Du Bois advocated, Subba Rao argues that the Negro must become a proper American, giving "a cultural content" to his "political citizenship," while the

Indian must receive "political rights" that recognize his existing "cultural status."[142] As discussed earlier in this chapter, Du Bois entertained separate agendas of advancement for each group in his novel *Dark Princess*, but he could do so precisely because of the suturing powers of his heterosexual romance plot: the Black American and the Indian Princess, differentiated by both sex and nation, could quite literally produce the brownie that would liberate the Global South. In the pages of nonfiction prose, as here in the *Aryan Path*, the articulation of divergence seems irreconcilable with the broader interlinkages enshrined in "the union of color"—or, as we would call it, the Global South.

This debate on whether Indians and Negroes should make common cause continued into a third issue of the *Aryan Path*, in which the "Correspondence" page ran a section once again titled "The Union of Colour." It opened with a letter from Du Bois, who positioned Subba Rao's response as anterior to contemporary African America: "We Negroes in the United States," he explains, "have repeatedly passed through this phase of reasoning," which he terms as a "self-denying attitude" with "easily disastrous" consequences.[143] While Subba Rao cautions against efforts to "unite or seem to unite against white people," Du Bois warns that "there is no hesitancy on the part of the European peoples in thinking of their own destiny and of their work and future without reference to the rest of the world."[144] Meaningful advancement, he argues, is "impossible" so long as "the children of India, Africa and Negro America are going to be brought up under the incubus of colour caste."[145] This final term, which surfaces increasingly in his writings in the 1930s, indicates a decisive shift in his understandings of race and caste. Seeking through his print internationalism to work in the prose of fact rather than that of fiction and fantasy, Du Bois moves from the caste-phobic antiracism of *Dark Princess* to arrive at a "color caste" model that interweaves divergent oppressions in search of worldwide commonality.

In this chapter, by focusing on the brownie of Du Bois and Fauset, we have examined an antiracist movement that departed decisively from racial logics by embracing both inclusivity and impurity. Leaving the racial identity of his decisive neologism undefined, Du Bois articulated a print internationalism of the global color line by espousing a transregional vision that echoes what we now term the Global South. This territorial imaginary was capable of accommodating differences both between political units and within them, yet it could not, in its fictive nature, avoid generating representations that ultimately served only local needs. We witnessed this repeatedly in Du Bois's depiction of India, which functioned at once as a treasured comrade in the fight against racism and as a convenient phobic object enabling Du Bois's castigation of U.S. racism as a distressingly Indian form of caste-based hierarchy.

In New York in December 1921, after two years of active publication, the *Brownies' Book* published its last issue, which opened with Yolande DuBois's story of "The Land behind the Sun," whose protagonist "looked like a little Japanese girl, with a dimpled face, golden-brown in color, and soft jet-black hair" and "pretty almond-shaped eyes."[146] It continued with a story about Mexico by Langston Hughes,[147] an explanation by "The Judge" of the publication's poor finances, and then pieces on "Olive Plaatje" and "'Saint' Gandhi: The Greatest Man in the World." Interspersed with riddles, very short stories by children, and plenty of photos, the final issue includes just one long feature that is set in the United States.[148] Fauset's valedictory note explains that the *Brownies' Book* was a response to "the great need that exists for literature adapted to colored children, and indeed to all children who live in a world of varied races," noting as well that they "have had an unusually enthusiastic set of subscribers."[149] The *world* of varied races, moreover, had been given material form. The children reading the final issue leaped from Japan to Mexico, and from South Africa to India, all through the print internationalism of the *Brownies' Book*.

For example, the essay "Olive Plaatje," written by the composer Sarah Talbert Keelan, provides an obituary of "one interested little subscriber, from Kimberley, South Africa."[150] Olive Schreiner Plaatje, the sixteen-year-old daughter of South African leader Sol Plaatje, died in 1919 on a South African railway platform, denied any succor on account of her race. Keelan concludes by suggesting that African American children, even under virulent U.S. racism, might be luckier than children elsewhere: "It will thus be seen that while Brownies are a 'problem' everywhere, in their own homeland—Africa—their troubles start rather early in life."[151] As this sentence suggests, her essay thus builds print internationalism even as it discourages international travel: the brownie who reads the *Brownies' Book* is likely reading from the United States, but nonetheless knows that there are brownies in Africa as well.

Turning the page, readers arrive at an article by Blanche Watson titled "'Saint' Gandhi." Whereas the article about Olive Plaatje fixates on tiny details at the expense of her biographical significance, the piece titled "'Saint' Gandhi" is, as the name suggests, fully invested in the singularity of the non-White person under discussion. Despite this juxtaposition, this article omits any mention of Gandhi's time in South Africa. The historical-geographical connection between Olive and Gandhi is passed up for a proximity that suggests connection without stating it outright—a connection that would have been obvious to the magazine's staff and to many of its readers. The gap between Olive and Gandhi is arguably one of orientation—Olive has died, whereas Gandhi persists—but it is also one of simple knowledge. Diligent readers of *The Crisis* would be familiar with Gandhi's South African agitations in the 1910s, and hence might find Gandhi's Indian work right after a story of South African injustice to be logical, appropriate, and even chronologically motivated. For other readers, however, the journal would have appeared random, and its internationalism more eclectic than connective. The connection between the features, after all, is no longer recognizable to most twenty-first-century scholars, who approach Olive's obituary as though she were simply an example of Africa's many neglected children, instead of the particular child of a famous South African political leader—the report of her death is intended to shock us precisely because of her relative privilege.[152]

As this example demonstrates, the text with intentional gaps makes a very specific—and powerful—demand on the reader, one akin to that of a neologism like gitanjali or satyagraha. In both instances, the feature that cannot be deciphered within the dominant code compels the reader to acknowledge, via the limits of her existing expertise, the beguiling opacity of future possibilities. In considering these two practices as analogous, my study of print internationalism bridges a theoretical divide between studies of the African diaspora, on the one hand, and of South Asia and its diasporas, on the other. One influential interpretive tradition within Black studies has theorized that these gaps signal the ruptures of the Afro-diasporic experience, which are then studied through histories of transatlantic travel, political translation, or musical collaboration.[153] In the prevailing scholarship, these gaps thereby come to be viewed as slippages within a connected but discontinuous history of Blackness. Within South Asian studies, by contrast, such semiotic interruptions have usually been addressed through the concepts of mimicry and hybridity, or even through the inner/outer dichotomies of (anti)colonial nationalism, whether in the subcontinent itself or in cultures shaped by Indian indenture. In approaching these interruptions, instead, as convergent strategies, I bring together, through my own print internationalism, what studies predicated on diaspora have frequently kept apart.

This divergence originates, at least in part, within the historical and the rhetorical inheritances of slavery in the Atlantic world. Ideas of the hybrid in the African diaspora point inexorably to those of interracial offspring; studies of hybridity in South Asia and its diaspora, by contrast, have frequently focused on cultural rather than reproductive intermixture. In this manner, the "mimic man" of South Asia and South Asian diasporic postcoloniality possesses a "not-quite-not-white" property that points, in the Black Atlantic, to the "passing plot" and the "tragic mulatto/a" story instead—yet this resemblance is quite literally superficial (because epidermal).

The "one-drop rule" of U.S. racism, after all, makes hybridity legally impossible even as it is repeatedly coerced. The raced individual rendered culturally hybrid under U.S. racism may also be racially "hybrid" through histories of sexual coercion—yet ideologies of White purity in a White supremacist slave society required that racial intermixture be disavowed. In this process, the person of African and European ancestry is categorized only as Black, and that repressed history of divided parentage, at once biological and cultural, may come to reverberate in the split of "double consciousness." Whereas the project of White supremacism in the United States thus facilitated the production of racially mixed yet officially Black persons, White rule in the Indian subcontinent sought to rework those non-White persons who already existed. In Macauley's famous 1835 "Minute on Indian Education," the British sought to produce "a class of persons Indian in blood and colour, but English in tastes, in opinions, in morals and in intellect" who could best serve the interests of a White supremacist state.[154] In the United States, White supremacy produced persons who were increasingly less Black "in blood and colour" even as it falsely insisted that they were fundamentally Black "in opinions, in morals and in intellect," perpetuating an essentialist racism in the service of a racist labor regime. In the Indian subcontinent, by contrast, White supremacy demanded purity of "blood and colour," both in race and in caste, even as it demanded cultural convergence for its own administrative convenience. The British Raj was also a White supremacist regime, but it was one that extracted wealth primarily through indirect rule and extractive trade, not primarily through plantation agriculture. (This schematization, I must note, is not universal: in South Africa, for instance, White supremacism sought both biological and cultural purity in its subjugated populations.) The centrality of South Asia to the theorization of the South Asian diaspora, and of the United States to that of the African diaspora, however, have predisposed these divergent histories to beget divergent theorizations: mimicry for one experience of racist subordination, double consciousness for the other.

The divergence becomes ever more explicable if one attends to the *kinds* of gaps that have captured scholarly attention: between Africa and its diaspora, in one case, and between the South Asian colonized and their colonizers, on the other. Even when the South Asian diaspora has drawn sustained conceptual attention, creative efforts have generally focused on the transformative effects of indenture and migration, not on the relations between South Asia and its diasporas. As a consequence, we have coinages like "migritude" and "coolietude," which draw on the Negritude of 1930s Black writers like Aimé Césaire and Léopold Sédar Senghor to articulate the South Asian diaspora through a visceral notion of displacement.[155] Racialization as expressed through migration becomes, thus, the object of theorization, whereas in recent studies of Black internationalism, it is often the connections of diaspora, rather than the transformations of migrancy, that attract critical attention.

The print internationalism, staged through narrative in *Dark Princess* and through juxtaposition in the *Brownies' Book*, can help us to denaturalize this implicit critical consensus, for the print internationalism of the brownie is very different, I would argue, from our contemporary approaches to the Global South. The brownie reaches its visual apotheosis in the image used to conclude the final issue of the *Brownies' Book*. In a full-page picture, captioned "Good-Bye!" (fig. 7), a young child gazes downward, facing toward us with dark skin, straight dark hair, and small eyes. The image resembles a Japanese woodblock print, and indeed the child's clothing and his environment, complete with bamboo, suggests a Japanese setting, in a representation evocative of Japanese art forms. Through its referent to another land, it suggests that the farewell of the *Brownies' Book* comes from elsewhere: it does not emanate from the adults running the magazine, nor is it representative of the magazine's primarily African American subscribers. Instead, the child that ends the children's magazine, much like the child that concludes *Dark Princess*, is a figure of racial ambiguity who betokens a future at the end of White supremacy: the ever-undefined, and hence ever-promising, brownie.

Fig. 7. “Good-bye,” from the *Brownies’ Book,* December 1921, 340. The style of the illustration suggests Japanese woodblock printing.

Conclusion

The solidarities forged through print internationalism may today appear hopelessly naive, but their strategies—and their optimism—may be more relevant than ever. All three of the great men featured in this book have experienced a curiously predictable trajectory in prestige over the last one hundred years. Our analysis began at the turn of the twentieth century, when Tagore, Gandhi, and Du Bois enjoyed great esteem both locally and globally, a status that persisted, with some minor variations, until around the end of the Second World War. During the Cold War, however, all three, whether living or dead, were reframed within its polarizing binaries. Tagore, who died in 1941, would have the singular distinction of becoming the posthumous author of two different national anthems—India's in 1950 and, in 1971, that of the newly created Bangladesh—despite, as we saw, his trenchant opposition to nationalism itself. Gandhi became known as the father of the Indian nation, even though he was assassinated in 1948 for his alleged betrayal of it. And Du Bois would be increasingly isolated from African American politics and aggressively persecuted by the U.S. government, moving to Ghana in 1961, two years before his death.

In the post–Cold War moment—and now, in our age of the War on Terror—the forms of internationalism advanced by these three men have come into both popular and academic fashion. Gandhi, Tagore, and Du Bois have all benefited from this revival—each in his own way has been reinvented by scholarly and popular commentary in the last quarter century as a sage figure warning us of the excesses of nationalism. The women featured in this monograph have fared rather worse. Of the three, only Jessie Redmon Fauset has gained from the changing priorities of our contemporary moment: she is increasingly recognized for her contributions to African American literature and culture, while Sister Nivedita and Sonja Schlesin feature peripherally, if at all, in either popular or scholarly awareness. Whereas the other historical figures in this volume can be, and are, celebrated as inspirations for young persons of Indian and African American heritage, I wonder when we will be able to celebrate Nivedita and Schlesin in similar terms: not in spite of their Whiteness, but because of what we can learn from it.

The discussions of this monograph's chapters end in the convulsions of the Second World War, and I will conclude with an essay, "The Seeds of the Fascist International" (1945), that speculated on the forms of internationalism in relation to that brutal conflict. Writing in the wake of the attempted Nazi genocide of the Jewish people, the German Jewish philosopher Hannah Arendt (1906–75) warned that "modern anti-Semitism was never a mere matter of extremist nationalism" but, as her essay's title declared, "a fascist international." Its operating "textbook," Arendt wrote, was the notorious *Protocols of the Elders of Zion*, a spurious document from nineteenth-century Russia that claimed to be the record of a widespread Jewish conspiracy.[1] Instead of solely celebrating the defeat of Nazi Germany, Arendt finds in its demise the proof of fascism's likely international resilience. The end of the Second World War may have led to widespread interrogation of the dangers of nationalism, but Arendt found in Hitler's Germany a warning of the danger of internationalism, for "only when fascism is understood as an anti-national international movement does it become intelligible why the Nazis . . . allowed their land to be transformed into a shambles."[2] Despite the many decades since Arendt's warning, we remain within the remit of her concern. Arendt feared that the fascist international's malicious conspiracy-mongering would remain palatable to those "who vaguely sense our worldwide interdependence but are unable to penetrate into the actual working of this universal relationship."[3] This condition, for better or worse, characterizes so many of us in the twenty-first century, which, as Arendt bemoaned of her own century, is also "a time when full political information, necessarily worldwide in scope, is available only to the professional."[4] Perhaps the most surprising continuity with our contemporary political climate lies in the widespread enthusiasm for internationalism, which forms a curious point of convergence between the contemporary Left and the contemporary Right: the former deplores globalization; the latter detests globalists; yet both insist on terming their worldwide organizations "international."

In the preceding chapters, I have sought new possibilities for the study of internationalism by describing its operations through the coining of new words. In doing so, I have coined a new term of my own: "print internationalism." Print internationalism, in my theorization, names a strategy within the worldwide hegemony of the English language (signaled in the moniker of "the global Anglophone") to create alternate geographies (such as "the Global South") and to summon new collectivities (such as "people of color") through the creation of new words. Reading Arendt's essay, we can recognize the operations of print internationalism, complete with its own fictionalized history (*Protocols of the Elders of Zion*) and catalyzing neologism (Nazi). I have focused my study on the print internationalisms of highly celebrated historical figures—but it would not be difficult, I suspect, to extend the analysis to include many of those whom history has condemned.

In choosing to call this phenomenon "print internationalism," I have intentionally echoed Benedict Anderson's "print nationalism," and I have reinforced that association by developing specific parallels. I have argued that print internationalism creates an interpretive community, rather than the imagined community of Anderson's model, and I have emphasized the centrality of the periodical and the fictionalized history as the genres of print internationalism, in contrast to Anderson's emphasis on the newspaper and the novel. By offering a vision of community formation through print media that diverges distinctly from Anderson's model, I have proposed a new avenue for literary and cultural studies that attends the differences between the national and the international. This new model can help us understand, for instance, Arendt's description of Nazism as "an anti-national international movement" that nonetheless appears to be extreme nationalism. The radical nationalist parties of many European nations, for instance, have found a curious internationalist solidarity in their mutual contempt: they will loudly decry each other's nations and, at the same time, support each other's national chauvinisms.

In developing these new possibilities for literary studies, I have proposed a dialectical reading practice that reads from two places at once—and, specifically, from the sites that a given text may render only as metaphor. Thus, we read Tagore's China through the interweaving of text and preface; Gandhi's South Africa through a literalization of parables; and Du Bois's India through the interplay of content and annotation. In developing this oscillating reading practice, I demonstrate a dialectical method for postcolonial reading that can hold multiple possibilities in suspension, reading at once through and from the figural portions of a text. Rather than resolving these contradictions, as in the political unconscious of Fredric Jameson's reading method, the reading method that I propose generates a divided consciousness: one that resides, as I have shown, in the relations among differently subjugated peoples.

This method is quite different from the reading modes foundational to postcolonial studies. In reading print internationalism, after all, we are not reading for the traces of British imperialism buried in nineteenth-century British fiction, or for the evidence of ordinary Indians' contributions to India's decolonization, or for the restoration of Africans' essential humanity.[5] I am fortunate to build on these works, and to assume readers who are, at the least, sympathetic to postcolonial critical practices. In reading print internationalism, we read, rather, for the relations among and across different colonial and semicolonial regions: to take the primary examples of this book, between India, China, South Africa, and African America. In writing *Imperfect Solidarities*, I have operated from the suspicion that the field has been ill-served by extending the methods developed for the study of relations between the colonizer and the colonized to that of relations among the colonized. Consequently, instead of the normative tone that such reading methods can enable, I offer a perhaps less definitive—one might say, imperfect—appraisal.

In deliberately constructing anachronistic applications for contemporary terms like "the global Anglophone," "people of color," and "the Global South," I aim to show that these unifying concepts have longer histories. The newness of the neologism is important precisely because that newness is manufactured: the coinage centralizes a latent meaning and puts it into newly effective circulation. A nonce word is truly new: it has no prior unarticulated meaning in cultural discourse and, partly as a consequence, it disappears after its immediate context of usage, never to be heard again. A neologism, by contrast, is a new coinage with a future—precisely because it also has a past, which enables it to outlast the immediate circumstances that led to its articulation. Much as the global Anglophone, in my theorization, exists before its explicit naming, so too did the concept of "people of color" exist before it is so named: it is the motivation behind Gandhi's initial South African concerns, as we saw in chapter 2, and it is the dream enshrined in Du Bois's brownie, as we saw in chapter 3. This preexistence, however, is not unlimited. Although the countries central to Gandhi's activism are both part of the Global South, that concept is not present in Gandhi's own work. The term "Global South" emphasizes the unequal worldwide distribution of material prosperity and industrialization, concerns that are fundamentally dissonant from Gandhi's own antimodernizing impulses. Instead, I argue, the Global South surfaces clearly in the work of Du Bois. As I demonstrated in chapter 3, Du Bois's reliance on a magical figure for childhood, the brownie, enables a suturing of divergent regions of the world in a manner that does not resolve their differences but instead reproduces them (quite literally). The brownie compresses differences across a worldwide gambit that we can recognize as "the Global South," while its magical quality means that it is not primarily indicative of actual "people of color."

Today's internationalisms are more likely to publish their insights on digital media platforms than in the print formats—the periodical, the pamphlet, and the codex—that were central to the internationalisms presented here. Yet their fundamental operating principles may well have much in common: then, as now, aspiring internationalists seek to create interpretive communities by generating new words. The internet abounds with neologisms coined within the global Anglophone, which likewise serve to create new geographies and summon new collectivities. It is my hope that the methods forged here for the study of print internationalism will help us to apprehend the neologisms of our own time, as we read among and across these interpretive communities to generate imperfect solidarities of our own.

Notes

INTRODUCTION

1. See, for instance, Wachal, "The Capitalization of *Black* and *Native American*"; Tharps, "The Case for Black with a Capital B." The Chicago, Associated Press, and Modern Language Association style guides all suggest that "black" and "white" should not be capitalized when referring to races, though the American Psychological Association disagrees. Du Bois, as I discuss briefly in chapter 3, once led a campaign for the capitalization of "Negro" in the 1920s: I imagine that he might support my formatting decision.

2. Borg, "Discourse Community," 398.

3. Stock, *The Implications of Literacy*; Fish, *Is There a Text in This Class?*

4. Borg, "Discourse Community," 398.

5. In Fish's famous anecdote, the question—"Is there a text in this class?"—while seemingly simple in its word-for-word comprehensibility, signifies differently depending on whether one utilizes the interpretive protocols of university instruction or those supplied in the pedagogy of deconstruction. This is an iconic example but a weak one for my purposes, not only because the institution in Fish's anecdote is literal—the university, the humanities disciplines—but also because the positionality is predictable—a female student asking a male professor.

6. Bernstein, *Racial Innocence*.

7. For a salutary demonstration of this approach to print culture, see Garvey, *Writing with Scissors*.

8. Ricoeur, *Freud and Philosophy*, 530–31.

9. Ricoeur, *Freud and Philosophy*, 28.

10. Ricoeur, *Freud and Philosophy*, 28.

11. Eve Kosofsky Sedgwick, "Paranoid Reading and Reparative Reading, or, You're So Paranoid, You Probably Think This Essay Is about You," in *Touching Feeling: Affect, Pedagogy, Performativity*.

12. Best and Marcus, "Surface Reading"; Freedgood and Schmitt, "Denotatively, Technically, Literally."

13. Anker and Felski, *Critique and Postcritique*.

14. Cheng, *Second Skin*.

15. Jameson, *The Political Unconscious*, 61.

16. For a longer discussion see Marling, "The Formal Ideologeme."

17. See, generally, Jameson, *The Political Unconscious*, 73.

18. I invoke here Louis Althusser's model of symptomatic reading, which has been particularly important for recent critics seeking to distance the practice from its synonymity with Jameson's version. See Bewes, "Reading with the Grain."

19. See Lahiri, "The Pose of the Author."

20. Dimock, "World Literature on *Facebook*"; Levine, "From Nation to Network"; Cooppan, "Net Work"; Cooppan, "World Literature between History and Theory."

21. Berman, *All That Is Solid Melts into Air*, 104.

22. Apter, *Against World Literature*, 235.

23. Turner, *Philology*; Ahmed, *Archaeology of Babel*; Chang, Elman, and Pollock, *World Philology*; Harpham, "Roots, Races, and the Return to Philology."

24. The *Oxford English Dictionary* dates the first use of "neurotypical" to 1994 and of "cisgender" to 1997. "neurotypical, adj. and n.," and "cisgender, adj. and n.," OED Online, March 2020, https://www-oed-com.proxy.lib.umich.edu/view/Entry/271429?redirectedFrom=neurotypical, https://www-oed-com.proxy.lib.umich.edu/view/Entry/35015487?redirectedFrom=cisgender.

CHAPTER 1

1. *Gitanjali: Song Offerings* was published in 1912 but initially distributed privately by subscription. The general public could first access Tagore's poems by purchasing the December 1912 issue of *Poetry* magazine or by waiting until 1913, when the *Gitanjali* collection became commercially available.

2. Pound, "Rabindranath Tagore."

3. G. Desai, "Postcolonial, by Any Other Name?"

4. Goyal, "Postcolonial, Still."

5. Panel at the Modern Language Association's annual conference in 2020; https://mla.confex.com/mla/2020/forum/extra/index.cgi?EntryType=Session&username=7342&password=134185.

6. Ganguly, *This Thing Called the World*; Walkowitz, "World Anglophone Is a Theory."

7. G. Desai, "Postcolonial, by Any Other Name?"

8. Lake and Reynolds, *Drawing the Global Colour Line*, 145.

9. Tagore, *Nationalism*.

10. Tagore and Chatterjee, "Rabindranath Tagore's Letter to the Viceroy," 105.

11. Tagore and Chatterjee, "Rabindranath Tagore's Letter to the Viceroy," 105.

12. Tagore and Chatterjee, "Rabindranath Tagore's Letter to the Viceroy," 105.

13. Tagore and Chatterjee, "Rabindranath Tagore's Letter to the Viceroy," 106.

14. Barbery et al., "Pour une 'littérature-monde' en français."

15. Tagore, *Nationalism*; Tagore, *The Home and the World.*

16. Rabindranath Tagore, preface to Lim, *The Li Sao*, xxiii.

17. William Radice has examined in archival and textual detail the correspondence between the English text of Gitanjali and its Bengali sources. He describes a pattern of radical transformations: within the poems, in paragraph structure, phrasing, and rhyme scheme, and across the collection, in the selection and ordering of poems. See his extended introduction in Tagore, *Gitanjali*, xvi.

18. The categories *tatsama*, *tadbhava*, and *desi* are used in the linguistics of South Asian languages to describe: words identical to their origins in Sanskrit; words traceable to Sanskrit that have been modified in the adaptation; and words that cannot be clearly traced to Sanskrit, respectively. By that measure, "Sanskritic" would probably cover both *tatsama* and *tadbhava* words, but the pattern I see veers quite strongly toward *tatsama.*

19. This account concurs with that of Inaga, "Sister Nivedita and her 'Kali the Mother, the Web of Indian Life.'" John Rosenfield claims that the lectures were "translated into English with the aid of Margaret Elizabeth Noble" and that MacLeod attended his lectures at the Japan Art Institute. Rosenfield, "Okakura Kakuzō and Margaret Noble (Sister Nivedita)," 58, 62.

20. See, for instance, Bharucha, *Another Asia.*

21. Sister Nivedita, introduction to Okakura, *The Ideals of the East*, xv.

22. Sister Nivedita, introduction to Okakura, *The Ideals of the East*, xv.

23. Okakura, *The Ideals of the East*, 1.

24. Okakura, *The Ideals of the East*, 19.

25. Okakura, *The Ideals of the East*, 3.

26. Okakura, *The Ideals of the East*, 3.

27. Okakura, *Collected English Writings*, 2:132; quoted in Inaga, "Okakura Kakuzō and India," 45.

28. Okakura, *The Ideals of the East*, 230.

29. The 1919 satyagraha was organized against the Rowlatt Act: legislation enacted in 1919 that extended the draconian emergency powers initially instated during the the First World War into perpetuity, rather than granting, as Indian leaders had hoped, greater political autonomy. The Khilafat movement was a worldwide agitation against the dismemberment of the Ottoman Empire and for the reinstatement of the Caliphate (Khilafat).

30. The entirety of Tagore and Gandhi's correspondence, from Gandhi's return to India in 1915 to Tagore's death in 1941, is available in Bhattacharya, *The Mahatma and the Poet.*

31. Tagore, "Letters from Rabindranath Tagore," 613.

32. Tagore, "Letters from Rabindranath Tagore," 613.

33. Tagore, "Letters from Rabindranath Tagore," 613.
34. Tagore, "The Call of Truth," 427.
35. Tagore, "Letters from Rabindranath Tagore."
36. The date and location of each letter are preserved in the 1928 collection edited by those letters' recipient, Charles Freer Andrews: see Tagore, *Letters to a Friend*, 127–37. The *Modern Review* version included the dates but not the locations, while neither are foregrounded in the versions in Bhattacharya, *The Mahatma and the Poet*, 54–62.
37. Tagore, "Letters from Rabindranath Tagore," 613.
38. Tagore, "Letters from Rabindranath Tagore," 615.
39. Tagore, "The Call of Truth," 428.
40. Tagore, "Letters from Rabindranath Tagore," 613–14.
41. Tagore, "The Call of Truth," 428.
42. Tagore, "Striving for Swaraj," 683.
43. Tagore, "The Call of Truth," 430.
44. Tagore, "Striving for Swaraj," 685.
45. Tagore, "The Call of Truth"; Tagore, "The Cult of the Charkha," 103.
46. Tagore, "The Call of Truth," 433.
47. Olivelle, *The Early Upanisads.*
48. Tagore, "Striving for Swaraj," 684.
49. Tagore, "Striving for Swaraj," 684–85.
50. Olivelle, *The Early Upanisads*, 453.
51. Gvili, "Pan-Asian Poetics," 185.
52. Lukács, "Tagore's Gandhi Novel."
53. A handwritten note (likely Leonard Elmhirst's) on a Tagore lecture manuscript from 1924 in the Visva Bharati archives tells us, "They had taken for granted he was a reactionary, saying 'go back,' have nothing to do with science. They clothed RT in the mantle of Gandhi whose works they'd read."
54. Zhou, "The Inseparable Dichotomy of Nationalism."
55. See, for instance, Anjaria, *Realism in the Twentieth-Century Indian Novel*; Hogan, *Empire and Poetic Voice*; Ray, *En-gendering India*; Walkowitz, *Cosmopolitan Style*; Nussbaum, "Patriotism and Cosmopolitanism"; Weidman, "Echo and Anthem."
56. In addition to the 1903 *Shishu*, the remaining poems were taken from *Kaḍi o Komal* (1886), *Sonār Tarī* (1894), *Kṣaṇikā* (1900), and *Gītimālya* (1914). Within the corpus of Tagore's Anglophone texts, three poems overlap between the *Gitanjali* and *Crescent Moon* collections: no. 60 becomes "On the Sea Shore," no. 61 becomes "The Source," and no. 9 becomes "When and Why." See Das, *The English Writings of Rabindranath Tagore*, 1, 603–5.
57. Signaling Tagore's fame, *The Crescent Moon* collection also advertises *Gitanjali*, described as "A Collection of Prose Translations Made by the Author from the Original Bengali," complete with effusive reviews; *The Gardener*, again "Translated by the Author from the Original Bengali," though with the caveat that "the translations are not always literal—the originals being sometimes abridged and sometimes paraphrased"; *Sādhanā: The Realisation of Life*, containing lectures were "delivered to large audiences" at Harvard and Oxford; and the autobiography of Maharishi Devendranath Tagore, Rabindranath's father.

58. Tagore, "The Hero," in *The Crescent Moon*, 62–65.

59. Quoted in Das, *The English Writings of Rabindranath Tagore*, I, 604.

60. Li Zhi, "Explanation of the Childlike Heart-Mind (Tongxin Shuo)," 110.

61. Wen, "Form in Poetry."

62. Gvili, "Pan-Asian Poetics," 191.

63. For extensive discussion of this trip and its implications, see Tan et al., *Tagore and China*.

64. Tagore, *Talks in China*.

65. P. C. M., publisher's note in Tagore, *Talks in China*, iii.

66. P. C. M., publisher's note in Tagore, *Talks in China*, i.

67. Liang Qichao, introduction to Tagore, *Talks in China*, 1.

68. Liang Qichao, introduction to Tagore, *Talks in China*, 2.

69. Liang Qichao, introduction to Tagore, *Talks in China*, 2.

70. Liang Qichao, introduction to Tagore, *Talks in China*, 2–3.

71. Liang Qichao, introduction to Tagore, *Talks in China*, 2–3.

72. Liang Qichao, introduction to Tagore, *Talks in China*, 3–4.

73. Liang Qichao, introduction to Tagore, *Talks in China*, 5–6.

74. Liang Qichao, introduction to Tagore, *Talks in China*, 17–18.

75. Liang Qichao, introduction to Tagore, *Talks in China*, 19–20.

76. Tagore, *Talks in China*, 23.

77. Tagore, *Talks in China*, 23-4.

78. Das, "The Controversial Guest."

79. Tagore, *Talks in China*, 59.

80. Tagore, *Talks in China*, 61.

81. Tagore, *Talks in China*, 42.

82. Tagore, *Talks in China*, 61.

83. Tagore, *Talks in China*, 40.

84. Tagore, *Talks in China*, 122, 124.

85. For a longer discussion see Lahiri, "Print for the People."

86. Owen, *An Anthology of Chinese Literature*, 156.

87. Hokkien refers to the people and the culture of China's southeastern Fujian province.

88. Chan, "The Case for Diaspora," 112.

89. Frost, "'Beyond the Limits of Nation and Geography'"; Hay, *Asian Ideals of East and West*.

90. Clifford, introduction to Lim, *The Li Sao*, xvi.

91. Clifford, introduction to Lim, *The Li Sao*, xvii.

92. Giles, preface to Lim, *The Li Sao*, xxii.

93. Lim Boon Keng, translator's preface to Lim, *The Li Sao*, xxx.

94. Lim Boon Keng, Translator's preface to Lim, *The Li Sao*, xxx.

95. Lim, *The Li Sao*, 52.

96. Lim, *The Li Sao*, 52.

97. Lim, *The Li Sao*, 52.

98. Lim, *The Li Sao*, 52.

99. Lim Boon Keng, translator's preface to Lim, *The Li Sao*, xxix.

100. Chan, "The Case for Diaspora," 117.

101. Owen, *An Anthology of Chinese Literature*, 156–57.

102. Tagore, preface to Lim, *The Li Sao*, xxiii.
103. Tagore, preface to Lim, *The Li Sao*, xxiii.
104. M. K. Gandhi, "The Poet and the Charkha," 376.
105. M. K. Gandhi, "The Poet and the Charkha," 376.
106. M. K. Gandhi, "The Poet and the Charkha," 376.
107. M. K. Gandhi, "The Great Sentinel," 326.
108. Tagore, *One Hundred Poems of Kabir*.
109. Arnold, *The Song Celestial*; Miller, *The Bhagavad Gita*.
110. M. K. Gandhi, "The Great Sentinel," 326.
111. Miller, *The Bhagavad Gita*, 45.
112. M. K. Gandhi, "The Great Sentinel," 326.
113. M. K. Gandhi, "The Charkha and the Gita," 329.
114. Arnold, *The Song Celestial*, 28; M. K. Gandhi, "The Charkha and the Gita," 329.
115. M. K. Gandhi, "The Charkha and the Gita," 329.
116. Brown, "Spinning without Touching the Wheel," 243–44.

CHAPTER 2

1. M. K. Gandhi, *Satyagraha in South Africa*, 93.
2. M. K. Gandhi, *Satyagraha in South Africa*, 95.
3. M. K. Gandhi, *Satyagraha in South Africa*, 93 (emphasis in the original).
4. M. K. Gandhi, *Satyagraha in South Africa*, 93.
5. M. K. Gandhi, *Satyagraha in South Africa*, 93.
6. Lake and Reynolds, *Drawing the Global Colour Line*, 9.
7. Safire, "People of Color" (emphasis in the original).
8. Biko, "The Definition of Black Consciousness."
9. M. K. Gandhi, *Satyagraha in South Africa*, 93.
10. M. K. Gandhi, *The Story of My Experiments with Truth*, 1:154.
11. M. K. Gandhi, *The Story of My Experiments with Truth*, 1:537–38.
12. M. K. Gandhi, *The Story of My Experiments with Truth*, 1:578.
13. M. K. Gandhi, *The Story of My Experiments with Truth*, 1:27.
14. "Boer," meaning "farmer" in Afrikaans (and Dutch), was used throughout much of the nineteenth and twentieth centuries to refer to Afrikaans-speaking settlers of mostly Dutch descent. The word is something of a slur in our time, though it would not have been in Gandhi's. Where possible here I use the more current term "Afrikaner," resorting to "Boer" only when necessary to prevent anachronism.
15. M. K. Gandhi, *Satyagraha in South Africa*, 16.
16. L. Gandhi, *The Common Cause*; Skaria, *Unconditional Equality*.
17. Written in Gujarati from Yeravada Central Jail from November 26, 1923, to February 5, 1924; and published serially in *Navajivan* from April 13, 1924, to November 22, 1925, *Satyagraha in South Africa* was also published in book form in two parts in 1924 and 1925. The English translation appeared in 1928 from S. Ganesan, Madras, and that is the volume to which I will chiefly refer. The text reprinted in volume 34 of the *Collected Works* of Mahatma Gandhi,

by contrast, is chiefly that of the third impression, issued by Navajivan Press in August 1961.

18. L. Gandhi, *Affective Communities*, 34–66, 86.

19. M. K. Gandhi, *The Grievances of the British Indians in South Africa* (*The Green Pamphlet*) (1896), Wilson Anti-slavery Collection, John Rylands University Library, University of Manchester (Manchester, U.K.), 31.

20. M. K. Gandhi, *The Grievances of the British Indians in South Africa*, Wilson Anti-slavery Collection, 30.

21. M. K. Gandhi, *The Grievances of the British Indians in South Africa*, Wilson Anti-slavery Collection, 2.

22. M. K. Gandhi, *The Story of My Experiments with Truth*, 1:253.

23. M. K. Gandhi, *The Story of My Experiments with Truth*, 1:80.

24. M. K. Gandhi, *The Story of My Experiments with Truth*, 1:253.

25. For a discussion of its sensibility, see Hofmeyr, *Gandhi's Printing Press*, 5; for a discussion of its constituency, see Mesthrie, "From Advocacy to Mobilization," 113.

26. *Indian Opinion*, June 4, 1903, 1.

27. Mesthrie suggests that the *African Chronicle*, which was written and published in English and Tamil, would have been the primary periodical for this community: the difference in its name, and its politics, is a notable contrast to Gandhi's explicitly diasporic formulation.

28. Bannerjee, *Becoming Imperial Citizens*, 27.

29. Scholarship on Indian-African exchanges and encounters has flourished in the last few decades. For a detailed discussion of this dynamic in the South African context, see Soske, *Internal Frontiers*. For a general overview of India as a subimperial center in the British Empire, see Metcalf, *Imperial Connections*. For these issues in East Africa, particularly as they impact print cultures, see G. Desai, *Commerce with the Universe*. For divergent interpretations of the political implications of Afro-Indian historical connections, see Burton, *Brown over Black*; Prashad, *The Darker Nations*.

30. Heather Hughes notes that "the first few editions" of John Dube's *Ilanga lase Natal*, a journal written in English and isiZulu, were published at the International Printing Press; this occurred, however, while the press was still in Durban and run by Madanjit Vijavaharik. Hughes, *First President*, 103.

31. M. K. Gandhi, *The Story of My Experiments with Truth*, 2:77.

32. For an example of the radicals-in-Britain argument, see Anthony Parel's 1997 introduction to the Cambridge edition of *Hind Swaraj* (2009). For the Indians-in–South Africa argument, see Hofmeyr, "Violent Texts, Vulnerable Readers."

33. M. K. Gandhi, *Hind Swaraj*, 10.

34. While the text itself thus presents a mostly European intellectual genealogy, Tridip Suhrud reads the foreword's claim of nonoriginality within a longer tradition of Indian authorship, wherein truth resides in the universal, rather than manifesting through individual innovation. He proves this claim by connecting this prefatory remark with Gandhi's statement in a private letter that he has "written an original book in Gujarati," which he suggests is "perhaps the

only instance of Gandhi making a claim . . . of authorship based on originality" (letter to Hermann Kallenbach, November 25, 1909, in Suhrud, "*Hind Swaraj: Translating Sovereignty*," 155). See also Suhrud and Sharma, *M. K. Gandhi's "Hind Swaraj,"* xiii.

35. M. K. Gandhi, *The Story of My Experiments with Truth*, 2:77.

36. M. K. Gandhi, *Hind Swaraj*, 89–90.

37. Leela Gandhi offers a somewhat different reading of this anecdote:

> The point is not only that history, à la Gandhi, is inattentive to small details but that it censors the creative leap of faith required to apprehend the extraordinary in the ordinary . . . . We can only grasp the mundane making up of quarrelsome siblings (or their putative "soul force") by simultaneously making up, or fictionalizing, its significance in a recklessly counterfactual or subjunctive appraisal. (L. Gandhi, *Affective Communities*, 156)

38. Suhrud, "*Hind Swaraj: Translating Sovereignty*."

39. The system of Indian indenture was put into place by the British after the abolition of slavery in 1833. It created a cheap and malleable migrant workforce for the colonies via the transportation of millions under coercive conditions: approximately 1.2 million Indians were shipped to nineteen colonies over the course of a hundred years. From 1860 to 1911 an estimated 152,184 Indians were brought to South Africa, primarily to work on the sugar plantations; most Indian South Africans today are descendants of those indentured arrivants. The terms of indenture were technically contractual, based on a five-year bond; in practice, the system was rife with abuses, and is generally now considered as a semislavery system. Despite its difference from slavery in the rhetoric of British imperialism, it was profoundly similar in its carceral labor regimes. For a comprehensive history of Indian indenture in South Africa, see Desai and Vahed, *Inside Indian Indenture*.

40. M. K. Gandhi, *Hind Swaraj*, 90.

41. M. K. Gandhi, *The Story of My Experiments with Truth*, 1:188.

42. M. K. Gandhi, *Collected Works of Mahatma Gandhi*, 29:6.

43. M. K. Gandhi, *Collected Works of Mahatma Gandhi*, 29:6.

44. M. K. Gandhi, *The Story of My Experiments with Truth*, 1:61.

45. M. K. Gandhi, *The Story of My Experiments with Truth*, 1:61.

46. M. K. Gandhi, *The Story of My Experiments with Truth*, 1:196.

47. M. K. Gandhi, *Collected Works of Mahatma Gandhi*, 29:6.

48. Ranajit Guha, *History at the Limit of World-History*, 51.

49. Ranajit Guha, *History at the Limit of World-History*, 53.

50. M. K. Gandhi, *Collected Works of Mahatma Gandhi*, 29:6.

51. M. K. Gandhi, *Collected Works of Mahatma Gandhi*, 29:6.

52. De Kock, *Civilising Barbarians*.

53. M. K. Gandhi, *Satyagraha in South Africa*, n.p.

54. Majeed, *Autobiography, Travel, and Postnational Identity*.

55. M. K. Gandhi, *The Story of My Experiments with Truth*, 1:2–3.

56. M. K. Gandhi, *The Story of My Experiments with Truth*, 1:3.

57. M. K. Gandhi, *The Story of My Experiments with Truth*, 1:63.

58. M. K. Gandhi, *The Story of My Experiments with Truth*, 1:64.
59. M. K. Gandhi, *Collected Works of Mahatma Gandhi*, 29:6.
60. Hofmeyr, "Violent Texts, Vulnerable Readers," 289.
61. M. K. Gandhi, *Satyagraha in South Africa*, 147.
62. M. K. Gandhi, *Satyagraha in South Africa*, 11.
63. M. K. Gandhi, *Satyagraha in South Africa*, 18.
64. Crais, "The Vacant Land"; McClendon, "Makwerekwere."
65. Vinson, "Providential Design," 133.
66. M. K. Gandhi, *Satyagraha in South Africa*, 18.
67. Kolge, "Was Gandhi a Racist?," 93; Burton et al., "The South African Gandhi," 104.
68. M. K. Gandhi, *Satyagraha in South Africa*, 19.
69. M. K. Gandhi, *Satyagraha in South Africa*, 20.
70. Chrisman, *Rereading the Imperial Romance*, 12.
71. M. K. Gandhi, *Satyagraha in South Africa*, 24.
72. M. K. Gandhi, *Satyagraha in South Africa*, 22–23.
73. The contemporary poles in this debate might arguably be mapped between the gentle approach of Ramachandra Guha's *Gandhi before India*, published in 2013, and the excoriating critique of A. Desai and Vahed's *The South African Gandhi*, published just two years later.
74. Plaut, *Promise and Despair*, 195–96.
75. M. K. Gandhi, *The Story of My Experiments with Truth*, 1:143, 147.
76. M. K. Gandhi, *The Grievances of the British Indians in South Africa*, Wilson Anti-slavery Collection, 9.
77. M. K. Gandhi, *The Grievances of the British Indians in South Africa*, Wilson Anti-slavery Collection, 31–32.
78. M. K. Gandhi, *The Story of My Experiments with Truth*, 1:278.
79. M. K. Gandhi, *The Story of My Experiments with Truth*, 1:263, 80.
80. M. K. Gandhi, *The Story of My Experiments with Truth*, 2:79.
81. M. K. Gandhi, *The Story of My Experiments with Truth*, 2:79.
82. M. K. Gandhi, *Satyagraha in South Africa*, n.p.
83. Although this conflict was initially called the "Anglo-Boer War," the non-White residents—neither "Anglo" nor "Boer"—of South Africa were profoundly affected, as indicated in the more recent nominalization of "South African War." Given their White supremacist views, both the Boer and British governments had hoped to keep the conflict "a white man's war"; as the war drew on, however, both sides relied on Black and Coloured fighters, as well as Indian noncombatants in supporting roles. Africans died in large numbers, not only during the regular course of combat but also within the British concentration camps (where African internees were deliberately mistreated even more than the Boer ones), and from Boer executions of Africans for their alleged disloyalty. See Plaut, *Promise and Despair*, 40, 44–45.
84. Plaut, *Promise and Despair*, 30–33.
85. Plaut, *Promise and Despair*, 133.
86. Plaut, *Promise and Despair*, 114.
87. M. K. Gandhi, *Satyagraha in South Africa*, 29.
88. M. K. Gandhi, *Satyagraha in South Africa*, 31.

89. M. K. Gandhi, *Satyagraha in South Africa*, 32.
90. M. K. Gandhi, *Satyagraha in South Africa*, 32.
91. M. K. Gandhi, *Satyagraha in South Africa*, 429.
92. M. K. Gandhi, *Satyagraha in South Africa*, 430.
93. M. K. Gandhi, *Satyagraha in South Africa*, 430.
94. M. K. Gandhi, *Satyagraha in South Africa*, 432.
95. Polak, "Women and the Struggle."
96. Polak, "Women and the Struggle," 25.
97. Polak, "Women and the Struggle," 25.
98. Polak, "Women and the Struggle," 26.
99. Polak, *Mr. Gandhi*, 132.
100. Polak, *Mr. Gandhi*, 134.
101. "Railway Travelling in the Transvaal," *Indian Opinion*, September 7, 1912; "Railway Travelling in the Transvaal," *Indian Opinion*, August 31, 1912.
102. Pirie, "Racial Segregation on South African Trains, 1910–1928," 83.
103. Paxton, *Sonja Schlesin*, 14.
104. Paxton, *Sonja Schlesin*, 4, 10.
105. The term "Colonial-born" was generally used for a person who was the subject of one British colony but was born in a different British colony. Gandhi would have certainly encountered this term in South Africa, where people of Indian descent who were born in South Africa were termed "Colonial-born Indians."
106. "The Mass Meeting," 20.
107. "Railway Travelling in the Transvaal," *Indian Opinion*, August 31, 1912, 292.
108. "Railway Travelling in the Transvaal," *Indian Opinion*, August 31, 1912, 292.
109. "Railway Travelling in the Transvaal," *Indian Opinion*, August 31, 1912, 292.
110. Pirie, "'A Most Difficult and Delicate Question,'" 116.
111. Pirie, "'A Most Difficult and Delicate Question,'" 122.
112. Pirie, "Rolling Segregation into Apartheid," 671.
113. "Railway Travelling in the Transvaal," *Indian Opinion*, August 31, 1912, 292.
114. "Railway Travelling in the Transvaal," *Indian Opinion*, August 31, 1912, 292.
115. "Railway Travelling in the Transvaal," *Indian Opinion*, August 31, 1912, 292.
116. "Railway Travelling in the Transvaal," *Indian Opinion*, August 31, 1912, 292.
117. Pirie, "'A Most Difficult and Delicate Question,'" 122; Pirie, "Racial Segregation on South African Trains, 1910–1928," 77, 90; Pirie, "Rolling Segregation into Apartheid," 677–78.
118. Pirie, "Racial Segregation on South African Trains, 1910–1928," 78–79; Pirie, "Rolling Segregation into Apartheid," 685–86.
119. "Railway Travelling in the Transvaal," *Indian Opinion*, August 31, 1912, 292.

120. "Railway Travelling in the Transvaal," *Indian Opinion*, August 31, 1912, 292.

121. "Railway Travelling in the Transvaal," *Indian Opinion*, August 31, 1912, 292.

122. "Railway Travelling in the Transvaal," *Indian Opinion*, September 7, 1912, 292–93.

123. "Railway Travelling in the Transvaal," *Indian Opinion*, September 7, 1912.

124. "Railway Travelling in the Transvaal," *Indian Opinion*, September 7, 1912.

125. M. K. Gandhi, "Indian Women as Passive Resisters."

126. M. K. Gandhi, "Indian Women as Passive Resisters."

127. Spivak, "Can the Subaltern Speak?," 298.

128. Trivedi, "Revolutionary Non-violence," 523–24.

129. Apter, *Against World Literature*, 235.

130. Melas, *All the Difference in the World*, 86.

131. Melas, *All the Difference in the World*, 89–90.

132. Melas, *All the Difference in the World*, 86–87.

CHAPTER 3

1. Du Bois, "The True Brownies," 285–86.

2. Du Bois, "The True Brownies," 285.

3. Du Bois, "The True Brownies," 285–86.

4. Levering-Lewis, *W. E. B. Du Bois*.

5. Banarsidas Chaturvedi to W. E. B. Du Bois, January 19, 1925, W. E. B. Du Bois Papers (MS 312), Special Collections and University Archives, University of Massachusetts Amherst Libraries (hereafter cited as Du Bois Papers).

6. Wilson M. Powell to *The Crisis*, March 6, 1925, Du Bois Papers.

7. J. Calloway to W. E. B. Du Bois, November 14, 1927, Du Bois Papers.

8. S. Muthray to W. E. B. Du Bois, March 19, 1925, Du Bois Papers.

9. *The Crisis* (India) to W. E. B. Du Bois, February 24, 1928, Du Bois Papers; Banarsidas Chaturvedi to W. E. B. Du Bois, September 15, 1925, Du Bois Papers.

10. Banarsidas Chaturvedi to W. E. B. Du Bois, January 19, 1925, Du Bois Papers.

11. Wilson M. Powell to *The Crisis*, March 6, 1925, Du Bois Papers.

12. Cummins, *Humorous but Wholesome*; Belleau, "Avant Walt Disney il y eut Palmer Cox."

13. See, for instance, Cox, *The Brownies: Their Book*, vii.

14. Cummins, *Humorous but Wholesome*, 56–57.

15. Cummins, *Humorous but Wholesome*, 65–66; Olivier, "George Eastman's Modern Stone-Age Family."

16. Cox, *The Brownies around the World*. Originally serialized in the *Ladies' Home Journal* from 1892 to 1893, the brownies in this story visit, in order, Canada, Ireland, Scotland, England, France, Spain, Italy, Turkey, Egypt, Arabia, Germany, Switzerland, Holland, Russia, China, Japan, and "the Polar regions." See also Cummins, *Humorous but Wholesome*, 78–79.

17. For example, according to the author of the only book-length study of Cox's Brownies, the Brownies are "thoroughly democratic," "utopian," and "embody the American dream." They impart, moreover, a message of diversity, for "through the Brownies a child learned that it was possible for a group of disparate members—the range of nationalities and occupations is large—to live together in harmony." Cummins, *Humorous but Wholesome*, 113.

18. Boehmer, "The Text in the World," 140.

19. This movement originated in a 1912 manual authored by Robert Baden-Powell's sister, Agnes Baden-Powell, *The Handbook for Girl Guides; or, How Girls Can Help Build the Empire*. The U.S. version would rename the imperial impetus as a nationalist project: Low, *How Girls Can Help Their Country*.

20. "The Grown-Ups' Corner," *Brownies' Book* 2, no. 1 (January 1921): 25.

21. For Fauset's work as a literary reviewer, see Wall, *Women of the Harlem Renaissance*, 55; as a nonfiction reporter, Sheehan, "Fashioning Internationalism in Jessie Redmon Fauset's Writing," 140; as a novelist, Popp, "Where Confusion Is"; and as an editor, Zackodnik, "Recirculation and Feminist Black Internationalism."

22. Popp, "Where Confusion Is," 131.

23. Ahmad, *Landscapes of Hope*; Ferguson, "W. E. B. Du Bois."

24. Stockton, *The Queer Child*, 41.

25. Kirschke, *Art in Crisis*; Carroll, *Word, Image, and the New Negro*.

26. Du Bois, "That Capital 'N,'" 28.

27. Du Bois, "That Capital 'N,'" 29.

28. Carroll, "Protest and Affirmation," 89.

29. Du Bois, "Gandhi and India," 205.

30. My argument focuses on Du Bois in the period before World War II; it thus does not reflect on his later writings, as for instance in his 1943 response to A. Philip Randolph's call for Gandhian resistance. For a discussion of that postwar debate, see Prashad, "Waiting for the Black Gandhi," 190.

31. Du Bois, *Dark Princess*, 286.

32. Bullard, "Global South," 726.

33. Meyers and Hunt, "The Other Global South."

34. The original U.S. naturalization law of 1790 made being a "free white person" a prerequisite for naturalization. The racial requirement was further enshrined in 1856 when, in *Dred Scott v. Sanford*, the U.S. Supreme Court ruled that no person of African descent could be considered a U.S. citizen. The Fourteenth Amendment, ratified in 1868 to protect African Americans after the abolition of slavery, defined legal criteria for citizenship on a *jus soli* basis, without any racial restrictions—and then the Naturalization Act of 1870 explicitly clarified that naturalization had only been extended to "aliens of African nativity and to persons of African descent." In 1898, the Supreme Court ruled in *Wong Kim Ark v. United States* that *jus soli* citizenship applied even to U.S.-born children of noncitizens who were neither White nor of African descent.

Explicitly racial restrictions on immigration began with the Page Act of 1875, which nearly eliminated the immigration of Asian women, and then the 1882 Chinese Exclusion Act, whose racial parameters were further expanded by the Asiatic Barred Zone Act of 1917. That "Asiatic Barred Zone" included all of

Asia except for Japan and the Philippines, then a U.S. colony; Japanese immigration was soon banned, however, in the more comprehensive 1924 Johnson-Reed Act (National Origins Quota Act). The introduction of a quota system in the early 1920s strongly favored White immigrants from Western Europe, even as the permissibility of immigration by those eligible for citizenship meant that immigration from Africa was never legally eliminated.

Other restrictions applied to women, whose citizenship could be revoked, and Native Americans, who gained citizenship with the 1924 Indian Citizenship Act. White immigrant women became capable of naturalization through marriage to U.S. citizens only in 1855, and with the 1907 Expatriation Act (repealed by the 1922 Cable Act) women who married non-U.S. citizens were automatically stripped of their U.S. citizenship. Even in the Cable Act, however, the U.S. made an anti-Asian exception: U.S. women who married noncitizens of Asian descent would still lose their citizenship.

Even expansions of naturalization rights often incorporated specifically anti-Asian exceptions. Some Asian Americans would become eligible for naturalization in the 1940s: Chinese Americans, with the 1943 repeal of the Chinese Exclusion Act, and then Indian and Filipino Americans, with the 1946 Luce-Celler Act. The United States would not move to a fully nonracial immigration and naturalization regime until 1965. While today by some measures Asian Americans are among the most prosperous of immigrant groups, the naturalization process for immigrants from the two most populous Asian nations—India and China—can easily take a decade longer than that for other applicants.

35. Freedgood and Schmitt, "Denotatively, Technically, Literally."

36. Cooppan, *Worlds Within*; Weinbaum, *Wayward Reproductions*.

37. M. Desai, *The United States of India*.

38. Lake and Reynolds, *Drawing the Global Colour Line*, 168–89.

39. Takao Ozawa v. United States, No. 260 U.S. 178 (1922); United States v. Bhagat Singh Thind, No. 261 U.S. 204 (1923).

40. United States v. Bhagat Singh Thind, No. 261 U.S. 204 (1923).

41. United States v. Bhagat Singh Thind, No. 261 U.S. 204 (1923).

42. Lake and Reynolds, *Drawing the Global Colour Line*, 313.

43. Du Bois, *The World and Africa*, 9.

44. Du Bois, *The World and Africa*, 9.

45. Du Bois, *The World and Africa*, 9–10.

46. Du Bois, *Dark Princess*, 311.

47. Du Bois, "Asia in Africa."

48. Du Bois, "The Negro Mind Reaches Out," 386.

49. Lahiri, "World Romance."

50. Ryan, "India and U.S. Cultures of Reform."

51. Du Bois, "Caste in America," Du Bois Papers, 4.

52. Du Bois, "Caste in America," Du Bois Papers, 4.

53. Du Bois, "Caste in America," Du Bois Papers, 7–8.

54. Du Bois, "Color Caste in the United States," 59.

55. Du Bois, *The Souls of Black Folk*, 5.

56. Du Bois, *Dark Princess*, 221.

57. Du Bois, *Dark Princess*, 245.

58. Du Bois, *Dark Princess*, 256–57.
59. Du Bois, *Dark Princess*, 311.
60. Wall, *Women of the Harlem Renaissance*, 46.
61. Fauset, "Dedication."
62. Fauset, "The Judge," *Brownies' Book* 1, no. 6 (June 1920): 176.
63. Fauset, "What to Read."
64. Fauset, "The Judge," *Brownies' Book* 1, no. 6 (June 1920): 176.
65. "Folk Tales."
66. Wall, *Women of the Harlem Renaissance*, 47; Zackodnik, "Recirculation and Feminist Black Internationalism," 439.
67. Wall, *Women of the Harlem Renaissance*, 48.
68. Wall, *Women of the Harlem Renaissance*, 57–58.
69. Poe, "Pumpkin Land."
70. Culbertson, "The Origin of White Folks."
71. Clifford, "Kindergarten Song."
72. See, for instance, an early tale translated by the fifteen-year-old Mary Cook: Cook, "The Story of Prince Jalma."
73. Fauset, "Over the Ocean Wave."
74. "The Merry Month of May."
75. Du Bois, "As the Crow Flies," 25.
76. Du Bois, "As the Crow Flies," 76.
77. Du Bois, "As the Crow Flies," 70–71.
78. Du Bois, "As the Crow Flies," 26.
79. Fauset, "The Judge," *Brownies' Book* 1, no. 3 (March 1920): 81.
80. Fauset, "The Judge," *Brownies' Book* 1, no. 3 (March 1920): 81.
81. Johnson, "The Ancestor."
82. In early issues, Fauset is listed as the literary editor and Du Bois as the managing editor, identical to the roles that they performed for *The Crisis*. By 1921, however, the masthead for the *Brownies' Book* proclaims Fauset as its managing editor, with Du Bois's name preceding as the person who "conducted" it.
83. Fauset, *There Is Confusion*, 14.
84. Bella Seymour, "The Grown-Ups' Corner," *Brownies' Book* 1, no. 2 (February 1920): 45.
85. Hattie Porter, "The Jury," *Brownies' Book* 1, no. 10 (October 1920): 308.
86. Easmon, "A Little Talk about West Africa."
87. Easmon, "A Little Talk about West Africa," 170.
88. Fauset, "The Judge," *Brownies' Book* 2, no. 5 (May 1921): 134.
89. Lake and Reynolds, *Drawing the Global Colour Line*, 143.
90. Simango, "Mphontholo Ne Shulo."
91. Simango, "Mphontholo Ne Shulo," 43–44.
92. For a longer discussion see Lahiri, "The Pose of the Author."
93. "Little People of the Month."
94. "The Grown-Ups' Corner," *Brownies' Book* 1, no. 3 (March 1920): 70.
95. "The Jury," *Brownies' Book* 2, no. 1 (January 1921): 62.
96. "The Grown-Ups' Corner," *Brownies' Book* 2, no. 1 (January 1921): 25.

97. Garvey, *Writing with Scissors.*

98. Ada Simpson, "The Jury," *Brownies' Book* 1, no. 4 (April 1920): 111.

99. "The Grown-Ups' Corner," *Brownies' Book* 2, no. 1 (January 1921): 25.

100. Smith, *Children's Literature of the Harlem Renaissance.*

101. Berlant, "The Theory of Infantile Citizenship"; Edelman, *No Future*; Stockton, *The Queer Child.*

102. Smith, *Children's Literature of the Harlem Renaissance*, 30.

103. W. E. B. Du Bois to Harcourt, Brace, and Company, October 13, 1927, Du Bois Papers; Harcourt, Brace, and Company to W. E. B. Du Bois, October 14, 1927, Du Bois Papers.

104. W. E. B. Du Bois to Adelbert H. Roberts, October 11, 1927, Du Bois Papers. Only the first page of this correspondence survives. W. E. B. Du Bois to Dr. Louis Wright, October 11, 1927, Du Bois Papers.

105. See, for instance, M. Desai, *The United States of India.*

106. Lala Lajpat Rai to W. E. B. Du Bois, October 6, 1927, Du Bois Papers.

107. W. E. B. Du Bois to Lala Lajpat Rai, November 9, 1927, Du Bois Papers.

108. Levering-Lewis, *W. E. B. Du Bois*; Mullen and Watson, *W. E. B. Du Bois on Asia*; Ahmad, "More Than Romance," 787.

109. W. E. B. Du Bois to Dhan Gopal Mukerji, October 29, 1927, Du Bois Papers.

110. Dhan Gopal Mukerji to W. E. B. Du Bois, November 4, 1927, Du Bois Papers.

111. W. E. B. Du Bois to Dhan Gopal Mukerji, November 7, 1927, Du Bois Papers.

112. W. E. B. Du Bois to Mahatma Gandhi, February 19, 1929, Du Bois Papers.

113. M. K. Gandhi to W. E. B. Du Bois, May 1, 1929, Du Bois Papers.

114. Du Bois and Gandhi, "To the American Negro," 225.

115. Du Bois and Gandhi, "To the American Negro," 225.

116. The Rowlatt Act of 1919 extended the regulations that Britain had placed on Indians during World War I, most notably extended detention without trial. The massacre on April 13, 1919, at Jallianwala Bagh in Amritsar resulted from a British army regiment firing on a crowd of peaceful and unarmed Indian civilians in a walled garden: at least 379 people were killed, and over 1,200 were injured.

117. Du Bois and Gandhi, "To the American Negro."

118. Tagore and Du Bois, "A Message to the American Negro from Rabindranath Tagore."

119. Tagore and Du Bois, "A Message to the American Negro from Rabindranath Tagore," 334.

120. Tagore and Du Bois, "A Message to the American Negro from Rabindranath Tagore," 334.

121. Tagore and Du Bois, "A Message to the American Negro from Rabindranath Tagore," 334.

122. Du Bois, "Indian Philosopher Hits Race Prejudice."

123. Tagore and Du Bois, "A Message to the American Negro from Rabindranath Tagore," 334.

124. Tagore and Du Bois, "A Message to the American Negro from Rabindranath Tagore," 334.

125. Du Bois obtained both 1929 notes through the intermediary services of C. F. Andrews. He sent letters to both Gandhi and Tagore under Andrews's cover, unsealed, on February 19, 1929. Tagore's secretary, A. C. Chakravarty, replied on March 1929; mentioning that he and Tagore had "read with much pleasure and interest" *The Crisis*, he adds "how deeply we are in sympathy with the broad human outlook which animates and illuminates its pages." Du Bois received the note in July 1929, publishing it in the October "Children's Number." Their correspondence, while sparse, continued for three years. In a letter dated December 27, 1930, Chakravarty praises Du Bois's "subtle (noble?) propaganda against racial discrimination"; on September 15, 1931, Du Bois reiterated his request for an article for *The Crisis*, this time explicitly voicing what he sought: "Could he not say a word concerning his experience in America and the little that he was able to see of the shadows of the color line?" We have no further record of their exchange. A. C. Chakravarty to W. E. B. Du Bois, March 1929, Du Bois Papers; A. C. Chakravarty to W. E. B. Du Bois, December 27, 1930, Du Bois Papers; A. C. Chakravarty to W. E. B. Du Bois, September 15, 1931, Du Bois Papers.

126. The editors of the *Aryan Path* to W. E. B. Du Bois, September 19, 1935, Du Bois Papers; W. E. B. Du Bois to the Editors of the *Aryan Path*, October 8, 1935, Du Bois Papers.

127. The editors of the *Aryan Path* to W. E. B. Du Bois, October 10, 1935, Du Bois Papers.

128. The editors of the *Aryan Path* to W. E. B. Du Bois, November 8, 1935, Du Bois Papers.

129. Viswanathan, *Outside the Fold*, 177–207.

130. "East and West."

131. "East and West."

132. Durtain, "The Clash of Ideals"; Watson, "The Emergence of Harmony."

133. Du Bois, "The Clash of Colour," 114.

134. M. K. Gandhi, *The Grievances of the British Indians in South Africa*, Wilson Anti-slavery Collection.

135. Du Bois, "The Clash of Colour," 111.

136. Du Bois, "The Clash of Colour," 111.

137. Du Bois, "The Clash of Colour," 112.

138. Du Bois, "The Clash of Colour," 112.

139. Du Bois, "The Clash of Colour," 113, mentions Lajpat Rai, *The United States of America*, as an exemplary text.

140. Du Bois, "The Clash of Colour," 114.

141. Du Bois, "The Clash of Colour," 115.

142. Subba Rao, "The Union of Colour," 216.

143. Du Bois, "Correspondence: the Union of Colour," 483.

144. Du Bois, "Correspondence: the Union of Colour," 483.

145. Du Bois, "Correspondence: the Union of Colour," 483–84.

146. Y. Du Bois, "The Land behind the Sun."

147. L. Hughes, "Up to the Crater of an Old Volcano."

148. Butler, "The Melody Man."

149. Fauset, "Valedictory."

150. Keelan, "Olive Plaatje," 342.

151. Keelan, "Olive Plaatje," 342.

152. Smith, *Children's Literature of the Harlem Renaissance*, 32–33; Corbould, *Becoming African Americans*, 104.

153. Gilroy, *The Black Atlantic*; Edwards, *The Practice of Diaspora*; Jaji, *Africa in Stereo*.

154. Macauley, "Minute."

155. Patel, *Migritude*; Torabully and Carter, *Coolietude*.

CONCLUSION

1. Arendt, "The Seeds of a Fascist International," 141.

2. Arendt, "The Seeds of a Fascist International," 144.

3. Arendt, "The Seeds of a Fascist International," 143.

4. Arendt, "The Seeds of a Fascist International," 143.

5. Spivak, "Three Women's Texts and a Critique of Imperialism"; Guha and Spivak, *Selected Subaltern Studies*; Fanon, *Peau noire, masques blancs*.

Bibliography

COLLECTIONS AND ARCHIVES

Historical Papers Research Archive, University of the Witwatersrand. Johannesburg, South Africa.

Rabindra-Bhavana Library, Viswa-Bharati University. Santiniketan, West Bengal, India.

W. E. B. Du Bois Papers (MS 312), Special Collections and University Archives, University of Massachusetts Amherst Libraries. Amherst, Mass., United States.

Wilson Anti-slavery Collection, John Rylands University Library, University of Manchester. Manchester, United Kingdom.

BOOKS AND ARTICLES

Ahmad, Dohra. *Landscapes of Hope: Anticolonial Utopianism in America*. Oxford: Oxford University Press, 2009.

———. "More Than Romance: Genre and Geography in *Dark Princess*." *ELH* 69, no. 3 (2002): 775–803.

Ahmed, Siraj. *Archaeology of Babel: The Colonial Foundation of the Humanities*. Stanford, Calif.: Stanford University Press, 2017.

Anjaria, Ulka. *Realism in the Twentieth-Century Indian Novel: Colonial Difference and Literary Form*. Cambridge: Cambridge University Press, 2012.

Anker, Elizabeth S., and Rita Felski, eds. *Critique and Postcritique*. Durham, N.C.: Duke University Press, 2017.

Apter, Emily. *Against World Literature: On the Politics of Untranslatability*. London: Verso, 2013.

Arendt, Hannah. "The Seeds of a Fascist International" (1945). In *Essays in Understanding: Formation, Exile, and Totalitarianism*, edited by Jerome Kohn, 140–50. New York: Schocken Books, 1994.

Arnold, Edwin. *The Song Celestial*. London: Trubner, 1886.

Baden-Powell, Agnes. *The Handbook for Girl Guides; or, How Girls Can Help Build the Empire*. London: Thomas Nelson and Sons, 1912.

Bannerjee, Sukanya. *Becoming Imperial Citizens*. Durham, N.C.: Duke University Press, 2010.

Barbery, Muriel, et al. "Pour une 'littérature-monde' en français." *Le Monde*, May 15, 2007. https://www.lemonde.fr/livres/article/2007/03/15/des-ecrivains-plaident-pour-un-roman-en-francais-ouvert-sur-le-monde_883572_3260.html#.

Belleau, Bernard. "Avant Walt Disney il y eut Palmer Cox." *Cap-aux-Diamants: La Revue d'Histoire du Québec* 48 (1997): 40–43.

Berlant, Lauren. "The Theory of Infantile Citizenship." *Public Culture* 5 (1993): 395–410.

Berman, Marshall. *All That Is Solid Melts into Air: The Experience of Modernity*. New York: Simon and Schuster, 1982.

Bernstein, Robin. *Racial Innocence*. New York: New York University Press, 2011.

Best, Stephen, and Sharon Marcus. "Surface Reading: An Introduction." *Representations* 108, no. 1 (2009): 1–21.

Bewes, Timothy. "Reading with the Grain: A New World in Literary Criticism." *Differences* 21, no. 3 (2010): 1–33.

Bharucha, Rustom. *Another Asia: Rabindranath Tagore and Okakura Tenshin*. New Delhi: Oxford University Press, 2009.

Bhattacharya, Sabyasachi. *The Mahatma and the Poet*. New Delhi: National Book Trust, 1997.

Biko, Stephen. "The Definition of Black Consciousness" (1971), 48–53. In *I Write What I Like: Selected Writings*. Chicago: University of Chicago Press, 2002.

Boehmer, Elleke. "The Text in the World." In *Ten Books That Shaped the British Empire*, edited by Isabel Hofmeyr and Antoinette Burton, 131–52. Durham, N.C.: Duke University Press, 2014.

Borg, Erik. "Discourse Community." *ELT Journal* 57, no. 4 (October 2003): 398–400.

Brown, Judith. "Spinning without Touching the Wheel: Anticolonialism, Indian Nationalism, and the Deployment of Symbol." *Comparative Studies of South Asia, Africa, and the Middle East* 29, no. 2 (2009): 230–45.

Bullard, Nicola. "Global South." In *Encyclopedia of Global Studies*, 725–27. Thousand Oaks, Calif.: Sage, 2019. https://doi.org/10.4135/9781452218557.

Burton, Antoinette. *Brown over Black*. Durham, N.C.: Duke University Press, 2012.

Burton, Antoinette, Faisal Devji, Mrinalini Sinha, Jon Soske, Ashwin Desai, and Goolam Vahed. "The South African Gandhi: Stretcher-Bearer of Empire." *Journal of Natal and Zulu History* 32, no. 1 (2018): 100–118.

Butler, James Alpheus, Jr. "The Melody Man." *Brownies' Book* 2, no. 12 (December 1921): 349–52.

Carroll, Anne Elizabeth. "Protest and Affirmation: Composite Texts in *The Crisis*." *American Literature* 76 (2004): 89–116.

———. *Word, Image, and the New Negro: Representation and Identity in the Harlem Renaissance*. Bloomington: Indiana University Press, 2005.

Chan, Shelley. "The Case for Diaspora: A Temporal Approach to the Chinese Experience." *Journal of Asian Studies* 74, no. 1 (2015): 107–28.

Chang, Ku-Ming Kevin, Benjamin A. Elman, and Sheldon Pollock, eds. *World Philology*. Cambridge, Mass.: Harvard University Press, 2015.

Cheng, Anne Anlin. *Second Skin: Josephine Baker and the Modern Surface*. Oxford: Oxford University Press, 2011.

Chrisman, Laura. *Rereading the Imperial Romance*. Oxford: Oxford University Press, 2000.

Clifford, Carrie W. "Kindergarten Song." *Brownies' Book* 1, no. 4 (April 1920): 124.

Cook, Mary, trans. "The Story of Prince Jalma." *Brownies' Book* 1, no. 3 (March 1920): 67–70.

Cooppan, Vilashini. "Net Work: Area Studies, Comparison, and Connectivity." *PMLA* 128, no. 3 (2013): 615–21.

———. "World Literature between History and Theory." In *The Routledge Companion to World Literature*, edited by Theo D'haen, David Damrosch, and Djelal Kadir, 194–203. New York: Routledge, 2011.

———. *Worlds Within: National Narratives and Global Connections in Postcolonial Writing*. Stanford, Calif.: Stanford University Press, 2009.

Corbould, Clare. *Becoming African Americans: Black Public Life in Harlem, 1919–1939*. Cambridge, Mass.: Harvard University Press, 2009.

Cox, Palmer. *The Brownies: Their Book*. New York: Century, 1887.

———. *The Brownies around the World*. New York: Century, 1894.

Crais, Clifton C. "The Vacant Land: The Mythology of British Expansion in the Eastern Cape, South Africa." *Journal of Social History* 25, no. 2 (Winter 1991): 255–75.

Culbertson, Annie Virginia. "The Origin of White Folks." *Brownies' Book* 1, no. 1 (January 1920): 7.

Cummins, Roger W. *Humorous but Wholesome: A History of Palmer Cox and the Brownies*. Watkins Glen, N.Y.: Century House, 1973.

Das, Sisir Kumar. "The Controversial Guest: Tagore in China." *China Report* 29, no. 3 (1993): 237–273.

———, ed. *The English Writings of Rabindranath Tagore*, vol. 1. New Delhi: Sahitya Akademi, 1994.

de Kock, Leon. *Civilising Barbarians: Missionary Narrative and African Textual Response in Nineteenth Century South Africa*. Johannesburg: Witwatersrand University Press, 1996.

Desai, Ashwin, and Goolam Vahed. *Inside Indian Indenture: A South African Story, 1860–1914*. Cape Town: Human Sciences Research Council Press, 2010.

———. *The South African Gandhi: Stretcher-Bearer of Empire*. Stanford, Calif.: Stanford University Press, 2015.

Desai, Gaurav. *Commerce with the Universe*. New York: Columbia University Press, 2013.

———. "Postcolonial, by Any Other Name?" *Interventions* 20, no. 3 (2018): 354–60.

Desai, Manan. *The United States of India: Anticolonial Literature and Transnational Refraction*. Philadelphia: Temple University Press, 2020.

Dimock, Wai Chee. "World Literature on *Facebook*." *PMLA* 126, no. 3 (2011): 730–36.

Du Bois, W. E. B. "Asia in Africa." In *W. E. B. Du Bois on Asia: Crossing the World Color Line*, edited by Bill V. Mullen and Cathryn Watson, 9–32. Jackson: University Press of Mississippi, 1947.

———. "As the Crow Flies." *Brownies' Book* 1, no. 1 (January 1920): 25–26.

———. "The Clash of Colour." *Aryan Path* 7, no. 3 (March 1936): 111–15.

———. "Color Caste in the United States." *The Crisis*, 40, no. 3 (March 1933): 59–60.

———. "Correspondence: The Union of Colour." *Aryan Path* 7, no. 10 (October 1936): 483–84.

———. *Dark Princess: A Romance* (1928). Jackson: University Press of Mississippi, 1995.

———. "Gandhi and India." *The Crisis* 23, no. 5 (March 1922): 203–7.

———. "Indian Philosopher Hits Race Prejudice: Hindu Poet and British Knight Declare America Has Contemptuous Attitude to All with Skins Not White." *Pittsburgh Courier*, April 27, 1929.

———. "The Negro Mind Reaches Out." In *The New Negro*, edited by Alain Locke, 385–414. New York: A. and C. Boni, 1925.

———. *The Souls of Black Folk*. New York: Penguin Books, 1903.

———. "That Capital 'N.'" *The Crisis* 10, no. 1 (May 1915): 28–29.

———. "The True Brownies." *The Crisis* 18, no. 6 (October 1919): 285–86.

———. *The World and Africa*. New York: Viking, 1946.

Du Bois, W. E. B., and Mohandas Karamchand Gandhi. "To the American Negro: A Message from Mahatma Gandhi." *The Crisis* 36, no. 3 (July 1929): 225–26.

Du Bois, Yolande. "The Land behind the Sun." *Brownies' Book* 2, no. 12 (December 1921): 331.

Durtain, Luc. "The Clash of Ideals: Analytical West and Synthesising East." *Aryan Path* 7, no. 3 (March 1936): 106–11.

Easmon, Kathleen. "A Little Talk about West Africa." *Brownies' Book* 2, no. 1 (June 1921): 170–73.

"East and West." *Aryan Path* 7, no. 3 (March 1936): 105.

Edelman, Lee. *No Future: Queer Theory and the Death Drive*. Durham, N.C.: Duke University Press, 2004.

Edwards, Brent Hayes. *The Practice of Diaspora: Literature, Translation, and the Rise of Black Internationalism*. Cambridge, Mass.: Harvard University Press, 2003.

Fanon, Frantz. *Peau noire, masques blancs*. Paris: Éditions du Seuil, 1952.

Fauset, Jessie Redmon. "Dedication." *Brownies' Book* 1, no. 1 (January 1920): 32.

———. "Valedictory." *Brownies' Book* 2, no. 12 (December 1921): 354.

———. "The Judge." *Brownies' Book* 1, no. 3 (March 1920): 81.

———. "The Judge." *Brownies' Book* 1, no. 6 (June 1920): 176.

———. "The Judge." *Brownies' Book* 2, no. 5 (May 1921): 134.

———. "Over the Ocean Wave." *Brownies' Book* 1, no. 2 (March 1920): 88.

———. "What to Read." *The Crisis* 3, no. 5 (March 1921): 211.

———. *There Is Confusion*. Boston: Northeastern University Press, 1989.

Ferguson, Roderik. "W. E. B. Du Bois: Biography of a Discourse." In *Next to the Color Line: Gender, Sexuality, and W. E. B. Du Bois*, edited by Alys Eve Weinbaum and Susan Gillman, 269–88. Minneapolis: University of Minnesota Press, 2007.

Fish, Stanley. *Is There a Text in This Class? The Authority of Interpretive Communities*. Cambridge, Mass.: Harvard University Press, 2003.

"Folk Tales." *Brownies' Book* 1, no. 2 (March 1920): 46–47.

Freedgood, Elaine, and Canon Schmitt. "Denotatively, Technically, Literally." *Representations* 125 (2014): 1–14.

Frost, Mark R. "'Beyond the Limits of Nation and Geography': Rabindranath Tagore and the Cosmopolitan Moment, 1916–20." *Cultural Dynamics* 24, nos. 2–3 (2012): 143–58.

Gandhi, Leela. *Affective Communities*. Durham, N.C.: Duke University Press, 2006.

———. *The Common Cause*. Chicago: University of Chicago Press, 2014.

Gandhi, Mohandas Karamchand. *The Story of My Experiments with Truth*. Vol. 1 of 2. Trans. Mahadev Desai. Madras: S. Ganesan, 1927.

———. *The Story of My Experiments with Truth*. Vol. 2 of 2. Trans. Mahadev Desai and Pyarelal Nair. Madras: S. Ganesan, 1929.

———. "The Charkha and the Gita." *Young India* 3, no. 42 (October 20, 1921): 329.

———. "The Great Sentinel." *Young India* 3, no. 41 (October 13, 1921): 324–26.

———. *Hind Swaraj*. Edited by Anthony Parel. Cambridge: Cambridge University Press, 2009.

———. "Indian Women as Passive Resisters." *Indian Opinion* 18, no. 11 (May 10, 1913): 109.

———. "The Poet and the Charkha." *Young India* 5, no. 45 (November 5, 1925): 376–77.

———. *Satyagraha in South Africa*. Madras: S. Ganesan, 1928.

———. *The Collected Works of Mahatma Gandhi*, vol. 29. New Delhi: Publications Division, Ministry of Information and Broadcasting, Government of India, 1968.

Ganguly, Debjani. *This Thing Called the World*. Durham, N.C.: Duke University Press, 2016.

Garvey, Ellen Gruber. *Writing with Scissors*. Oxford: Oxford University Press, 2013.

Gilroy, Paul. *The Black Atlantic: Modernity and Double Consciousness*. Cambridge, Mass.: Harvard University Press, 1993.

"The Grown- Ups' Corner," *Brownies' Book* 1, no. 2 (February 1920): 45.

Goyal, Yogita. "Postcolonial, Still." *Post45*, February 22, 2019. http://post45.research.yale.edu/2019/02/postcolonial-still/.

Guha, Ramachandra. *Gandhi before India*. London: Penguin Books, 2013.

Guha, Ranajit. *History at the Limit of World-History*. New York: Columbia University Press, 2002.

Guha, Ranajit, and Gayatri Chakravorty Spivak, eds. *Selected Subaltern Studies*. Oxford: Oxford University Press, 1988.

Gvili, Gal. "Pan-Asian Poetics: Tagore and the Interpersonal in May Fourth New Poetry." *Journal of Asian Studies* 77, no. 1 (2018): 181–203.

Harpham, Geoffrey. "Roots, Races, and the Return to Philology." *Representations* 106 (2009): 34–62.

Hay, Stephen. *Asian Ideals of East and West*. Cambridge, Mass.: Harvard University Press, 1970.

Hofmeyr, Isabel. *Gandhi's Printing Press: Experiments in Slow Reading*. Cambridge, Mass.: Harvard University Press, 2013.

———. "Violent Texts, Vulnerable Readers: *Hind Swaraj* and Its South African Audiences." *Public Culture* 23, no. 2 (Spring 2011): 285–97.

Hogan, Patrick Colm. *Empire and Poetic Voice: Cognitive and Cultural Studies of Literary Tradition and Colonialism*. Albany: State University of New York Press, 2004.

Hughes, Heather. *First President: A Life of John L. Dube, Founding President of the ANC*. Auckland Park: Jacana Media, 2011.

Hughes, Langston. "Up to the Crater of an Old Volcano." *Brownies' Book* 2, no. 12 (December 1921): 334–38.

Inaga, Shigemi. "Okakura Kakuzō and India: The Trajectory of Modern National Consciousness and Pan-Asian Ideology across Borders." Translated by Kevin Singleton. *Review of Japanese Culture and Society* 24 (2012): 39–57.

———. "Sister Nivedita and her 'Kali the Mother, the Web of Indian Life,' and Art Criticism: New Insights into Okakura Kakuzō's Indian Writings and the Function of Art in the Shaping of Nationality." *Japan Review* 16 (2004): 129–59.

Jaji, Tsitsi. *Africa in Stereo: Modernism, Music, and Pan-African Solidarity*. Oxford: Oxford University Press, 2014.

Jameson, Fredric. *The Political Unconscious*. London: Routledge, 2002.

Johnson, Georgia Douglas. "The Ancestor." *Brownies' Book* 1, no. 4 (April 1920): 106.

Keelan, Sarah Talbert. "Olive Plaatje." *Brownies' Book* 2, no. 12 (December 1921): 342–43.

Kirschke, Amy Helene. *Art in Crisis*. Bloomington: Indiana University Press, 2003.

Kolge, Nishikant. "Was Gandhi a Racist?" *Economic and Political Weekly* 51, no. 5 (January 2016): 88–93.

Lahiri, Madhumita. "The Pose of the Author: Colonial Africa and the Operations of Genre." *Social Dynamics* 45, no. 1 (2019): 53–74.

———. "Print for the People: Tagore, China, and the Bengali Vernacular." *Comparative Literature* 70, no. 2 (June 1, 2018): 145–59.

———. "World Romance: Genre, Internationalism, and W. E. B. Du Bois." *Callaloo* 33, no. 2 (2010): 537–52.

Lajpat Rai, Lala. *The United States of America.* Calcutta: R. Chatterjee, 1916.

Lake, Marilyn, and Henry Reynolds. *Drawing the Global Colour Line: White Men's Countries and the International Challenge of Racial Equality.* Cambridge: Cambridge University Press, 2008.

Levering-Lewis, David. *W. E. B. Du Bois: A Biography.* New York: Henry Holt, 2009.

Levine, Carolyn. "From Nation to Network." *Victorian Studies* 55, no. 4 (Summer 2013): 647–66.

Lim Boon Keng. *The Li Sao.* Shanghai: Commercial Press, 1929.

"Little People of the Month." *Brownies' Book* 1, no. 2 (February 1920): 58.

Li Zhi. "Explanation of the Childlike Heart-Mind (Tongxin Shuo)." In *A Book to Burn and a Book to Keep (Hidden): Selected Writings of Li Zhi*, edited by Haun Saussy, Pauline C. Lee, and Rivi Handler-Spitz, translated by Pauline C. Lee and Rivi Handler-Spitz, 106–10. New York: Columbia University Press, 2016.

Low, Juliette Gordon. *How Girls Can Help Their Country: A Handbook for Girl Scouts.* Savannah, Ga.: Press of M. S. and D. A. Byck, 1916.

Lukács, Georg. "Tagore's Gandhi Novel." In *Essays and Reviews.* 1922. Reprint, London: Merlin Press, 1983.

Macauley, Thomas Babington. "Minute by the Hon'ble T.B. Macaulay, dated the 2nd February 1835." In Bureau of Education, India. *Selections from Educational Records, Part I, 1781–1839*, edited by H. Sharp, 107–17. Calcutta: Superintendent Government Printing, India, 1920.

Majeed, Javed. *Autobiography, Travel, and Postnational Identity: Gandhi, Nehru, and Iqbal.* Basingstoke: Palgrave Macmillan, 2007.

Marling, William. "The Formal Ideologeme." *Semiotica* 98, nos. 3–4 (2009): 277.

"The Mass Meeting." *Indian Opinion* 6, no. 2 (January 11, 1908): 19–20.

McClendon, Thomas V. "Makwerekwere: Separating Immigrants and Natives in Early Colonial Natal." In *The Demographics of Empire: The Colonial Order and the Creation of Knowledge*, edited by Karl Iittmann, Dennis D. Cordell, and Gregory H. Maddox, 113–29. Athens: Ohio University Press, 2010.

Melas, Natalie. *All the Difference in the World: Postcoloniality and the Ends of Comparison.* Stanford, Calif.: Stanford University Press, 2007.

"The Merry Month of May." *Brownies' Book* 1, no. 5 (May 1920): 142–4.

Mesthrie, Uma. "From Advocacy to Mobilization: *Indian Opinion*, 1903–1914." In *South Africa's Alternative Press: Voices of Protest and Resistance,*

1880s–1960s, edited by Les Swizer, 99–126. Cambridge: Cambridge University Press, 1997.

Metcalf, Thomas. *Imperial Connections*. Berkeley: University of California Press, 2008.

Meyers, Todd, and Nancy Rose Hunt. "The Other Global South." *The Lancet* 384, no. 9958 (2014): 1921–22.

Miller, Barbara Stoler, trans. *The Bhagavad Gita: Krishna's Counsel in Time of War*. 1986. Reprint, New York: Bantam Books, 2004.

Mullen, Bill V., and Cathryn Watson, eds. *W. E. B. Du Bois on Asia: Crossing the World Color Line*. Jackson: University Press of Mississippi, 2005.

Nussbaum, Martha. "Patriotism and Cosmopolitanism." *Boston Review*, October 1, 1994.

Okakura, Kakuzō. *Collected English Writings*. Vol. 2. Tokyo: Heibonsha Limited, 1984.

———. *The Ideals of the East*. London: John Murray, 1902.

Olivelle, Patrick, ed. *The Early Upanisads: Annotated Text and Translation*. Translated by Patrick Olivelle. Oxford: Oxford University Press, 1998.

Olivier, Marc. "George Eastman's Modern Stone-Age Family: Snapshot Photography and the Brownie." *Technology and Culture* 48, no. 1 (2007): 1–19.

Owen, Stephen, ed. *An Anthology of Chinese Literature: Beginnings to 1911*. New York: W. W. Norton, 1996.

Patel, Shailja. *Migritude*. Los Angeles: Kaya Press, 2008.

Paxton, George. *Sonja Schlesin: Gandhi's South African Secretary*. Glasgow: Pax Books, 2006.

Pirie, Gordon H. "'A Most Difficult and Delicate Question': Racial Segregation on the Central South African Railways, 1902–10.'" *Journal of Transport History* 10, no. 2 (1989): 113–27.

———. "Racial Segregation on South African Trains, 1910–1928: Entrenchment and Protest." *South African Historical Journal* 20, no. 1 (1988): 75–93.

———. "Rolling Segregation into Apartheid: South African Railways, 1948–53." *Journal of Contemporary History* 27, no. 4 (October 1992): 671–93.

Plaut, Martin. *Promise and Despair: The First Struggle for a Non-racial South Africa*. Athens: Ohio University Press, 2016.

Poe, Peggy. "Pumpkin Land." *Brownies' Book* 1, no. 1 (January 1920): 3.

Polak, Millie. *Mr. Gandhi: The Man*. Bombay: Vora & Co., 1931.

———. "Women and the Struggle." In *Souvenir of the Passive Resistance Movement in South Africa, 1906–1914 (Golden Number of* Indian Opinion*)*, edited by Mohandas Karamchand Gandhi, 25–26. Phoenix, South Africa: International Printing Press, 1914.

Popp, Valerie. "Where Confusion Is: Transnationalism in the Fiction of Jessie Redmon Fauset." *African American Review* 43, no. 1 (Spring 2009): 131–44.

Pound, Ezra. "Rabindranath Tagore." *Fortnightly Review*, new series 93, no. 555 (March 1913): 572–79.

Prashad, Vijay. *The Darker Nations*. New York: New Press, 2007.

———. "Waiting for the Black Gandhi: Satyagraha and Black Internationalism." In *From Toussaint to Tupac: The Black International since the Age of Revolution*, edited by Michael O. West, William G. Martin, and Che Wilkins, 179–96. Chapel Hill: University of North Carolina Press, 2009.

"Railway Travelling in the Transvaal." *Indian Opinion* 20, no. 35 (August 31, 1912): 292–93.

"Railway Travelling in the Transvaal." *Indian Opinion* 20, no. 36 (September 7, 1912): 301.

Ray, Sangeeta. *En-gendering India: Woman and Nation in Colonial and Postcolonial Narrative*. Durham, N.C.: Duke University Press, 2000.

Ricoeur, Paul. *Freud and Philosophy: An Essay on Interpretation*. Translated by Denis Savage. New Haven, Conn.: Yale University Press, 1970.

Rosenfield, John. "Okakura Kakuzō and Margaret Noble (Sister Nivedita): A Brief Episode." *Review of Japanese Culture and Society* 24 (2012): 58–69.

Ryan, Susan M. "India and U.S. Cultures of Reform: Caste as Keyword." In *India in the American Imaginary, 1780s–1880s*, edited by Anupama Arora and Rajender Kaur, 199–228. Cham, Switzerland: Palgrave Macmillan, 2007.

Safire, William. "People of Color." *New York Times Magazine*, November 20, 1988.

Sedgwick, Eve Kosofsky. *Touching Feeling: Affect, Pedagogy, Performativity*. Durham, N.C.: Duke University Press, 2003.

Sheehan, Elizabeth M. "Fashioning Internationalism in Jessie Redmon Fauset's Writing." In *A Companion to the Harlem Renaissance*, edited by Cherene Sherrard-Johnson, 137–53. Malden, Mass.: John Wiley & Sons, 2015.

Simango, C. Kamba. "Mphontholo Ne Shulo: The Lion and the Hare." *Brownies' Book* 2, no. 2 (1921): 42–44.

Skaria, Ajay. *Unconditional Equality: Gandhi's Religion of Resistance*. Minneapolis: University of Minnesota Press, 2016.

Smith, Katherine Capshaw. *Children's Literature of the Harlem Renaissance*. Bloomington: Indiana University Press, 2006.

Soske, Jon. *Internal Frontiers: African Nationalism and the Indian Diaspora in Twentieth-Century South Africa*. Columbus: Ohio University Press, 2017.

Spivak, Gayatri Chakravorty. "Can the Subaltern Speak?" In *Marxism and the Interpretation of Culture*, edited by Lawrence Grossberg and Cary Nelson, 271–314. Urbana: University of Illinois Press, 1988.

———. "Three Women's Texts and a Critique of Imperialism." *Critical Inquiry* 12, no. 1 (1985): 243–61.

Stock, Brian. *The Implications of Literacy: Written Language and Models of Interpretation in the Eleventh and Twelfth Centuries*. Princeton, N.J.: Princeton University Press, 1983.

Stockton, Kathryn Bond. *The Queer Child, or Growing Sideways in the Twentieth Century*. Durham, N.C.: Duke University Press, 2009.

Subba Rao, D. S. "The Union of Colour." *Aryan Path* 7, no. 4 (May 1936): 214–16.

Suhrud, Tridip. "*Hind Swaraj*: Translating Sovereignty." In *Ten Books That Shaped the British Empire*, edited by Isabel Hofmeyr and Antoinette Burton, 153–67. Durham, N.C.: Duke University Press, 2014.

Suhrud, Tridip, and Suresh Sharma, eds. *M. K. Gandhi's "Hind Swaraj": A Critical Edition*. New Delhi: Orient Blackswan, 2010.

Tagore, Rabindranath. "The Call of Truth." *Modern Review* 30, no. 4 (October 1921): 423–33.

———. *The Crescent Moon*. London: Macmillan, 1913.

———. "The Cult of the Charkha." *Modern Review* 38, no. 3 (September 1925): 263–70.

———. *Gitanjali: Song Offerings*. Translated by William Radice. New Delhi: Penguin Books, 2011.

———. *The Home and the World*. London: Macmillan, 1916.

———. "Letters from Rabindranath Tagore." *Modern Review* 29, no. 5 (May 1921): 612–17.

———. *Letters to a Friend*. Edited by C. F. Andrews. London: George Allen & Unwin, 1928.

———. *Nationalism*. New York: Macmillan, 1917.

———. *One Hundred Poems of Kabir*. London: Macmillan, 1915.

———. "Striving for Swaraj." *Modern Review* 38, no. 6 (December 1925): 681–85.

———. *Talks in China*. Calcutta: Visva-Bharati, 1925.

Tagore, Rabindranath, and Ramananda Chatterjee. "Rabindranath Tagore's Letter to the Viceroy." *Modern Review* 26, no. 1 (July 1919): 105–6.

Tagore, Rabindranath, and W. E. B. Du Bois. "A Message to the American Negro from Rabindranath Tagore." *The Crisis* 35, no. 6 (October 1929): 333–34.

Tan Chung, Amiya Dev, Wang Bangwei, and Wei Liming, eds. *Tagore and China*. New Delhi: Sage, 2011.

Tharps, Lori L. "The Case for Black with a Capital B." *New York Times*, November 19, 2014. https://www.nytimes.com/2014/11/19/opinion/the-case-for-black-with-a-capital-b.html.

Torabully, Khal, and Marina Carter. *Coolietude: An Anthology of the Indian Labor Diaspora*. London: Anthem, 2002.

Trivedi, Harish. "Revolutionary Non-violence: Gandhi in Postcolonial and Subaltern Discourse." *Interventions* 13, no. 4 (2011): 521–49.

Turner, James. *Philology: The Forgotten Origins of the Modern Humanities*. Princeton, N.J.: Princeton University Press, 2014.

Vinson, Robert. "Providential Design: American Negroes and Garveyism in South Africa." In *From Toussaint to Tupac: The Black International since the Age of Revolution*, edited by Michael O. West, William G. Martin, and Che Wilkins, 130–54. Chapel Hill: University of North Carolina Press, 2009.

Viswanathan, Gauri. *Outside the Fold: Conversion, Modernity, and Belief*. Princeton, N.J.: Princeton University Press, 1998.

Wachal, Robert S. "The Capitalization of *Black* and *Native American*." *American Speech* 75, no. 4 (2000): 364–65.

Walkowitz, Rebecca. *Cosmopolitan Style: Modernism beyond the Nation*. New York: Columbia University Press, 2000.

———. "World Anglophone Is a Theory." *Interventions* 20, no. 3 (2018): 361–65.

Wall, Cheryl. *Women of the Harlem Renaissance*. Bloomington: Indiana University Press, 1995.

Watson, Miller. "The Emergence of Harmony." *Aryan Path* 7, no. 3 (March 1936): 115–16.

Weidman, Amanda. "Echo and Anthem: Representing Sound, Music, and Difference in Two Colonial Modern Novels." In *Audible Empire: Music, Global Politics, Critique*, edited by Ronald Radano and Tejumola Olaniyan, 314–33. Durham, N.C.: Duke University Press, 2016.

Weinbaum, Alys Eve. *Wayward Reproductions: Genealogies of Race and Nation in Transatlantic Modern Thought*. Durham, N.C.: Duke University Press, 2004.

Wen Yiduo. "Form in Poetry." In *Modern Chinese Literary Thought*, edited by Kirk Denton, translated by Randy Turnbull, 318–27. Stanford, Calif.: Stanford University, 1996.

Zackodnik, Teresa. "Recirculation and Feminist Black Internationalism in Jessie Fauset's 'The Looking Glass' and Amy Jacques Garvey's 'Our Women and What They Think.'" *Modernism/Modernity* 19, no. 3 (September 2012): 437–59.

Zhou, Xingyue. "The Inseparable Dichotomy of Nationalism: The Readings of *The Home and the World* in China and the Reconsiderations." *Rupkatha* 2, no. 4 (2010): 366–72.

Index

Page numbers in italics refer to figures.

FLASHPOINTS

1. *On Pain of Speech: Fantasies of the First Order and the Literary Rant*, Dina Al-Kassim
2. *Moses and Multiculturalism*, Barbara Johnson, with a foreword by Barbara Rietveld
3. *The Cosmic Time of Empire: Modern Britain and World Literature*, Adam Barrows
4. *Poetry in Pieces: César Vallejo and Lyric Modernity*, Michelle Clayton
5. *Disarming Words: Empire and the Seductions of Translation in Egypt*, Shaden M. Tageldin
6. *Wings for Our Courage: Gender, Erudition, and Republican Thought*, Stephanie H. Jed
7. *The Cultural Return*, Susan Hegeman
8. *English Heart, Hindi Heartland: The Political Life of Literature in India*, Rashmi Sadana
9. *The Cylinder: Kinematics of the Nineteenth Century*, Helmut Müller-Sievers
10. *Polymorphous Domesticities: Pets, Bodies, and Desire in Four Modern Writers*, Juliana Schiesari
11. *Flesh and Fish Blood: Postcolonialism, Translation, and the Vernacular*, S. Shankar
12. *The Fear of French Negroes: Transcolonial Collaboration in the Revolutionary Americas*, Sara E. Johnson
13. *Figurative Inquisitions: Conversion, Torture, and Truth in the Luso-Hispanic Atlantic*, Erin Graff Zivin
14. *Cosmopolitan Desires: Global Modernity and World Literature in Latin America*, Mariano Siskind
15. *Fiction beyond Secularism*, Justin Neuman
16. *Periodizing Jameson: Dialectics, the University, and the Desire for Narrative*, Phillip E. Wegner
17. *The Practical Past*, Hayden White
18. *The Powers of the False: Reading, Writing, Thinking beyond Truth and Fiction*, Doro Wiese
19. *The Object of the Atlantic: Concrete Aesthetics in Cuba, Brazil, and Spain, 1868–1968*, Rachel Price
20. *Epic and Exile: Novels of the German Popular Front, 1933–1945*, Hunter Bivens
21. *An Innocent Abroad: Lectures in China*, J. Hillis Miller
22. *Form and Instability: East Europe, Literature, Postimperial Difference*, Anita Starosta
23. *Bombay Modern: Arun Kolatkar and Bilingual Literary Culture*, Anjali Nerlekar
24. *Intimate Relations: Social Reform and the Late Nineteenth-Century South Asian Novel*, Krupa Shandilya
25. *Media Laboratories: Late Modernist Authorship in South America*, Sarah Ann Wells
26. *Acoustic Properties: Radio, Narrative, and the New Neighborhood of the Americas*, Tom McEnaney

27. *The New Woman: Literary Modernism, Queer Theory, and the Trans Feminine Allegory*, Emma Heaney
28. *Civilizing War: Imperial Politics and the Poetics of National Rupture*, Nasser Mufti
29. *Late Colonial Sublime: Neo-epics and the End of Romanticism*, G. S. Sahota
30. *Globalizing Race: Anti-Semitism, Empire, and the Politics of Scale in Modern French and European Culture*, Dorian Bell
31. *Domestications: American Empire, Literary Culture, and the Postcolonial Lens*, Hosam Mohamed Aboul-Ela
32. *Behold an Animal: Four Exorbitant Readings*, Thangam Ravindranathan
33. *Capital Letters: Hugo, Baudelaire, Camus, and the Death Penalty*, Ève Morisi
34. *Immaterial Archives: An African Diaspora Poetics of Loss*, Jenny Sharpe
35. *Figures of the World: The Naturalist Novel and Transnational Form*, Christopher Laing Hill